Prophet and Teacher

Other Westminster John Knox Press books by William R. Herzog II

Parables as Subversive Speech
Jesus, Justice, and the Reign of God
The Faith of Fifty Million (with Christopher H. Evans)

Prophet and Teacher

An Introduction to the Historical Jesus

WILLIAM R. HERZOG II

WESTMINSTER
JOHN KNOX PRESS
LOUISVILLE · KENTUCKY

Scripture quotations from the New Revised Standard Version of the Bible are copyright © 1989 by the Division of Christian Education of the National Council of the Churches of Christ in the U.S.A. and are used by permission.

Scripture quotations from the Revised Standard Version of the Bible are copyright © 1946, 1952, 1971, and 1973 by the Division of Christian Education of the National Council of the Churches of Christ in the U.S.A. and are used by permission.

Some Scripture quotations are translated by the author.

Book design by Sharon Adams
Cover design by Lisa Buckley

First edition
Published by Westminster John Knox Press
Louisville, Kentucky

This book is printed on acid-free paper that meets the American National Standards Institute Z39.48 standard. ♾

PRINTED IN THE UNITED STATES OF AMERICA

05 06 07 08 09 10 11 12 13 14 — 10 9 8 7 6 5 4 3 2 1

Library of Congress Cataloging-in-Publication Data

Herzog, William R.
    Prophet and teacher : an introduction to the historical Jesus / William R. Herzog II.
      p. cm.
    Includes bibliographical references and index.
    ISBN 0-664-22528-4 (alk. paper)
    1. Jesus Christ—Historicity.   I. Title.

BT303.2.H445 2005
232.9'08—dc22   2005042235

This study is dedicated to

Nancy Carolyn Smith
&
Benjamin Lawson Smith

of blessed memory

Contents

Preface

It is appropriate that one should write the preface last even though it will introduce the book. Only at the close of a work like this can one contemplate and appreciate the many people who made it possible. Every student of the historical Jesus necessarily works surrounded by "a great cloud of witnesses" (Heb. 12:1) who can testify to the impossibility of the task while confessing its inevitable lure. This study is caught in that common dilemma.

The inception of this project traces to a conversation I had with Carey Newman, who was then my editor at Westminster John Knox. After I had completed two projects devoted to the study of the historical Jesus, *Parables as Subversive Speech* (1994) and *Jesus, Justice, and the Reign of God* (2000), he suggested that I combine the two works into one to integrate the common project that they seemed to imply. In addition, he urged me to think of this project as a textbook that would introduce pastors, students, seminarians, and laity to the historical Jesus using the tools and perspectives developed in those two earlier studies. That conversation laid the foundation for this book as the final work in this trilogy. This origin of the present work means that attentive readers will find some duplication of materials found in the earlier volumes as well as some new material. Readers will also notice a greater level of integration of materials and perspectives in this current effort.

No one reaches the end of a project like this without a deep sense of gratitude and indebtedness. I am thankful for the generations of students at Colgate Rochester Crozer Divinity School who took my courses on the historical Jesus and added their perspectives to my own growing work. I am also grateful for the pastors and laity who have been interested enough in the historical Jesus to attend the seminars and lectures that I have given in a variety of settings. Their earnest engagement has been a source of encouragement and a challenge to sharpen areas that seemed obscure and unclear. It has been a privilege to work with the faculty members at Colgate Rochester Crozer Divinity School and to experience their collegial support. A special word of thanks must go to the Dean of the Faculty, Dr. Melanie May, who has been supportive of my scholarship in ways too numerous to mention. I also appreciate the president of the school, Dr. Thomas Halbrooks, and the board of trustees of this divinity school who continue to value the scholarly contributions of faculty members and support those endeavors.

This entire project is a multilayered conversation with a number of conversational partners. The footnotes will begin to identify the extent of my indebtedness to these colleagues but they cannot express my full indebtedness. Richard Horsley has been a steadfast friend and critic of my work who has improved everything he has read. In addition, he encouraged me to continue the earlier work I had done on Paulo Freire as a model for understanding Jesus as a pedagogue of the oppressed. I will not soon forget a memorable evening of dinner and conversation around his dining room table. His own work continues to scout new terrain in biblical studies and open up fresh perspectives for dealing with familiar texts. I continue to be indebted to the work of the members of the Context Group and rely on their work. It was Bruce Malina who introduced me to the use of the social sciences and their relevance for biblical interpretation. The work of persons like Scott Bartchy, Jack Elliott, K. C. Hanson, Halvor Moxnes, Jerry Neyrey, Douglas Oakman, John Pilch, and Richard Rohrbaugh have proven the worth of using the social sciences to interpret the New Testament. I am fortunate to be doing this work at a time when they have opened so many doors that were previously closed.

I have worked with a different editor for each of the works I have published with Westminster John Knox Press. Mr. Harold Twiss edited the study of the parables, Dr. Carey Newman edited the book on Jesus, and Dr. Jon Berquist edited this volume. Each editor proved to be extraordinarily competent, thorough, and gifted in improving the manuscript and saving me from a number of embarrassing errors. Any errors that remain are my responsibility alone.

I have designed this volume so that students can begin reading any chapter that catches their interest. This has entailed a certain amount of repetition that will be more noticeable if one reads the volume through from beginning to end. I hope it will not prove to be distracting. This study attempts to develop an interpretation of the public work of the historical Jesus and indicate why it led to his show trial and crucifixion. In light of the recent popularity of the movie *The Passion of the Christ*, a serious, historical approach may be needed now more than ever.

This work places special emphases on the political, economic, and social aspects of Jesus' public activity, and it develops Jesus' theology and ethics as a response to the context of his activity in Galilee, Samaria, and Judea. Since so many studies of the historical Jesus emphasize his theological teachings and ethical insights, I have chosen "the road less traveled by," and it has certainly made a difference, whether for good or ill its readers will decide. Like any historical study, this one raises more questions than it answers. It is said that the great physicist Niels Bohr used to begin his seminars by saying to his students, "you are to regard my every sentence as a question in disguise." The same could be said of this book.

Finally, this volume is dedicated to the memory of my sister, Nancy Smith, and her husband, Ben Smith. Ben was my pastor for several years during which he was the very embodiment of the thoughtful preacher and teacher of the Bible. He was in touch with the Scripture's emphasis on justice and taught that to a not always attentive youth group. My sister lived the justice message of the Bible in her work and in her participation at all levels of the United Church of Christ. Their passionate commitment to the gospel and to justice continues to sustain me, although it cannot adequately compensate for their loss.

WILLIAM R. HERZOG II

Abbreviations

Ann.	Tacitus, *Annals*
ANRW	*Aufstieg und Niedergang der römischen Welt*
Ant.	Josephus, *Jewish Antiquities*
ATR	*Anglican Theological Review*
BA	*Biblical Archaeologist*
BAGD	Walter Bauer, William Arndt, F. Wilbur Gingrich, Frederick Danker, *Greek English Lexicon of the New Testament*
Bib Res	*Biblical Research*
BR	*Bible Review*
BTB	*Biblical Theology Bulletin*
CBQ	*Catholic Biblical Quarterly*
Hist.	Tacitus, *Histories*
IDB	*The Interpreter's Dictionary of the Bible*
JAAR	*Journal of the American Academy of Religion*
JBL	*Journal of Biblical Literature*
JJS	*Journal of Jewish Studies*
JRS	*Journal of Roman Studies*
JSNT	*Journal for the Study of the New Testament*
NTS	*New Testament Studies*
Sat.	Juvenal, *Satires*
SBLSP	*Society of Biblical Literature Seminar Papers*
TDNT	G. Kittel, *Theological Dictionary of the New Testament*
Vita	Josephus, *Life*
War	Josephus, *The Jewish War*

1

The Historical Jesus

A Modern Quest for an Ancient Figure

This book is an introduction to the quest for the historical Jesus and the resources scholars have used to pursue that quest, but it is more than a survey of other scholars' work or a summary of various views. This study also develops a proposal for understanding Jesus' public activity,[1] from its beginning in Galilee to its culmination in Jerusalem, while suggesting how his public activity led almost inevitably to his crucifixion. The figure we discover through this kind of research is called "the historical Jesus." The historical Jesus with whom we are concerned is the Jesus we can know through historical research as both recovery and discovery, the Jesus whose public work can be reconstructed through historical analysis and constructed through the use of the historical imagination. As we shall see, both inquiry and imagination are needed for the task.

THE FACTS, JUST THE FACTS, AND NOTHING BUT THE FACTS

The historical Jesus belongs to the world of first-century Palestine. He was born around the turn of the eras, most likely between 4 BCE and 6 CE,[2] and

---

1. Throughout this study, I will refer to Jesus' "public activity" or "public work" in preference to the phrase "Jesus' ministry." The use of ministry to describe Jesus' activities implies that the model for understanding Jesus is Christian ministry. While this model might be useful in a number of theological or ecclesiastical contexts, it assumes too much and is anachronistic when applied to the historical Jesus. For this reason, we will use the more neutral phrases "public activity" or "public work."

2. This study will use the abbreviations CE (Common Era) and BCE (Before the Common Era) instead of the earlier AD and BC designations. It is also important to

he was crucified around 30 or 33 CE when Pontius Pilate was prefect of Judea and Caiaphas was high priest of the temple in Jerusalem. His public activity in Galilee was conducted during the reign of Herod Antipas, one of Rome's client kings. Listing facts such as these is one way to begin a search for the historical Jesus, and this is the way at least one scholar has attempted to proceed. In two studies of Jesus in his first-century context, E. P. Sanders has developed two different lists of what he calls "indisputable facts" that could be used to construct a view of Jesus' life and its aftermath.[3] In his earlier work *Jesus and Judaism*, Sanders listed eight such facts:

1. Jesus was baptized by John the Baptist.
2. Jesus was a Galilean who preached and healed.
3. Jesus called disciples and spoke of there being twelve.
4. Jesus confined his activity to Israel.
5. Jesus engaged in controversy about the temple.
6. Jesus was crucified outside Jerusalem by Roman authorities.
7. After his death, Jesus' followers continued as an identifiable movement.
8. At least some Jews persecuted at least parts of the new movement.[4]

Eight years later in a more popular treatment of the subject, Sanders had expanded the list to include fifteen facts on which a study of the historical Jesus and the early Jesus movement could be based:

1. Jesus was born c. 4 BCE, near the time of the death of Herod the Great.
2. He spent his childhood and early adult years in Nazareth, a Galilean village.
3. He was baptized by John the Baptist.
4. He called disciples.
5. He taught in the towns, villages, and countryside of Galilee (but not in its cities).
6. He preached the "kingdom of God."
7. About the year 30, he went to Jerusalem for Passover.
8. He created a disturbance in the temple area.

---

note that Jesus' birth can be located within a range of dates rather than a specific date. The range reflects the conflicting clues in the material in the birth narratives in Matthew and Luke. Matthew associates the birth with the final years and the death of Herod the Great, who died around 4 BCE. By contrast, Luke associates the birth of Jesus with the census undertaken when Quirinius was legate of Syria. This occurred about 6 CE. It is not uncommon to have a range of dates for significant events in the ancient world where calendars were local, were sometimes lunar rather than solar, and often lacked precision.

3. E. P. Sanders, *Jesus and Judaism* (Minneapolis: Fortress Press, 1985); and *The Historical Figure of Jesus* (London: Penguin, 1993).

4. Sanders, *Jesus and Judaism*, 11.

9. He had a final meal with his disciples.
10. He was arrested and interrogated by Jewish authorities, specifically the high priest.
11. He was executed on the orders of the Roman prefect, Pontius Pilate.
12. His disciples fled at first.
13. They saw him (in what sense is not certain) after his death.
14. As a consequence, they believed he would return to found the kingdom.
15. They formed a community to await his return and sought to win others to faith in him as messiah.[5]

If we remove the references to the movement that emerged after Jesus' death and collate the "indisputable facts" about the historical Jesus found in the two lists, we can then, following Sanders's lead, identify thirteen facts about Jesus and his public activity:

1. Jesus was born about 4 BCE, near the time of the death of Herod the Great.
2. He was raised in a Galilean village called Nazareth.
3. Jesus was baptized by John the Baptist.
4. He called disciples and spoke of there being twelve.
5. Jesus was a Galilean who preached and healed.
6. He preached the kingdom of God.
7. He taught in the towns, villages, and countryside of Galilee, but not in cities.
8. Jesus confined his activity to Israel.
9. About 30 CE he went to Jerusalem to celebrate Passover.
10. He created a disturbance in the temple area and/or engaged in controversy about the temple.
11. He shared a final meal with his disciples.
12. He was arrested and interrogated by Jewish authorities, specifically the high priest.
13. He was executed on the orders of the Roman prefect, Pontius Pilate, and crucified outside Jerusalem.

While, at first glance, these facts might seem to provide a substantial starting point for seeking the historical Jesus, they actually provide a rather problematic starting place, because facts by themselves do not tell us as much as we would like to know about Jesus of Nazareth. Typically, facts raise as many questions as they answer. What is the significance of the fact that Jesus limited his activity to the towns, villages, and countryside of Galilee but avoided the cities? This question is especially important in light of the urbanization of Galilee that occurred during Jesus' boyhood and youth when Herod Antipas rebuilt Sepphoris and then built a new city on the shore of the Sea of Galilee

5. Sanders, *Historical Figure of Jesus*, 10–11.

that he named Tiberius, in honor of the emperor Tiberius, his Roman patron. Did Jesus avoid the two dominant cities in Galilee and, if so, why?

Is it important to know that Jesus was raised in a peasant artisan family in the village of Nazareth? What can be learned about Jesus by studying village life in Galilee or by studying peasant societies and values? Who was John the Baptist, and why was Jesus baptized by him? What was the meaning of baptism in general and of John's baptism in particular? Why did Jesus call disciples? Did he single out twelve for special recognition and, if he did, why? If he confined his activity to Israel, why did he do so?

Similarly, it is one thing to know that Jesus created a disturbance in the temple but quite another to ask why he followed that course of action and what he intended to communicate by doing it. Was the temple controversy related to his teaching, to his public activity, or to his crucifixion? If so, in what ways? If Jesus preached, what did he preach, and if he preached about "the kingdom of God," what did he mean by it? For that matter, isn't it anachronistic to speak about Jesus "preaching"? He was quite likely more like a rabbi, a teacher of Torah, than a "Christian" preacher. Were Jesus' healings and exorcisms related to his preaching and teaching? If so, in what ways? Why was Jesus arrested? Why did Romans and Jerusalem elites collude to execute him? On what charges was he condemned and crucified? Since crucifixion was a punishment reserved for political subversives, does the manner of his death indicate that he was politically subversive? Why was the high priest so prominent in the show trial in Jerusalem? Why did Pilate either order or permit the execution of Jesus? How was he protecting or representing Roman interests?

Clearly, facts about Jesus of Nazareth do not even begin to tell the story of the historical Jesus. They provide a place to start our investigation, but facts do not interpret themselves, and in some cases what counts as an "indisputable fact" can be hotly debated. What Sanders may accept as an unquestioned fact may be disputed by other Jesus scholars. For example, take the calling of the twelve disciples (Mark 3:13–19a; Matt. 10:1–4; Luke 6:12–16). Sanders thinks it is an established fact in part because it fits his understanding of Jesus as a teacher of "restoration eschatology." Although he does have some reservations about the matter, he judges it likely that Jesus called twelve disciples to symbolize the restoration of the twelve tribes of Israel.[6] By contrast, John Dominic Crossan thinks that the calling of the twelve disciples is a creation of the early church, placed in the Gospels to justify the church's claim about the apostolic

---

6. Sanders, *Jesus and Judaism*, 103–4. Sanders acknowledges that the calling of the twelve is the least certain fact on which he builds his study, and he confesses that we can no longer know why Jesus called disciples or what their role was. Yet he does think the number twelve refers to Israel and therefore fits his model of restoration eschatology.

roots of its leadership and mission.[7] Just as Sanders finds the calling of the twelve likely because it fits his larger framework of "restoration eschatology," so Crossan finds the same fact unlikely because it does not accord with his view of Jesus as a Jewish cynic-like teacher who practices what he calls "open commensality," that is, table fellowship open to all "nuisances and nobodies." The calling of the twelve, as well as the hierarchy implied by it, would undermine Crossan's view of Jesus as a teacher of a radical egalitarianism.[8]

N. T. Wright accepts the historicity of the twelve even though the lists of the twelve cannot be harmonized. He sees the twelve representing "the inner circle" who symbolize the "the reconstitution of Israel" for the purpose of judging Israel, a theme congruent with Wright's view of Jesus as a prophet who announces the end of Israel's long exile[9] (see Q: Luke 22:28–30). In similar fashion, John Meier finds the calling of disciples a natural correlate of Jesus' prophetic and teaching activity.

> All this simply states the obvious: prophesying and teaching are exercises in social communication. A prophet or teacher who had absolutely no receptive audience would have a slim chance of even being remembered as a prophet or teacher. . . . Having disciples simply jibes with Jesus' job description in 1st century Jewish Palestine.[10]

Once again, facts can accommodate a variety of interpretations, depending on the larger interpretive framework in which they are placed. Any reconstruction of the historical Jesus must remain cognizant of the dialogical and dialectical relationship between facts and their interpretive frameworks.

In other words, simply compiling facts about Jesus produces minimal results and creates far more questions than the facts themselves can answer as well as more confusion than clarity. This might be why Meier rightly notes that the historical Jesus is not "the real Jesus."[11] The real Jesus is the full reality of the historical person only a vestige of which can be captured through historical inquiry and investigation. This means quite simply that "the real

7. John Dominic Crossan, *Jesus: A Revolutionary Biography* (San Francisco: Harper-Collins, 1994), 108–10.

8. John Dominic Crossan, *The Historical Jesus: The Life of a Mediterranean Peasant* (San Francisco: HarperSanFrancisco, 1991), see chaps. 12, 13; also see Crossan, *Jesus: A Revolutionary Biography*, chap. 3.

9. See N. T. Wright, *Jesus and the Victory of God* (Minneapolis: Fortress Press, 1996), 298–300.

10. John P. Meier, *A Marginal Jew: Rethinking the Historical Jesus*, vol. 3, *Companions and Competitors* (New York: Doubleday, 2001), 46–47.

11. For a fuller discussion of the real Jesus and the historical Jesus, see John P. Meier, *A Marginal Jew: Rethinking the Historical Jesus*, vol. 1, *The Roots of the Problem and the Person* (New York: Doubleday, 1991), 21–40.

Jesus is not available and never will be,"[12] a forceful reminder of one of the inevitable and inescapable conditions of historical research, namely, that "what really occurs in history is much broader than the history recoverable by a historian."[13] What we call the historical Jesus is the composite of the recoverable bits and pieces of historical information and speculation about him that we can assemble, construct, and reconstruct. For this reason, the historical Jesus is, in Meier's words, "a modern abstraction and construct."[14] This seemingly pessimistic conclusion need not mean that the quest for the historical Jesus is not worth pursuing, but it does counsel humility and a clear recognition of the limited nature of any attempt to paint a picture of the public work of Jesus. It is an ever-present temptation, to which this study will succumb from time to time, to claim too much on the basis of too little evidence.

FRAMING THE FACTS:
PARADIGMS AND HYPOTHESES

At the beginning of the last century, Albert Schweitzer recognized this same basic problem though he stated it in different terms.[15] Commenting on the value of the Synoptic Gospels as historical sources,[16] Schweitzer lamented

> the lack of any connecting thread in the material which they offer us. [They are] only collections of anecdotes. [F]rom these materials we can get only a Life of Jesus with yawning gaps. How are these gaps to be filled? At the worst with phrases, at the best with historical imagination. There is no other means of arriving at the order and inner

---

12. Ibid., 22.
13. Ibid., 23.
14. Ibid., 25.
15. Albert Schweitzer, *The Quest of the Historical Jesus*, ed. John Bowden and trans. W. Montgomery, J. R. Coates, Susan Cupitt, and John Bowden (Minneapolis: Fortress Press, 2001. German original, 1906).
16. The Synoptic Gospels refer to Matthew, Mark, and Luke. The Fourth Gospel, or the Gospel of John, is not included. The three Synoptics were so designated because it was thought that they "see together" (syn-optic) the events they describe. We now know that the Synoptics have significant differences from one another, but they are still very different from John. We also need to add that the Synoptics are no less theological in their portrayal of Jesus than the portrayal of Jesus in John. The difference between the Synoptics and John is one of degree, not one of kind. Still, the Synoptics remain, by general consensus, more useful sources for dealing with the task at hand than the Gospel of John. One notable exception to this general rule will be John's description of the show trial in Jerusalem, and we will use John's narrative to augment the Synoptics in reconstructing the events in Jerusalem. See chap. 10.

connexion of the facts of the life of Jesus than the making and testing of hypotheses.[17]

Of course, Schweitzer believed that the search for the historical Jesus should result in something like a biography of Jesus (the life of Jesus or *Leben Jesu*), whereas contemporary scholars seek more modest results, such as an account of Jesus' public activity or his teaching. Yet, however the outcome of the project may be conceived, it is clear that facts require hypotheses that can make sense out of the fragmentary nature of the materials of the Synoptic tradition. But where do such hypotheses originate? What guarantees their value and validity?

In the light of this dilemma, it will not be surprising to learn that scholars studying the historical Jesus have been working with both facts and larger hypotheses. Sooner or later, all interpreters need to propose a holistic image or paradigm or Gestalt that captures the hypothesis contained in their work. A few examples will illustrate this point. Marcus Borg has developed something of a typology of such larger frameworks that he uses to interpret the various dimensions of Jesus' public work. In particular, he proposes four ways of viewing Jesus:

1. As a spirit-filled figure who mediates the presence of the holy in human experience
2. As a prophet with a political and social agenda
3. As a sage and teacher of subversive wisdom (as opposed to conventional wisdom)
4. As a founder of a revitalization movement[18]

But Borg's typology is by no means exhaustive, and his larger categories are as debatable as any list of facts.

In recent times, Crossan has proposed that Jesus can be understood as a Jewish version of a cynic philosopher, a visionary teacher, a peasant protester, a magician and prophet, as the one who ushers in a brokerless kingdom of nuisances and nobodies.[19] Richard Horsley depicts Jesus as a "social revolutionary," rather than a political revolutionary, who worked among the villages and towns of Galilee to restore the foundations of Israel as a covenant community,[20] and E. P. Sanders finds in Jesus a teacher of "Jewish restoration eschatology"

17. Schweitzer, *Quest*, 7.
18. See Marcus Borg, *Jesus: A New Vision. Spirit, Culture and the Life of Discipleship* (San Francisco: Harper & Row, 1987), 39–171, for a fuller discussion of these categories.
19. See Crossan, *The Historical Jesus*, 89–224, 265–353, 421–22. A shorter version of his portrayal of Jesus can be found in *Jesus: A Revolutionary Biography*.
20. Richard Horsley, *Jesus and the Spiral of Violence: Popular Jewish Resistance in Roman Palestine* (San Francisco: Harper & Row, 1987), 147–317.

focusing on the destruction and rebuilding of the temple.[21] N. T. Wright develops a view of Jesus as the messianic prophet who announces the end of Israel's exile and the beginning of a new chapter in the ongoing story and historical journey of the people of God.[22] Geza Vermes argued that Jesus could be seen as a Galilean holy man (*ḥasid*) and charismatic healer, much like Hanina ben-Dosa or Honi the Circle Drawer.[23] Other portrayals pick up more traditional views of Jesus as a proclaimer of the kingdom of God,[24] while still other studies emphasize Jesus as an apocalyptic figure.[25] Even after all of this is noted, these comments hardly begin to illustrate the many views of the historical Jesus that have emerged in the past twenty-five years.[26]

Schweitzer was so impressed with the scope and depth of the problem of searching for the historical Jesus in light of the fragmentary nature of the sources that he judged the complexity of the task to be unprecedented.

> For the problem of the life of Jesus has no analogy in the field of history. No historical school has ever laid down the canons for the investigation of this problem. . . . Every ordinary method of historical investigation proves inadequate to the complexity of the conditions. . . . The historical study of the life of Jesus has had to create its own methods for itself.[27]

It was for this reason that Schweitzer thought the only way forward in these historical investigations of Jesus of Nazareth was the making and testing of hypotheses, but he failed to propose any means for judging the value of the hypotheses being generated or the validity of the materials of the Synoptic tra-

---

21. Sanders, *Jesus and Judaism*, and a shorter statement of his thesis in *Historical Figure of Jesus*.

22. Wright, *Jesus and the Victory of God*. For another study of Jesus as a prophet, see R. David Kaylor, *Jesus the Prophet: His Vision of the Kingdom on Earth* (Louisville, Ky.: Westminster John Knox Press, 1994).

23. Vermes has developed this view in three studies: *Jesus the Jew: A Historian's Reading of the Gospels* (Philadelphia: Fortress Press, 1973); *Jesus and the World of Judaism* (Philadelphia: Fortress Press, 1983); and *The Religion of Jesus the Jew* (Minneapolis: Fortress Press, 1993).

24. See, for example, Jurgen Becker, *Jesus of Nazareth* (New York: Walter de Gruyter, 1998); and Joachim Gnilka, *Jesus of Nazareth: Message and History* (Peabody, Mass.: Hendrickson Publishers, 1997).

25. See Dale C. Allison, *Jesus of Nazareth: Millenarian Prophet* (Minneapolis: Fortress Press, 1998); and Bart D. Ehrman, *Jesus, Apocalyptic Prophet of the New Millenium* (New York: Oxford University Press, 1999).

26. For a fuller discussion, see Ben Witherington III, *The Third Quest for the Jew of Nazareth* (Downers Grove, Ill.: InterVarsity, 1995); and Mark Allen Powell, *Jesus as a Figure in History: How Modern Historians View the Man from Galilee* (Louisville, Ky.: Westminster John Knox Press, 1998).

27. Schweitzer, *Quest*, 7.

dition on which they were based. The situation described by Schweitzer may have obtained in 1906 when he wrote his epochal volume, but it is no longer the case. In the years since Schweitzer recorded his observations, scholars have developed a variety of criteria for dealing with the historical sources as we have them in the Gospels and for testing hypotheses about the historical Jesus. We will turn to this task in the next chapter.

These dilemmas are significant enough to discourage many historians and some scholars conclude that the entire enterprise is useless and futile. Luke Johnson has recently made the case that all efforts to find the historical Jesus are misguided quests based on the illusion that one can extract sayings and events from the Gospels for the purpose of rearranging them to form different yet coherent depictions of the historical Jesus. For Johnson, the problem is that individual sayings and deeds do not (indeed cannot) provide a portrait of the historical Jesus because they are without both context and interpretive controls. The only framework that can make sense of the Gospel portraits, he argues, is the framework adopted by all four of the Gospel writers. The canonical Gospels alone can provide narrative context and interpretive controls for the individual units of tradition. As Johnson put it in his own words, "whether plausible or implausible, all such constructions lack any real claim to historical probability once the given narrative framework has definitively been abandoned."[28] The effort to evaluate the historical credibility of individual items from the Gospel traditions only makes matters worse because it leaves the impression that discrete units of tradition may have a claim to historical standing even when read outside of the Gospels' narrative framework. Again, to quote Johnson,

> It is *not* legitimate on the basis of demonstrating the probability of such items [what Jesus said or did] to then connect them, arrange them in sequence, infer causality, or ascribe special significance to any combination of them. . . . Once the narrative control is gone, the pieces can be (and have been) put together in multiple ways.[29]

But what exactly is that common framework provided by the Gospels' narrative of Jesus' public activity? Johnson summarizes it as "radical obedience to God and selfless love toward other people."[30] The value of this framework for Johnson is that it reflects the creeds of the church as well as the canonical Gospels. It may go without saying that Johnson's summary of the common

28. Luke Timothy Johnson, *The Real Jesus* (San Francisco: Harper, 1996), 125.
29. Ibid., 124–25.
30. Robert Miller has provided an extensive critique of Johnson's thesis in two articles: "The Jesus of Orthodoxy and the Jesuses of the Gospels: A Critique of Luke Timothy Johnson's *The Real Jesus*," *JSNT* 68 (1997): 101–20; and "History is Not Optional: A Response to 'The Real Jesus' by Luke Timothy Johnson," *BTB* 28 (1998): 27–34.

framework shared by the Gospels is as disputable as any "undisputed fact"or, for that matter, any larger framework for interpreting the work of Jesus. Numerous other possibilities could have been and have been suggested.

Johnson has provided a useful critique of one essential aspect of the effort to discern and discover the Jesus of history. To do so requires that the materials of the Gospel traditions be removed from their present narrative context and placed in a different context created by the interpreter, just as the materials now present in the Gospels were taken out of their earlier contexts, both oral and written, by the evangelists[31] and placed in the current Gospel narratives. Does the fact that an oral saying or parable has been written down by a Gospel writer and incorporated into his narrative preclude any and all further use of these materials, as Johnson seems to imply? It would be equally reasonable to argue that the work and methods of the Gospel writers can serve as a prototype for the ways that we will work with their materials in our ongoing search for the historical Jesus. After all, the Gospel writers took finely fashioned units of tradition, honed by telling and retelling or shaped and reshaped before being incorporated into collections of written materials, and changed them from final products into the raw materials of their Gospel narratives. Scholars now repeat that process, using the final products of the Gospels as the raw materials for their contemporary constructs of the historical Jesus. Deconstructing their narratives teaches us not only how they pursued their task but also how we can construct new historical narratives that reuse their materials by removing them from their present narrative context and recontextualizing them in new patterns. Will such efforts produce multiple proposals, as Johnson fears? The answer is, "Yes, of course they will," as surely as the earliest efforts to undertake this task yielded four (canonical) Gospels, not one, and a group of extracanonical gospels as well. Why should we expect or demand our efforts to produce different results? The diversity of outcomes that will ensue from following this procedure only reminds us that final answers will continue to elude us in our quest for the historical Jesus but will not prevent us from pursuing limited and partial outcomes.

Staking out a position nearly diametrically opposed to Johnson, Crossan has argued that the quest for the historical Jesus must be undertaken in every generation: "[N]o generation ever gets it right forever. The best we can do, and it is more than enough, is to get it adequately right for here and now. That is not personal or individual humility but structural and systemic destiny."[32]

---

31. "Evangelists" is just another word to describe the Gospel writers, perhaps emphasizing their shaping hands in using the traditions they inherited to fashion the present narratives and their ethical and theological concerns.

32. John Dominic Crossan, "The Historical Jesus," *BR* 12, no. 1 (1996): 45.

Every attempt to portray the historical Jesus will, in the nature of things, be incomplete, yet every effort will contribute to our understanding of Jesus. This exploration seeks to make a small contribution to this continuing task by emphasizing the political, social, and economic dimensions of Jesus' teaching and public activity. Before proceeding, we will give a preview of coming attractions by outlining the view of Jesus' work examined in this study, keeping in mind Crossan's caution and Johnson's warning while accepting the systemic destiny that encompasses all attempts to describe the historical Jesus.

"JUST WHAT SORT OF MAN IS THIS . . . ?" (MATT. 8:27)

If we take the Gospel traditions as our guide, it is obvious we are not the first to ask about Jesus. Following the stilling of the storm (Mark 4:35–41; Matt. 8:23–27; Luke 8:22–25), the disciples began to ask questions about Jesus' identity and ponder who he was. Even though the current versions of this incident have been crafted to emphasize christological themes, they still record the disciples' growing curiosity about Jesus. In an incident somewhere around the villages near Caesarea Philippi, the Gospels report that Jesus turned the tables and asked his disciples what people were saying about him. When he did, he discovered that he was being compared to the likes of John the Baptist, Elijah, Jeremiah, or one of the old prophets (Mark 8:27–30; Matt. 16:13–20; Luke 9:18–21). As Rohrbaugh has noted, the question "Who do people say that I am?" is a question about Jesus' "public self," that is, about his public identity and the social role or roles he is perceived to be fulfilling. In contrast, the question "Who do you say that I am?" is a question about his "in-group" identity, that is, the self that emerges "as one internalizes the values, expectations and descriptions of an in group in which one is embedded."[33] Note that neither question addresses the issue of Jesus' "private self," the internalized self at the core of Western individualism and the self at the heart of the search for Jesus' self-consciousness. This study will focus on Jesus' "public self," because that gives us a glimpse of his public persona when he is, in James C. Scott's language, "on stage" in the presence of his adversaries, and his "in-group" self, because that gives us a glimpse of how he appeared when he was "off stage," out of the reach and out of the view of the scribes and the authorities who were

33. Richard Rohrbaugh, "Ethnocentrism and Historical Questions about Jesus," in Wolfgang Stegemann, Bruce Malina, and Gerd Theissen, eds., *The Social Setting of Jesus and the Gospels* (Minneapolis: Fortress Press, 2002), 33–35.

trying to trap him and neutralize him.[34] It will not deal with Jesus' "private self," which is inaccessible to us and was not a subject of much interest in a dyadic society.[35]

More specifically, this study brings together four ways of viewing the historical Jesus, each one as inadequate as the answers proposed by the people of Jesus' day, and each one as inadequate as "Peter's confession," which reflected as much confusion as insight. The four approaches employed in this study of the historical Jesus are as follows:

1. Jesus as a prophet in the tradition of Israel's prophetic figures
2. Jesus as a teacher and rabbi, or subversive pedagogue of the oppressed
3. Jesus as a traditional healer and exorcist, a shamanistic figure
4. Jesus as a reputational leader who brokers the justice of Yahweh's covenant and coming reign

The remainder of this chapter will spell out, in preliminary fashion, each of these ways of understanding Jesus.

"ONE OF THE OLD PROPHETS"
(MATT. 16:14; LUKE 9:19)

The answers to the question "Who do people say that I am?" make one thing clear: Jesus was perceived to be a prophet. Insofar as he was understood to be a prophet in the tradition of Israel this would mean that Jesus, like his great prophetic predecessor Moses, was called to interpret the Torah and mediate between Yahweh and the people (Exod. 20:18–21; Deut. 5:23–29; 18:15–19). A prophet in the Deuteronomic tradition was a prophet of the Sinai covenant who made its meaning clear for the people and disclosed the consequences of disobeying or abandoning the covenant (Deut. 18:9–22). Moses was the prototypical figure in this tradition, and every subsequent prophet was understood to be cut out of Moses' cloth (Deut. 18:15). The tradition that began with

34. For fuller descriptions of onstage and offstage behavior, see James C. Scott, *Weapons of the Weak: Everyday Forms of Peasant Resistance* (New Haven, Conn.: Yale University Press, 1985); and *Domination and the Arts of Resistance: Hidden Transcripts* (New Haven, Conn.: Yale University Press, 1990). Scott's perspectives will be pursued later in this study. See especially chaps. 8 and 9.

35. For a discussion of the dyadic personality, see Bruce J. Malina and Jerome H. Neyrey, "First-Century Personality: Dyadic, Not Individualistic," in Jerome Neyrey, ed., *The Social World of Luke-Acts: Models for Interpretation* (Peabody, Mass.: Hendrickson Publishers, 1991), 67–96.

Moses concluded with Jeremiah, the end of whose prophetic career coincided with the exile. Notice that Matthew's version of Peter's confession includes Jeremiah as one of the figures to whom Jesus was being compared (Matt. 16:14). Standing in this tradition, Jesus can be seen as a "prophet of the justice of the reign of God," as I have argued elsewhere in more detail.[36]

As the history of prophecy in Israel and Judah reveals, prophets were often involved in conflict with the ruling authorities. They could take aim at the rulers or the holy places that legitimated their rule because they saw how the emergence of the monarchy adversely affected peasant villagers whose lands could be confiscated to support the political aims of the monarchy and its growing ruling class (e.g., Amos 2:6–8; 4:1–5; 5:4–7; 7:10–17; Mic. 2:1–5; 3:1–12; Isa. 1:12–17; 5:1–13). The emergence of the centralized state created hardship for the vast majority of the population because it broke up the tribe and clan structure of Israel, and, from its inception, it generated a strong prophetic protest. Samuel captured this dissent in his speech to the elders who approached him to ask for a king to rule over them so that they could be like the nations (1 Sam. 8:1–22). When the rulers enlisted the support of the priests and Levites, the custodians of holy sites, to justify their economic and political policies, the prophets arose in protest to remind the ruling class that kings were subject to Yahweh every bit as much as the poorest peasant.

Indeed, it was in response to the crisis caused first by the emergence of the united monarchy (Saul, David, and Solomon) and later by the divided kingdoms of Israel (Northern Kingdom) and Judah (Southern Kingdom) that the prophets emerged as a counterweight to the centralized authority and power of the monarchy. They became voices speaking on behalf of those who had been silenced and marginalized by the increasingly oppressive and exploitive practices of petty tyrants and their aristocrats. Although the framers of the Torah attempted to limit the power of the king and subject him to Yahweh, the momentum caused by the centralization of power and wealth in a ruler and ruling class remained unchecked (see Deut. 17:14–20 for an effort to turn the king into a ruler obedient to the covenant). What made the public activity of Amos, Hosea, Micah, and Isaiah of Jerusalem so distinctive in the ancient world is that they were all insiders who advocated for outsiders, power brokers interceding for the powerless, voices speaking for the voiceless. They became intellectual dissidents who judged Israel and Judah by the standards of the covenant.[37]

36. William R. Herzog II, *Jesus, Justice, and the Reign of God* (Louisville, Ky.: Westminster John Knox Press, 2000), esp. chap. 3.

37. See Joseph Blenkinsopp, *Sage, Priest, Prophet: Religious and Intellectual Leadership in Ancient Israel* (Louisville, Ky.: Westminster John Knox Press, 1995), chap. 3.

When Jesus was called a prophet, he was quite likely being associated with the prophets in this great tradition stretching from Moses to Jeremiah, "one of the ancient prophets" (Luke 9:19) as Luke puts it. But Jesus was also a prophet in the tradition of Israel, the northern kingdom. The two great exemplars of this prophetic tradition were Elijah and Elisha, although the figure of Micaiah ben Imlah (1 Kings 22) is as impressive as he is overlooked. It is possible that Jesus called a group or formed a faction of disciples because he wanted to evoke the tradition of the prophet surrounded by a prophetic conventicle. Elijah and Elisha were known for their mighty acts as well as their words and, in his public activity, so was Jesus. In his public work, Jesus not only revived the prophetic voice but, through his healings and exorcisms, renewed the prophetic act as well. He was a prophet like unto Elijah as well as Moses. The early church would recognize this in their shaping of the story of the transfiguration (Mark 9:2–10; Matt. 17:1–9; Luke 9:28–36).

In spite of all that has been said to this point, it should be noted that Jesus does not exactly resemble the prophets we have been discussing. He does not use the formula "thus says the Lord" like the prophets of old, and he does not address the rulers of his day the way that the prophets, during the monarchy, spoke the truth to the face of power, such as Micaiah ben Imlah in 1 Kings 22, Elijah in 1 Kings 21, or Nathan before David in 2 Samuel 7 and 11. Nor does Jesus have access to the corridors of power characteristic of Isaiah and Jeremiah. Why does he look so different? Part of the answer lies in the changed context and circumstances of Jesus' life. Jesus lived in a Palestine controlled by a colonial power, the Roman Empire, and its client rulers, like Herod Antipas and the high priestly houses in Jerusalem. The challenge that faced Jesus was to articulate the meaning of the Sinai covenant in this context of colonial rule and to do so in a way that represented the interests of the peasant villagers in Galilee. This is what we mean when we speak of a "little-tradition" reading of the Torah or the covenant. Like his illustrious predecessors, Jesus advocated for the poor and the marginalized but not from a position of power. Rather, he embodied the values of those on whose behalf he spoke and acted. He was, in Robert Wilson's language, a peripheral prophet (peripheral intermediary), not a central prophet (central intermediary).[38] Whether from the margins in the villages of Galilee or from the center in the streets of Jerusalem, Jesus was a prophetic figure crying out in the wilderness of Roman occupation and local client rulers who were ever ready to sacrifice the interests of the peasants under their control to advance and enhance their ties with Rome.

---

38. Robert R. Wilson, *Prophecy and Society in Ancient Israel* (Philadelphia: Fortress Press, 1980), 69–86.

TEACHER, NOT RABBI?

Jesus was also called rabbi and teacher (*didaskalos*). Interestingly enough, Jesus is called rabbi only in the Gospel of John (1:38, 49; 3:2, 26; 4:31; 6:25; 9:2; 11:8). In the sole passage from the Synoptics where "rabbi" appears (Matt. 23:7–8), Jesus rejects the title because it is associated with the status-seeking "Pharisees" who "sit on Moses' seat." The use of the title "rabbi" as a term of respect and deference was evidently a part of the Pharisees' agenda for enhancing the authority surrounding the title. Therefore, it would have been inappropriate to apply the term to Jesus or his disciples, who were living together as a kinship group without distinctions. "But you are not to be called rabbi, for you have one teacher, and you are all kin [*adelphoi*]" (Matt. 23:8 RSV). Perhaps more to the point, the title is associated with the figures who bind "heavy burdens, hard to bear"and place them on the backs of the common people (23:4). The unanswered question remains whether these comments in Matthew 23 reflect the time of Matthew or the time of Jesus. It is difficult not to see the rejection of the title as a part and parcel of the larger rejection of the synagogue by the fledgling house church in the 80s or 90s of the first century. If these sayings in Matthew 23 trace to the time of Jesus, the rejection of the title "rabbi" might relate to its being coopted by the representatives of the great tradition that did lay heavy burdens on peasant shoulders, especially in the area of tithes and offerings to the temple. In order to surround the title with an aura of authority consonant with the increasingly important role of rabbis in propagating the great tradition, the title may have been associated with rituals (phylacteries and fringes), public recognition (places of honor at feasts, prominent seats in the synagogue service), and displays of honor and deference (salutations in the *agora* or market place). By contrast, the role of teacher was associated with the little tradition in which the teacher taught as a member of his kinship group ("you are all kin to one another"). If rabbi was to the great tradition as teacher was to the little tradition, then it is possible to speculate why Jesus was called teacher but not addressed as rabbi. However, in this instance, it seems more likely that the Gospel of John may convey a genuine historical reminiscence of Jesus being addressed as rabbi, a custom that was suppressed after the split of house church from the synagogue.

What is clear is that, in the rest of the Gospel traditions, Jesus is called "teacher" (twelve times in Matthew; twelve times in Mark; sixteen times in Luke for a total of twenty-six separate instances or sayings, not counting overlaps; he is also called teacher eight times in John). Does this mean simply that Jesus was a prophetic teacher or does it imply more? Is the title teacher just another way of speaking of Jesus as a prophet or does it speak of a role compatible but complementary to the work of a prophet? It is certainly possible to interpret

these titles as pointing to yet another role of the historical Jesus as a subversive pedagogue of the oppressed.[39]

To understand this role, we must look briefly at the life of a modern figure,
Paulo Freire, whose "pedagogy of the oppressed"[40] defined the scope and role
of a subversive teacher and will open another window onto the world of Jesus
and his teaching. Freire was raised in Brazil in a middle-class family who lost
everything in the depression of the 1930s, forcing them to relocate to an
impoverished area of Brazil. There, Freire formed new friendships with the
poor and became acquainted with the "culture of silence" in which they were
immersed. Once a promising student, he had a difficult time studying because
he was constantly hungry, and he began to observe how social class determines
whether students succeed or fail. After a time, Freire's family regained their
previous position in society, and Paulo's academic work began to improve.
Eventually, he graduated from the local university, but he never forgot the
lessons he had learned as an impoverished, hungry student. In spite of the fact
that their experiences differ in many ways, both Jesus and Paulo came out of
an experience of severe poverty. Jesus was the son of a village handyman (*tektōn*) who may have held a small plot of land and even worked as a day laborer
during harvest times to augment the family's slender resources. General conditions in Galilee would suggest that Jesus and his family lived at the subsistence level and struggled to make ends meet.[41] They both lived in the midst
of extreme poverty.

Freire eventually became a teacher but left his job to teach illiterate rural
peasants how to read. This commitment led to the literacy campaigns he was
invited to conduct on behalf of the Brazilian government. Unfortunately, his
work began just when the coup of 1964 terminated all literacy programs and
the democratic reforms that they were intended to support. Freire himself was
imprisoned before being deported and, after his departure, his program of
educational reforms was destroyed. No one would argue that Jesus was a first-
century version of Paulo Freire conducting a literacy campaign in Galilee and
Judea in preparation for the removal of Herod Antipas and the introduction
of democratic reforms. But Jesus does share some life circumstances with
Freire. Both men worked with illiterate peasants living under a harsh, authoritarian, militaristic regime interested only in keeping peasants quiescent and

39. William R. Herzog II, *Parables as Subversive Speech: Jesus as Pedagogue of the
Oppressed* (Louisville, Ky.: Westminster John Knox Press, 1994), see part 1, chap. 1.

40. Paulo Freire, *Pedagogy of the Oppressed*, 9th ed., trans. Myra Bergman Ramos
(New York: Seabury, 1973, orig. pub. 1968).

41. The most thorough discussion of Jesus' family and circumstances can be found
in Meier, *A Marginal Jew*, vol. 1, 205–371.

politically uninvolved, but even more substantial similarities arise when we look at the details of the pedagogy that Freire devised to teach the illiterate how to read their world. Both Jesus and Paulo realized that what we call education is a political process that can alter in small ways balances of power, and they both believed that the peasants whom they taught were capable of learning to read their world.

When Freire began his work with peasant villagers, he discovered that they were under the spell of an ideology that had been impressed upon them and implanted in them by the ruling class of Brazil. In this "social construction of reality,"[42] peasants were little more than objects in their oppressors' reality with no history to call their own (past), no way make sense of their own experience (present), and no vocation to remake their world (future). Rather, they were locked in an eternally unchanging and hopeless present. Freire discovered that the peasants with whom he was working had internalized the world of their oppressors and, as they did, they were submerging themselves into a self-imposed culture of silence in which they had neither voice nor vision. They were mute in the face of their own oppression, forced to collaborate with the very people who dehumanized them. In light of this dilemma, Freire decided that, in order to teach these peasants to read, he first had to teach them how to read their world and diagnose their condition.

To accomplish this, Freire developed a four-stage pedagogy, three stages of which are germane to the work of the subversive pedagogue from Nazareth. First, Freire believed that any effort to teach peasants must begin with their context and their world, so he sent teams of participant observers to live with peasant villagers. Through participant observation they were able to see the world through peasant eyes by studying their characteristic vocabulary, habits of speech, and peculiar expressions. Out of this immersion experience, the teams began to assemble "generative words" that provided a glimpse of the peasants' "thematic universe." It was in the pursuit of this task that Freire discovered how completely the peasant villagers had internalized the great tradition being propagated by the elites. This construct justified the domination of the elites and the deprivation of the poor as a divine ordering of the world. Since people could not change what God had ordained, the peasants' task was to adjust to this world and to adapt to the limits it imposed on them. The purpose of the exercise was to justify the unimaginable wealth of the rulers and the indescribable poverty of the ruled. To the degree that elites took an interest in

---

42. The phrase is taken from Peter L. Berger and Thomas Luckmann, *The Social Construction of Reality: A Treatise in the Sociology of Knowledge* (Garden City, N.Y.: Doubleday/Anchor Books, 1967). The use of the phrase emphasizes that social structures and institutions are human constructions.

educating the poor, it was for the purpose of depositing this view of the world in their minds and hearts, a form of teaching and learning that Freire called "banking education." It perpetuated the sense of hopelessness engendered by the unending struggle to maintain a subsistence existence. This "deposit" is what we will call elsewhere "the great tradition" (chapter 8).

Freire began his pedagogy by identifying the generative words that came out of daily life in the peasant villages in order to construct a thematic universe different from the one propagated by the ruling elites. This could also be called the beginning of "the little tradition" (chapters 8 and 9). But how did Freire break the power of the great tradition of the elites so that the little tradition of the peasants could emerge? Having identified generative words, Freire moved into the second phase of his pedagogy, preparing "codifications" of these words, usually in visual form. Then the peasants formed "culture circles" to study the codifications. Each codification posed a problem and objectified some aspect of the peasants' lives. By examining aspects of their everyday lives in this fashion, peasants became interpreters of their world and began to experience social, political, and economic realities not as divine givens but as human constructions capable of being changed. Freire believed that codifications contained both a surface structure and a deep structure. The longer the peasants attended to the codifications, the more likely it was that they would move from understanding the surface structures to grasp the deep structures that revealed how their social world and the world of the elites were intimately related. For example, they began to realize that their poverty was one consequence of the wealth amassed by the elites. Social description moved into social analysis.

The third phase of his pedagogy involved "decoding, problematizing, and recodifying" the world. Decoding removed the efforts to mystify the current arrangements, a task that revealed the peasants were much more aware of the realities of their world than one might have expected. Problematizing takes previous fixities and re-presents them as problems to be solved. Engaging in this very process discloses that the world is not a final fact or divinely structured reality but a series of problems to be posed, examined, and acted on. As peasants discover their own power and ability to remake the world, they emerge from the culture of silence imposed on them and begin to discover their vocation as subjects capable of making and remaking their own history. This process Freire called "conscientization." Since learning leads to action, Freire realized that it was not enough just to codify problems. It was necessary to codify "limit situations" and "limit acts," those moments when the oppressed could challenge the world of the elites and change their own in the process. Social analysis was leading to social action. This educational process contrasted sharply with the banking model of the elites because it led to a transformation of the world rather than maintaining the status quo. In this sense, his pedagogy was utopian, looking to create a future different from the oppressive and repressive past. This utopian function may be found in the apocalyptic imagery and sayings of Jesus, since his apocalyptic teaching envisions a transformed world. Conscientization described a movement from a consciousness dominated by an alien ruling class to a critical consciousness capable of interpreting and changing a world previously thought to be immutable. When followed, this pedagogy encouraged peasants to break the culture of silence in which they had been immersed and inspired them to reimagine their world. The pedagogy of the oppressed led to a liberating praxis and, for Freire, the meaning of praxis was unambiguous and clear; it is "reflection and action upon the world in order to transform it."[43]

Other aspects of Freire's pedagogy are not relevant to understanding Jesus' role as a teacher, but there is enough evidence to argue that Jesus functioned as a pedagogue of the oppressed who not only advocated for the peasants of Galilee but, in his parables, provided something like Freire's codifications. In a visual modern society, codifications would naturally assume the form of visual pictures, but in an illiterate oral culture, such as first-century Galilee, stories and vivid oral images could serve the same purpose. Jesus the parabler is also Jesus the pedagogue of the oppressed, and this function of his work may emerge in the Gospels when he is called teacher. At least, this is the proposal we will pursue here.

HEALER AND EXORCIST

In his massive study of the historical Jesus, John Meier notes a curious paradox. As an element in the Jesus tradition, exorcisms and healings are well attested. In fact, it is, historically speaking, a virtual certainty that Jesus performed mighty works that we call healings and exorcisms.

> To sum up: the historical fact that Jesus performed extraordinary deeds deemed by himself and others to be miracles is supported most impressively by the criterion of multiple attestation of sources and forms and the criterion of coherence.[44]

The difficulty comes when interpreters move from their general conclusion about Jesus to the evaluation of specific incidents, the accounts of healings and exorcisms. None of these seem to pass the test of historical plausibility. So we

---

43. Freire, *Pedagogy of the Oppressed*, 36.
44. Meier, *A Marginal Jew: Rethinking the Historical Jesus*, vol. 2, *Mentor, Message, and Miracles* (New York: Doubleday, 1994), 630.

find ourselves affirming, in general, that Jesus healed and exorcized but cannot credit any specific account of a healing or exorcism.

It may help to survey the exorcisms and healing narratives in the Gospel tradition to see what materials we are referring to in this study.

Exorcisms

Mark 1:23–28 par. Luke 4:33–37	exorcism in the synagogue
Mark 5:1–20 pars. Matt. 8:28–34; Luke 8:26–39	the Gerasene/Gadarene demoniac(s)
Mark 9:14–29 pars. Matt. 17:14–21 and Luke 9:37–43a	the possessed boy
Mark 3:22–27 pars. Matt. 12:22–30; 9:32–34; Luke 11:14–15, 17–23	the Beelzebul controversy
Luke 8:2	Mary Magdalene exorcized
Mark 7:24–30 par. Matt. 15:21–28	Syrophoenician woman's daughter

Related material includes the saying about the return of the evil spirit (Matt. 12:43–45 par. Luke 11:24–26) and the story of the strange exorcist (Mark 9:38–41 par. Luke 9:49–50).

The complex nature of the healing material poses a number of dilemmas for anyone studying the historical Jesus. The following list of healing stories reflects some critical decisions that need to be mentioned briefly, though there is not enough space to justify them fully. First, I have omitted the miracles from the Gospel of John and concentrated on materials from the Synoptic Gospels. This decision reflects a general conviction that the materials in John are less suited for studying the historical Jesus than their counterparts in the Synoptics, although there are some notable exceptions to this tendency. In addition, I have omitted the so-called nature miracles, such as the feeding miracles (Mark 6:32–44 pars.; 8:1–10 par. Matt. 15:32–39), the stilling of the storm (Mark 4:35–41 and pars.), walking on the water (Mark 6:45–52 par. Matt. 14:22–33), the miraculous catch of fish (Luke 5:1–11), and the cursing of the fig tree (Mark 11:12–14, 20–21; Matt. 21:18–19, 20–22) since they lead too readily to post-Enlightenment questions about the natural and supernatural that do not advance the topic of this study. Next, I have omitted the raising-from-the-dead stories, such as the raising of Jairus's daughter (Mark 5:21–43 and pars.) and the raising of the widow's son at Nain (Luke 7:11–17) for similar reasons. My final decision was to omit the summaries in which Jesus' miracles are mentioned (e.g., Mark 1:32–34 pars.; 3:7–12 pars.) since they do not advance the discussion stimulated by the healing narratives and exorcisms. After we have bracketed this material, the following list of healings could be considered as part of the discussion of Jesus as a healer and exorcist.

Healings

Mark 1:29–31 pars. Matt. 8:14–15; Luke 4:38–39	Peter's mother-in-law
Mark 1:40–45 pars. Matt. 8:1–4; Luke 5:12–16	leper cleansed
Mark 2:1–12 pars. Matt. 9:1–8; Luke 5:17–26	healing paralytic
Mark 3:1–6 pars. Matt. 12:9–14; Luke 6:6–11	withered hand restored
Matt. 8:5–13 par. Luke 7:1–10 (Q)	the centurion at Capernahum
Mark 5:21–43 pars. Matt. 9:18–26; Luke 8:40–56	two women healed
Matt. 9:27–31; 20:29–34 pars. Mark 10:46–52; Luke 18:35–43	the blind healed
Mark 7:31–37 par. Matt. 15:29–31	Jesus heals a deaf mute
Mark 8:22–26	blind man at Bethsaida healed
Luke 13:10–17	healing the bent woman
Luke 14:1–6	healing the man with dropsy
Luke 17:11–19	cleansing ten lepers
Matt 21:10–17	healing in the temple
Luke 22:51	Jesus restores ear of a servant

How are we to sort this material? What does it tell us about Jesus as an exorcist and a healer?

Jesus was a traditional healer who was interested in healing both illness and disease. Disease refers to what is physically wrong with a person (e.g., leprosy) while illness refers to the social consequences of the disease (e.g., isolation, being cut off from friends and family).[45] This explains why Jesus' exorcisms and healings so often lead to the restoration of those who have been healed. The Gerasene demoniac is freed to return to his community, "go home to your friends" (Mark 5:20), and the possessed boy is restored to his father (Mark 9:14–29). In similar fashion, the woman with the hemorrhage is restored to her family (Mark 5:25–33), and the bent woman can live like the daughter of Abraham she is (Luke 13:10–17). Every leper healed, from one to ten, implies a restoration to family and kin as well as to the covenant people of Israel (Mark 1:40–45; Luke 17:11–19). So healing is a means not an end, and Jesus is not a healer or an exorcist who conducts his work to gain public support. Wright observes that the healings and exorcisms parallel Jesus' activity in welcoming the sinners and the outcasts, since Jesus' healing work is often carried out among folks like Bartimaeus, a blind beggar (Mark 10:46–52), a paralytic (Mark 2:1–12), a deaf mute (Mark 7:31–37), and a Syrophoenician woman

45. See John J. Pilch, *Healing in the New Testament: Insights from Medical and Mediterranean Anthropology* (Minneapolis: Fortress Press, 2000), esp. chap. 2.

(Mark 7:24–30). When Jesus touches a leper, the leper comes clean, but Jesus does not catch the infection. His touch redraws the boundary between clean and unclean, and, by the finger of God, Jesus releases the power of the reign of God to reconstitute the people of God. Every healing or exorcism was a gathering of the exiles. So Wright says,

> This means that Jesus' healing miracles must be seen clearly as bestow-ing the gift of *shalom*, wholeness, to those who lacked it, bringing not only physical health but renewed membership in the people of YHWH.[46]

It was not enough to heal disease; Jesus had to address the matter of illness as well.

It is also true that many of Jesus' healings and exorcisms were part of larger conflict situations. The healing of the paralytic occurred in the midst of a dis-pute about blasphemy and forgiveness (Mark 2:1–12), while at least four heal-ings or exorcisms occur in the midst of disputes about the sabbath (Mark 3:1–6 pars.; Luke 13:10–17; 14:1–6; Mark 1:23–28). In these synagogue settings, the healing or exorcism becomes part of the larger dispute. Once again, neither healing nor exorcism is an end in itself. Wright has argued that Jesus' healings and exorcisms were an integral part of what he calls "the prophetic praxis" of Jesus.[47] Jesus the traditional healer is closely identified with Jesus the prophet, and the healings and exorcisms could also be interpreted as prophetic signs in the tradition of Elijah and Elisha.

BROKER OF THE REIGN OF GOD
AND REPUTATIONAL LEADER

It is probably true that these mighty works also confirmed Jesus' role as a reliable broker of God's power. They illustrated and validated his claim that "if it is by the finger of God that I cast out demons, then the reign of God has come upon you" (Luke 11:20, cf. Matt. 12:28).[48] In the context of Roman imperial domination and Herodian rule, the claim to broker another reign that was, in fact, the reign of Yahweh, was a claim subversive to the powers that be. In a world where the priests and their retainers controlled access to Yahweh

46. Wright, *Jesus and the Victory of God*, 192.
47. Ibid., chap. 5.
48. For a thorough discussion of the presence of patron and client in the Gospels, see Bruce J. Malina, "Patron and Client: The Analogy Behind Synoptic Theology," in Bruce J. Malina, *The Social World of Jesus and the Gospels* (New York: Routledge, 1996), 143–75.

through the temple, the claim to be a broker of God's power independent of
the temple and priesthood was not welcome but would serve as a source of
conflict and sharp disagreements.

Reputational leaders emerge because they embody the values of the group
they represent. Jesus, for instance, emerges out of the village life of Galilee, a
peasant artisan steeped in the prophetic traditions of Israel and the little tradition of peasant villages like Nazareth. In his teaching and through his
actions, he challenged the higher-order norms and institutions represented by
the Torah as it came from Jerusalem and the temple system, controlled as it
was by the high priestly houses serving their Roman masters.

Not surprisingly, scribal Pharisees and Pharisees challenged his role as reputational leader and broker of God's power, which was centered in temple and
Torah. The Beelzebul controversy provides a glimpse of some of the dynamics
of that conflict (Mark 3:22–27 pars. Matt. 12:22–30; Luke 11:14–15, 17–23 cf.
Matt. 9:32–34). The conflict begins when Jesus exorcizes a "dumb demoniac."
Using Freire's language, we could say that Jesus' exorcism lifts the possessed
man out of the "culture of silence" in which he has been immersed. Jesus brokers God's redeeming power to retrieve the demoniac from his enforced silence
and, through his exorcism, returns the gift of speech by restoring his voice. In
the agonistic world of Palestine, the exorcism is a challenge, and the scribes of
the Pharisees respond to Jesus' action by labeling and libeling him: "He casts
out demons by Beelzebul, the ruler of the demons" (Luke 11:15). By shaming
and stigmatizing Jesus, the scribes hope to destroy his reputation and social
standing with his followers. After all, who wants to be found following Satan?
This assault represents the scribes' riposte to the challenge Jesus has issued by
exorcizing the man.[49] Having been aggressively attacked by the scribes, Jesus
must respond if he is to retain his honor. Although he has several tactical
options before him, Jesus rejects and ridicules the charge leveled against him.
If it were true, it would establish an intolerable contradiction, for it would be
setting Satan against Satan. Jesus then appeals to his hearers' experience of the
impossibility of maintaining such a division. In agrarian societies, all social systems (the economy, religion, etc.) are embedded in politics and kinship, so
Jesus' appeal to a kingdom divided against itself (politics) and a house divided
against itself (kinship) is an appeal to the most basic elements of his social setting. Divided houses (and here there may also be an allusion to the powerful

---

49. For a fuller discussion of the passage and its labeling strategies, see Bruce J.
Malina and Jerome H. Neyrey, *Calling Jesus Names: The Social Value of Labels in Matthew*
(Sonoma, Calif.: Polebridge Press, 1988), see chap. 2; and Santiago Guijarro, "The Politics of Exorcism," in Stegemann, Malina, and Theissen, eds., *The Social Setting of Jesus
and the Gospels*, 159–74.

houses of the ruling elites) and divided kingdoms cannot endure, so it is impossible for Satan to be attacking his own kingdom. "How can Satan cast out Satan?" Common wisdom teaches this obvious lesson.

It is one thing to ridicule his attackers and reject their charge, but Jesus is still not off the hook. He must find a way to reframe the effort to label him a deviant, dedicated to Satan. Jesus does this by appealing to a higher power: "If it is by the finger of God [Spirit of God in Matthew] that I cast out demons, then the reign of God has come upon you" (Q: Luke 11:20 par. Matt. 12:28). Jesus reveals that the source of the power he is brokering is not Satan but God. Now he can complete his counterriposte by reinterpreting the initial exorcism that triggered the debate (Q: Luke 11:14–15 par. Matt. 12:22–23). The exorcism was not some guerilla warfare or fractious fighting between Satan and Satan, but God's reign attacking Satan's domain. Jesus is binding the strong man (Satan) so that he can plunder his house by liberating those who have been possessed (Mark 3:27). Here, "house" may carry the connotation of a ruling house, in this case Satan's ruling house, so that house implies kingdom. Jesus is plundering Satan's kingdom by striking at its ruling house. In this response, Jesus emerges as the broker of that powerful reign of God, a theme present from the very beginning of Jesus' appearance on stage in Galilee (Mark 1:14–15 pars. Matt. 4:13–17; Luke 4:14b–15). Every figure that Jesus healed or exorcized was invited to "repent and trust."

CONCLUSION

The figure that we call the historical Jesus can be viewed in many ways. This study proposes to examine Jesus through four different but related lenses. We will interpret him as a prophetic figure, a subversive pedagogue, a healer and exorcist, and a broker of God's reign and reputational leader. In truth, although it is possible to separate these four approaches for analytical purposes, they actually overlap in numerous ways and, taken together, do provide a coherent interpretation of the historical Jesus. This introductory study is neither an exhaustive nor a completely convincing proposal because it remains subjected to the systemic destiny of which Crossan spoke so eloquently. But it is an effort to get a portion of it adequately right for today.

As Johnson has noted, this effort entails evaluating and interpreting the Gospel materials in ways that go beyond their meaning in their current Gospel settings. This process requires a set of critical tools. The next chapter will explore some of the tools that scholars have developed to assist in this task.

2

Jesus and the Gospels

One of the perennial problems in the study of the historical Jesus is how to weigh and evaluate the traditions in the Gospels, especially the Synoptic Gospels, but the extracanonical gospels and sayings as well. In short, how can we use the current materials in the Gospels as a means to look behind them in order to glimpse the elusive figure of Jesus to whom they bear witness? It is a bit like doing archaeology. Archaeologists begin at the end, at the surface of the tell, and then excavate backwards in time as they dig deeper and establish the stratigraphy of the site. The Gospels are like literary tells. We begin at the end, with the canonical form of the text, but work backwards to earlier forms of the units of tradition found in the Gospel texts. It is a process replete with complexity and uncertainty, and it only yields disputable results. How we pursue this study is the subject of this chapter.

ORAL TRADITIONS IN WRITTEN TEXTS: THE RIDDLE OF THE GOSPELS

As Schweitzer suspected, the Gospels are essentially collections of oral traditions and written sources organized by the Gospel writers. This meant that every unit of tradition (called a pericope) most likely had a history prior to its use in the Gospels, and this history had left its imprint on the text. Put differently, every text contained layers of tradition that had been laminated together to form the text as it appears in the Gospel narrative. Insofar as these traditions carried echoes of earlier uses, a text might speak with multiple voices. An example may illustrate the problem and one tool for dealing with it.

Let's look at the familiar story of Jesus healing the ten lepers (Luke 17:11–19). This story may have three layers of tradition folded into the text as we have it. At the core of the text is a healing story.

core healing story	17:12–14	(the ten)

In the core healing story, the earliest level of the traditions contained in the text, ten lepers approach Jesus and appeal for healing. Jesus tells them to go to the temple and show themselves to the priests in order to have their healing confirmed in the chamber of the lepers, and because all ten believe that he will heal them, they leave. As a reward for their faith in Jesus and their confidence that he would heal them, they are cleansed as they journey toward Jerusalem. At this stage of the tradition, the ten are undifferentiated. They all believe, and they all are cleansed. The core cleansing story has all the elements found in the typical form of a miracle story. The story introduces the supplicants and the healer (v. 12), then describes their appeal for help and the healer's response (vv. 13–14a). Finally, the story recounts the outcome of the encounter (v. 14b). It is a complete miracle story as it stands, and its focus is on all ten lepers.

At the next stage of the tradition, one leper is singled out and distinguished from the rest. This is the first expansion of the story.

core healing story	17:12–14	(the ten)
first expansion	17:15, 16a, 17	(the nine)

In the core healing story, all ten lepers trusted that Jesus would heal them, and their faith was rewarded, but in the first expansion, one leper "when he saw that he was healed" (17:15) returned to prostrate himself at Jesus' feet and give thanks for his healing. These are the actions of a believer confessing his faith in Jesus, which suggests that the healing has been transformed into a parable of faith. It is one thing to be healed, but it is quite another to "see" that one is healed and acknowledge the source of healing. Jesus then asks two questions: "Were not ten cleansed? Where are the nine?" Both change the status of the nine from faithful believers who trust Jesus to heal them into ungrateful recipients of grace. Now the nine are cast in a negative light. Why? What historical context or change in the church's situation might account for the shift in emphasis? One answer is that the church was struggling with the phenomenon that many were being healed in their house church gatherings but not many returned to become part of the community that healed them.[1] They simply went their way, failing to see

1. Hans Dieter Betz, "The Healing of the Ten Lepers (Luke 17:11–19)," *JBL* 90 (1971): 314–28.

that they were healed and ignoring the one who had healed them. Healing did not lead to gratitude and discipleship. If this reflects the problem being addressed, then the early church might have expanded the healing story so that it became a reflection on the problematic relationship between healing and ingratitude.

When Luke received these materials, he put them to yet another purpose by adding more material to the growing tradition and refocusing the story to communicate yet another theme.

core healing story	17:12–14	(the ten)
first expansion	17:15, 16a, 17	(the nine)
Lukan expansion	17:11, 16b, 18, 19	(the one)

Luke added the connective in verse 11 to stitch this story into his travel narrative (9:51–19:44). Then he refocused the story again, this time shifting its previous emphasis from the nine ungrateful lepers to the one grateful leper whom he identified as a Samaritan (16b). The reason that Luke identified the leper who returned as a Samaritan may be found in the third, long question that Jesus asks in verse 18: "Was none of them found to return and give praise to God except this foreigner [*allogenēs*]?" We might well ask why Luke has transformed the grateful Samaritan into a "foreigner." One possible answer is that Luke was writing for a largely Gentile audience and may have used the healing of the lepers as a paradigm for portraying the faith of outsiders or Gentiles like those for whom he is writing. In this way, Luke provides an opportunity for his audience to locate themselves in the stories of the Jesus tradition.

This example shows how complex a seemingly simple story can be. In this example, one text may contain three distinct layers of tradition, each of which addresses a different issue. If one were to incorporate this text into a study of the historical Jesus, one would need to use it with care, since it is not clear whether the two expansions reflect Jesus traditions or the traditions of the early church. The emphasis on Samaritans, for instance, may be found in the text because Luke inserted it or because it was already present in the earlier Jesus traditions. So the first problem with the Gospels is that their narratives and sayings may reflect multiple layers of tradition and, for this reason, they need to be analyzed circumspectly. With the use of form criticism and traditiohistorical criticism this can be done, allowing for the fact that all such interpretive judgments are debatable and arguable.[2]

2. Both form criticism and traditiohistorical criticism perform similar tasks. Form criticism analyzes the oral or literary forms in which the Gospel traditions have been placed while tradition criticism studies the development of traditions over time. See P. H. Davids, "Tradition Criticism," and C. L. Blomberg, "Form Criticism," in Joel B. Green and Scot McKnight, eds., *Dictionary of Jesus and the Gospels* (Downers Grove, Ill.: InterVarsity Press, 1992), 243–50, 831–34.

If the Gospels are composed of materials that reflect their prior history, then the Gospels can be used to reconstruct the historical Jesus by arguing and inferring backwards from the text as we have it to its earlier forms. In his classic study of Jesus' parables, Joachim Jeremias characterized the problem as "The Return to Jesus from the Primitive Church."[3] Once again, an example may prove helpful in showing how the process works. Since it is found with an interpretation already attached to it, the parable of the sower (Mark 4:1–9 pars. Matt. 13:1–9; Luke 8:4–8) provides an example of how a parable of Jesus was appropriated and applied by the early church (Mark 4:13–20 pars. Matt. 13:18–23; Luke 8:11–15). The allegorical language of the parable's interpretation strongly suggests that it traces to the early church. The church read the sower as a parable about four different ways that people either received or resisted the gospel. The hard path became a symbol for those hearers of the Word whose response was aborted by Satan. The rocky ground represented those whose initial enthusiasm was tempered when persecution arose so that they became fair-weather followers who faded away. The thorny ground represents those who could not detach themselves from the values and reward systems of the Roman empire and so fell away. The good soil symbolizes those who both hear and accept the Word, thereby becoming fruitful and productive disciples. The parable appears to be a straightforward allegory about the mixed results of sowing the Word in a hostile world by highlighting the four most common responses. It was a reading that Jeremias characterized as "psychological" and "hortatory,"[4] since it focused on human motivation and response while appealing to the church to persevere in its work in spite of discouraging results.

The problem with this reading is that it seems to presuppose the presence of something like the church with a mission in the world. This circumstance fits the birth of the early church after the resurrection, but it does not describe very well the situation of the historical Jesus. It is equally important to note that oral storytelling (and Jesus spoke the parables; he did not write them down) usually works by threes. The interpretation of the parable uses a four-fold format for reading the parable, and although a four-fold scheme is not impossible, it is improbable. Can the parable be seen as an oral form organized around a three-fold pattern? The answer is, yes it can. When viewed through these lenses, the parable contains two sequences of three, outlined below.

---

3. Joachim Jeremias, *The Parables of Jesus*, 6th ed., trans. S. H. Hooke (New York: Charles Scribner's Sons, 1963), 11–114.
    4. Ibid., 149–51.

three unpromising sowings	three promising yields
sowing/beginning	harvest/end
1. the hardened path (v. 4)	1. 30-fold (v. 8c)
2. the rocky ground (vv. 5–6)	2. 60-fold (v. 8c)
3. the thorny ground (v. 7)	3. 100-fold (v. 8c)

The parable of Jesus presents two scenes, *beginning* (sowing) and *end* (harvest). The allegorical reading of the parable focused on the unfolding experience of the church in the *middle* of time, the very time frame omitted in the oral parable. One other oddity is noticeable: the section devoted to the second seed (vv. 5–6) is longer than the other two sections. Why might this be the case? Most likely, because the Gospel writer is trying to explain the horticulture of Palestine to outsiders. So he includes an explanation of the rocky ledges that lie beneath the soil and choke the seeds that fall in the shallow soil on top of them.

There are other indications of oral performance in the parable. The verbs follow a pattern: seed is sown; a predator is introduced; and a violent outcome ensues. Knowing this can help us to reconstruct the story of the rocky ground so that it fits the pattern of the other two seeds, in which case it would read, "other seed fell on rocky ground, and the sun rose and scorched it." The pattern is noted below.[5]

Pattern	*First Seed*	*Second Seed*	*Third Seed*
sowing	seed fell	other seed fell	other seed fell
predator appears	birds came	sun rose	thorns grew
violent outcome	devoured	scorched	choked

The oral parable raises questions. Why does violence enter the apparently pastoral parable about sowing a field? If the parable is about sowing the reign of God, then it is evident that the reign of God has enemies and, if Jesus is telling this story as a reflection on his own work as Jeremias speculated, then it is clear that he has enemies willing to use violence to frustrate and defeat his work (see also Mark 3:6). If the parable is a coded way of speaking about resistance to the reign of God, or at least the reign of God proclaimed by Jesus, then it speaks a word of hope in the face of increasing opposition. The sowing may appear to be a lost cause, but God will ensure a bountiful harvest. This theological theme heightens the contrast between the scenes in the parable.

One thing seems obvious. If this reconstruction of the parable of the sower is possible, then the parable Jesus told had a purpose somewhat different from

5. This pattern was first called to my attention by Theodore Weeden's article, "Recovering the Parabolic Intent in the Parable of the Sower," *JAAR* 47, no. 1 (1979): 97–120.

the parable as it was used by the early church, but it also shows that it is possible to construct a parable of Jesus by working backwards from the parable found in the Gospel of Mark. Of course, the interpreter who follows this course would also have to propose a framework within which the parable makes sense. In this instance, it would need to be a conflict-laden situation in which the stakes are high enough to warrant either resorting to violence or maintaining the threat of violence. This makes it important to identify the parties in conflict and the issues over which they are at odds in terms that make sense in the 20s and 30s of the first century in Galilee and Judea. Jeremias thought he had accomplished this feat by reading the parable in eschatological terms, that is, as referring to the coming of the reign of God. For Jeremias, the parable announces Jesus' "great assurance"[6] that, appearances notwithstanding, the reign of God is at hand. At this remove from Jeremias's superb work, it is apparent that his reading of the parable was in the service of a larger holistic reading of Jesus' ministry, and he believed that he had found that larger framework in Jesus' announcement of the coming reign of God. As time passed, the church turned to a psychological and hortatory reading of the parable that missed its eschatological import, although there still remains continuity between Jesus' parable and its appropriation by the early church. Both versions of the parable place the sowing of the reign of God (or the Word) in the context of conflict, opposition, and even rejection, and both versions proclaim a confidence rooted in God's promise to produce a bountiful harvest under the most difficult of circumstances.

In the parable just examined, the problem of inferring backwards from the Markan parable to the parable of Jesus was made easier by the fact that Mark recorded both the parable (4:1–9) and the early church's interpretation of it (4:13–20). Sometimes the interpretation and the parable are wrapped together through the artistry of the evangelist, and each evangelist[7] may have his own agenda that may or may not relate to the circumstances of the historical Jesus. Another example will demonstrate how the Gospel writer's agenda can shape a particular text and why it must be taken into consideration when determin-

---

6. Jeremias organized the parables around a cluster of theological themes set in an eschatological context, one of which he called "The Great Assurance." He placed the parable of the sower in this category. Other themes were as follows: now is the day of salvation; God's mercy for sinners; the imminence of catastrophe; it may be too late; the challenge of the hour; and realized discipleship. See Jeremias, *Parables*, 115–219.

7. The authors of the Gospels are often called "evangelists." The designation indicates that they were interested in proclaiming a theological message though their work. See John 20:31, "But these [things] are written so that you may come to believe that Jesus is the Messiah, the Son of God, and that through believing you may have life in his name."

ing what traces to Jesus and what reflects the Gospel writer's point of view. The parable of the widow and the judge (Luke 18:1–8) illustrates the problem very well. The core parable of Jesus is found in verses 2b–5. But Luke has added a preface that frames the meaning of the parable for his readers (v. 1) and appended some sayings to the parable (vv. 7–8) as further attempts to determine and circumscribe its meaning. In addition, he has added a connective comment joining the sayings to the parable (v. 6). The connective comment begins with a typical attachment formula ("and the Lord said"). The description of Jesus as "the Lord" suggests that these are the words of the risen One addressing the church, not the words of the historical Jesus. If Luke had intended these words to be from Jesus, he would most likely have used the phrase "and he said" or "and Jesus said." Diagramed, the parable and its reworking by Luke appear as follows:

Lukan framing	v. 1
attachment formula 1 (he said)	v. 2a
parable of Jesus	vv. 2b–5
attachment formula 2 (and the Lord said)	v. 6a
connective comment	v. 6b
questions about delay of vindication (parousia)	v. 7
attachment formula 3 (I tell you)	v. 8a
statement of reassurance	v. 8b
generalizing conclusion and implicit exhortation	v. 8c

Luke has taken a parable of Jesus (vv. 2b–5) and framed it as an exhortation to the church to persevere in prayer in the face of the delay of God's final vindication (sometimes called the "parousia" which means the "appearing" of the Lord). This is clear in Luke's initial framing (v. 1), in the questions posed by the Lord (v. 7), and in the word of reassurance (v. 8a). The widow in the parable is meant to serve as a role model of such prayerful perseverance, and she illustrates what "faith on earth" might look like. But Luke's reading of the parable does pose some problems, mainly in the way it portrays God as a "judge of injustice" (or unrighteousness) who "neither fears God nor regards human status!" (author's trans.). How can God not fear God? Even worse, insofar as the judge is viewed as a God figure, the parable portrays God as one who dallies and delays when petitioned, not as a God who "will vindicate them speedily." Moreover, the sayings and questions attached to the parable stand in some tension with the parable itself. Of course, it is entirely possible that Luke is arguing from the lesser to the greater. If an unjust judge will eventually respond to the desperate widow, how much more will God respond to the prayers of the faithful.

If one were using the parable of the widow and the judge as a parable of Jesus, it would be necessary to remove the Lukan framing and its concerns so that one could ask what a parable about a widow petitioning a judge in a Torah court might reveal about conditions in Galilee or Judea during the time of Jesus, as we shall do later in this study. To do this, we would need to know the status of widows, the nature of the "court system," and the role of Torah in the lives of the villagers of Galilee. We would also need to know why a widow is petitioning the court without the support of male family members and what issue she is bringing before the judge. Likewise, we would need to know who the judge is and what it means to say that "he neither feared God nor regarded human status." Answering these queries might lead us to a reading of the parable as a codification of the weak (the widow) seeking justice at the gate from an unjust system that threatens her life and a judge more concerned with soliciting a bribe than dispensing righteousness. Yet the parable shows the widow not only refusing to be silenced but shouting her distress for all to hear and, through her efforts, forcing the judge, against his own nature, to act justly. Such a reading is a far cry from Luke's parable about persistent prayer, but it may open a door into the world of the historical Jesus. Once we remove the Lukan framework, then we will be obliged to provide another framework in which the new reading of the parable of Jesus fits.

Before turning the parable into an incident report, we need to remind ourselves that a parable is not a newspaper account of a specific event but an imaginative creation. Yet even parables will reflect the realities of the social world in which they are told, and their narratives will contain recognizable social scripts and familiar situations. If they did not, then they would be ineffective as a means of communication. For this reason, parables may provide us glimpses into typical situations and stereotypical characters from the first century and, if used with care and corroborating materials, may provide information for historical reflection.

THE CRITERIA FOR AUTHENTICITY

As the three previous examples illustrate, it is possible to work backwards from the Gospels to the time of Jesus though the results of such work will always be provisional and debatable. But form criticism and traditiohistorical criticism are not the only tools for determining what may trace to the historical Jesus. Most studies of Jesus' teachings include a discussion of the criteria that are used to sort the materials of the Jesus tradition, but identifying and applying the criteria are not easy jobs. The difficulty of working with the criteria of authenticity can be illustrated in an article by Robert Funk,[8] known more

---

8. Robert W. Funk, "Rules of Evidence," in Robert W. Funk and Mahlon Smith, *The Gospel of Mark: Red Letter Edition* (Sonoma, Calif.: Polebridge Press, 1991), 29–52.

recently for his work in founding the controversial Jesus Seminar. The Jesus Seminar has made at least two major contributions to the study of the historical Jesus. First, the Seminar's members compiled an exhaustive database of Jesus' sayings and sayings attributed to him, and second, they sought to evaluate those sayings by applying the criteria of authenticity to them. In his essay, Funk identifies six kinds of evidence used by the Seminar: (1) "the wit and wisdom of Jesus"; (2) "oral evidence"; (3) "written evidence"; (4) "attestation"; (5) "narration"; and (6) "general rules."[9] The essay is not only comprehensive but also illustrates the difficulties encountered when we try to develop criteria of authenticity. The first category, "the wit and wisdom of Jesus," provides an illustration of these problems. In this section, Funk defines eight tests that can be applied to the sayings of Jesus.

1. The oral test: "Jesus said things that were short, provocative and memorable."
2. The form test: "Jesus' best remembered forms of speech were aphorisms and parables."
3. Distinctive talk: "Jesus' talk was distinctive."
4. Against the grain: "Jesus' sayings and parables cut against the social and religious grain."
5. Reversal and frustration: "Jesus' sayings and parables surprise and shock; they characteristically call for a reversal of roles or frustrate ordinary, everyday expectations."
6. Extravagance, humor, and paradox: "Jesus' sayings and parables are often characterized by exaggeration, humor and paradox."
7. Vivid images, unspecified application: "Jesus' images are concrete and vivid, his sayings and parables customarily metaphorical and without specific application."
8. The serene, self-effacing sage: "Jesus does not as a rule initiate dialogue or debate, nor does he offer to cure people; Jesus rarely makes pronouncements or speaks about himself in the first person."[10]

Even a cursory reading of the criteria reveals that they are not simply a list of objective rules impartially applied. They are, in part, an enumeration of conclusions about who Jesus was, and they probably reflect some portion of Funk's larger framework for understanding Jesus. In Funk's view, Jesus was a wordsmith who spoke in witty aphorisms and told vivid parables, usually with a countercultural tendency. He was, in this view, something like a first-century "shock jock" or a late-night comedian delivering one-liners about American life, sort of a cross between David Letterman and Jay Leno. Translate this social role into first-century Palestine, and Jesus begins to look like a cynic

9. Ibid., 29.
10. Ibid., 30–35.

sage, a talking head with a habit of surprising and frustrating his audience. However, while this image of Jesus may appeal to Funk and others, it is problematic when applied to Jesus of Nazareth in first-century Galilee.

The following example will illustrate the problem. Funk makes a distinction between proverbs and aphorisms. Proverbs reflect collective, commonplace wisdom, while aphorisms reflect "personal insight, individual authority."[11] Marcus Borg makes a similar distinction between conventional wisdom and a more radical, subversive wisdom.[12] Both Funk and Borg assume that Jesus should be associated with subversive wisdom and the personal authority and individual insight of aphorisms. But Jesus moved through the villages, towns, and rural countryside of Galilee, havens for peasant life where the very conventional wisdom devalued and despised by modern commentators was valued and nurtured as part of the "little tradition" that guided village life and held the clues for survival in an oppressive world. If Jesus had any credibility in the villages and towns of Galilee, it was because he articulated the meaning of the Torah in ways that were congruent with this popular "little tradition" and the Israelite folk traditions that shaped their lives. It is unlikely that a radical, individualistic voice would have been either valued or heeded in the village culture of Galilee. It is also difficult to imagine how a "serene self-effacing sage" who failed to engage people in conversation would be remembered for forms of speech that were either antithetical to his character or incompatible with it. Extravagance and paradox do not seem to be particularly self-effacing forms of speech, nor does the desire to shock and frustrate for no specific purpose seem particularly sage-like. In short, Jesus' speech and his reputed character do not seem to match each other.

To further complicate matters, Funk's criteria seemingly contradict each other. His seventh test of evidence suggests that Jesus spoke in vivid images but without specific or explicit application. If so, then how can he conclude that Jesus' sayings and parables cut against the grain or called for a reversal of roles or frustrated everyday expectations? All of these are explicit and specific applications. As types of speech, humor, exaggeration, and paradox usually imply applications of some kind. That is, in part, what it means to "get it" or catch the punch line. Why would Jesus' speech be "provocative" and "memorable" if it related to nothing in particular in his hearers' world? It would more likely have been forgotten and discarded. However, the criteria articulated by Funk do make sense if he already assumed that Jesus was something like a Jewish cynic philosopher and then selected his criteria to support his prior con-

---

11. Ibid., 31.

12. Marcus Borg, *Meeting Jesus Again For the First Time: The Historical Jesus and the Heart of Contemporary Faith* (San Francisco: HarperCollins, 1994), 69–95.

viction, but, methodologically speaking, that is to put the cart before the horse. Funk and the Jesus Seminar seemed to indicate that they were doing empirical research, inductively building up a picture of Jesus from the pieces of evidence found to be genuine after they were judged according to the criteria of authenticity. It would appear that the Jesus Seminar was following Schweitzer's advice after all; they were making and testing hypotheses. But this should not surprise us; this is what we all do when we study the historical Jesus.

A more nuanced approach to the question of the criteria has been proposed by Dennis Polkow.[13] After surveying a number of attempts to identify and define appropriate criteria, he distills a total of more than twenty-five criteria into eight and organizes them into three levels of importance. They can be organized as follows:

Preliminary Criteria:	1. discounting redaction
	2. discounting tradition
Primary Criteria:	1. dissimilarity
	2. coherence
	3. multiple attestation
Secondary Criteria:	1. Palestinian context
	2. style
	3. scholarly consensus

The meaning of these eight criteria may be understood if we apply them to the texts we have already studied above: the cleansing of the ten lepers (Luke 17:11–19), the parable of the sower (Mark 4:1–9), and the parable of the widow and the judge (Luke 18:1–8). Discounting redaction refers to eliminating the redactional work of the Gospel writers themselves. In the healing of the ten lepers, this would refer to the Lukan additions to the healing story with their emphasis on the Samaritan who returned to give thanks (Luke 17:11, 16b, 18, 19). These materials reflect Luke's concerns. Discounting tradition refers to the middle layers of tradition found between Jesus and the Gospel writer. In the account of the ten lepers, this would be the first expansion of the healing that shifts attention from the ten to the nine (Luke 17:15, 16a, 17). In the parable of the sower, the Markan redaction can be seen in 4:1, 2, 3a, 9. Discounting tradition would focus on the second seed (4:5, 6), which seeks to clarify Palestinian agriculture for a non-Palestinian audience. Discounting redaction

13. Dennis Polkow, "Method and Criteria for Historical Jesus Research," *SBLSP* (1987): 336–56. See also the volume edited by Bruce Chilton and Craig A. Evans, *Authenticating the Words of Jesus* (Leiden: E. J. Brill, 1999) and the companion volume also edited by Chilton and Evans, *Authenticating the Activities of Jesus* (Leiden: E. J. Brill, 1999).

in the parable of the widow and the judge would mean removing Lukan additions (18:1, 2a, 6–8) although some of the questions in 18:6–8 may trace to a pre-Lukan source and would count as discounting tradition.

We are now left with a core healing story (Luke 17:12–14) and two parables (Mark 4:3b–8 with a simplified version of 4:5–6 and Luke 18:2b–5) to which the primary criteria can be applied. The criterion of dissimilarity contends that to be genuinely from Jesus, a saying or parable must be so distinctive that it reflects neither the teachings of first-century Judaism nor the theology of the early church. It must show a double dissimilarity. Norman Perrin modified the criterion by noting that the materials must be dissimilar to "the characteristic emphases" of Judaism and the early church.[14] For example, the parables of the sower and the widow and the judge are unlike contemporary rabbinic parables. Nor did the early church use parables in its teaching. So the parables used here (and by extension many of Jesus' parables) pass the test of dissimilarity, at least as regards their form. But the teaching of "the Lord" in Luke 18:1, 6–8 reflects the concerns of the early church as it struggled to understand its continuing role in history in light of the apparent "delay of the parousia."

As many scholars have recognized, the criterion of dissimilarity, if rigorously applied, would yield an odd picture of Jesus because it would emphasize only his discontinuity with the faith that nurtured him, first-century Judaism, and the developing theologies of the early church that were inspired by his teaching. To correct this tendency to focus only on what is discontinuous between Jesus and his environment, N. T. Wright has proposed a criterion of double similarity and dissimilarity.[15] By this, he means that a saying or parable must be dissimilar enough from formative Judaism and the teachings of the early church to show the distinctive presence and context of Jesus yet similar enough to Judaism and early Christianity to show how Jesus' teaching relates to distinctively Jewish emphases and the developing theologies of the early church. In other words, how can we trace Jesus' indebtedness to Judaism so we can see his teaching as a development of it yet related to it, and how can we see his teaching as contributing to the developing theology of the early church? The parable of the sower may provide a good illustration of this expanded version of the criterion of dissimilarity. The voice of the eschatological prophet proclaiming the coming of the reign of God is Jesus' own voice (dissimilarity). Yet the phrase "reign of God" is found in formative Judaism (similarity) yet not in the ways Jesus seems to use it (dissimilarity). The para-

14. Norman Perrin, *Rediscovering the Teaching of Jesus* (New York: Harper & Row, 1967), 39.
15. N. T. Wright, *Jesus and the Victory of God* (Minneapolis: Fortress Press, 1996), 131–33.

ble was appropriated by the early church which saw Jesus' announcement of the reign of God (dissimilarity) analogous to its sowing of the "Word" (the gospel) in history and the typical ways in which the Word was received or resisted (similarity). In this view, Jesus' teachings become examples of the normal range of discontinuity in the midst of continuity that is characteristic of the historical process, especially during times of ferment and turmoil.

The next primary criterion is multiple attestation. Are the materials we have been studying found in more than one level of tradition? At first glance, it might seem that the parable of the sower is found three times since it is part of the triple tradition (texts found in all three Synoptic Gospels). But if Matthew and Luke both used Mark as a source, then the parable of the sower can only be counted as found in Mark. Matthew and Luke both used Mark's version of the parable. However, the parable of the sower is found in the extracanonical *Gospel of Thomas* (*Gospel of Thomas* 9), a second-century Coptic gospel found in Egypt. So the parable of the sower does meet the criterion of multiple attestation. The cleansing of the ten lepers (Luke 17:11–19) and the parable of the widow and the judge (Luke 18:1–8) are found only in Luke. They are "special L" materials.[16]

The third primary criterion is coherence. Do the materials in question cohere with other materials found to be authentic based on the criterion of dissimilarity? This criterion was introduced, to some extent, because a rigorous application of the criterion of dissimilarity left the researcher with a rather small amount of material. How could one expand the materials to be considered? One answer was to add to the hard core of materials established on the basis of double dissimilarity other sayings that could not, on their own, pass the criterion of dissimilarity but cohered with those materials that could. In the case we are following, can we argue that the special Lukan materials cohere with the parable of the sower or other materials that meet the criterion of dissimilarity? It is evident that this is a problematic criterion because it is not always clear just what it means or what it adds to the core of "authentic" Jesus materials. If coherence means that one adds only new materials that repeat what has already been said by the hard core of sayings established by the criterion of dissimilarity, then why bother? If, on the other hand, the criterion

16. The discussion of the criteria assumes the consensus solution to the relationship among the Synoptic Gospels (Matthew, Mark, and Luke). Using this solution, Mark is the earliest Gospel, and both Matthew and Luke used Mark but did not use each other. In addition, Matthew and Luke have in common about 200–250 verses that are not found in Mark. For this reason, scholars assume that, since these verses exhibit verbatim and nearly verbatim agreement, they were drawn from a common written sayings source called Q (for the German word *Quelle*, which means "source"). Finally, Matthew and Luke each have distinctive materials found nowhere else, and these are called (originally enough) special M (for Matthew) and special L (for Luke).

means that one can add new materials that enlarge what the core materials say, then isn't the historian smuggling into the acceptable core of sayings some materials that do not meet the stringent criterion of dissimilarity, thereby circumventing it? If one must do an end run around the criterion of dissimilarity, then perhaps the criterion is not as useful as it was once thought to be. Indeed, Wright's reformulation of the criterion as "the criterion of double similarity and dissimilarity" provides a more flexible and realistic framework for assessing the materials of the Jesus tradition and may render the criterion of coherence superfluous.

Of the three secondary criteria, the most useful may be Palestinian context. This criterion originally applied to language. Did the Greek of Jesus' sayings or parables reflect the influence of Aramaicisms or Semiticisms? But Charles Carlston enlarged the criterion to include the social world of Palestine when he observed,

> An authentic parable will reflect or fit into the conditions (social, political, ecclesiastical, linguistic, etc.) prevailing during the earthly ministry of Jesus, rather than (or, in some cases, as well as) conditions which obtained in the post-resurrection church.[17]

If the sayings or parables reflect the context of Palestine in the 20s and 30s of the first century, then they must be examined carefully. In the examples we have been using, if the parable of the sower reflects tensions surrounding Jesus' proclamation of the reign of God and the threats of violence it engendered, eventually leading to the cross, then the parable must be taken seriously as a parable of Jesus. In similar fashion, if the parable of the widow and the judge reveals social dynamics at work in Galilee and Judea, then it, too, merits serious consideration. Of course, just because parables may reflect the historical circumstances surrounding Jesus' public activity does not mean that they are authentic Jesus materials. The fact is that many of the same social, political, and economic conditions apply throughout the first century. This makes it difficult to know with certainty if we are seeing materials that reflect Jesus' time or a later period. So the criterion must be applied in conjunction with others.

The criterion of style was taken by Jeremias to mean that he could identify the "characteristics of the *ipsissima vox Jesu* [the very voice of Jesus]."[18] In similar fashion, James Breech applied the criterion in his reconstruction of some of Jesus' parables.[19] As noted earlier, Funk appealed to this same criterion to

---

17. Charles E. Carlston, "A Positive Criterion for Authenticity?" *Bib Res* 7 (1951): 34.
18. Joachim Jeremias, *The Prayers of Jesus*, trans. John Bowden, Christoph Burchard, and John Reumann (London: SCM Press, 1967), 108–15.
19. James Breech, *The Silence of Jesus* (Philadelphia: Fortress Press, 1983), 81–85.

identify the distinctive "wit and wisdom of Jesus." If we turn our attention again to the two parables we have been studying, we might ask whether we can discern a distinctive style to the parables, a voice that is neither Mark's nor Luke's but traces back to Jesus. The issue is important. Are we seeking to discover the very words of Jesus (*ipsissima verba Jesu*) or to identify the characteristics of his speech? Like all the criteria, this one can also involve circular reasoning. A scholar could posit a distinctive voice and then use this assumed voice as a criterion by which to judge the material.

Finally, Polkow identifies "scholarly consensus" as the last of the secondary criteria. Is the saying or parable widely accepted by scholars from a variety of persuasions as tracing to the historical Jesus? The problems with this criterion are evident. First, what counts as a consensus? How many scholars out of what database would be required to claim a consensus? Second, how do we account for the constant shifts in consensus that are a normal part of scholarly work? What is judged to be authentic at one time may be thought to be inauthentic at another. For example, if we read the parable of the sower through the lens of the early church's interpretation of it, we might judge the parable to be the work of the early church. But if we read it as a proclamation of the reign of God, then we might view it as a parable of Jesus. Finally, scholarly consensus is a function of the worldviews of the scholars being cited. For instance, scholars may dismiss the cleansing of the ten lepers on the grounds that such healings do not, indeed cannot, occur. Others might argue for its authenticity based on either an understanding of the role of traditional healers in agrarian cultures or on christological grounds.

The criteria for authenticity may be helpful tools for sifting and sorting the materials of the Jesus tradition. They are not objective criteria, and they all involve circular forms of reasoning. We need to make assumptions to govern our inquiry, and without hypotheses we have no larger framework for facts and information. This means that the criteria are not guides for inductive or empirical research on the Jesus traditions, but they encourage us to ask questions about these materials and subject them to scrutiny. That the criteria have limited value does not mean that they are without value. They are part of a larger task.

PUTTING THE PIECES TOGETHER TO GLIMPSE THE PICTURE IN THE PUZZLE

What do these discussions of facts, hypotheses, and criteria mean for the study of the historical Jesus? Is there any way to integrate the various approaches surveyed here and find a way forward? Crossan has devoted considerable attention to the question of method, and in his work *The Historical Jesus: The*

Life of a Mediterranean Jewish Peasant, he proposes[20] following what he calls a "triadic" method, involving as it does, three levels of research. On the *macrocosmic* level, Crossan uses cross-cultural and cross-temporal models taken from anthropology and macrosociology complemented by studies of more specific aspects of first-century Palestinian culture, such as peasant studies. On the *mesocosmic* level, he uses historical studies specific to the era and area, like the histories of Josephus as well as modern scholarly works such as Richard Horsley's and Sean Freyne's studies of Galilee. Finally, on the *microcosmic* level, he works with a database of specific texts that have to be subjected to thorough scrutiny. When dealing with the sayings of Jesus, Crossan employs an elaborate inventory of the sayings based on his dating of the various documents in which they are found.[21]

This essay will follow a similar approach though it will not employ Crossan's stratigraphy of Jesus' sayings. However, we will assume the consensus solution to the so-called Synoptic problem. This solution proposes that Mark served as a source for Matthew and Luke. Matthew used Mark, and Luke used Mark, but Matthew and Luke were composed independently of each other. The materials that Matthew and Luke have in common derive from a sayings source called Q. This means that Mark and Q are the two primary sources used by Matthew and Luke. In addition, both Matthew and Luke contain materials found only in their Gospels. These sources are designated L (for special Lukan materials) and M (for special Matthean materials). Not very original, but easy to remember.

To provide an adequate introduction to the historical Jesus, any study must use materials from each of the three levels identified by Crossan. At the highest level of abstraction, this study will draw on models from cultural anthropology and macrosociology to describe Palestine in the first century.[22] Palestine was an example of an advanced agrarian society whose political fortunes were largely determined by the presence of the Roman Empire, an aristocratic empire and colonial ruler. These studies will be supplemented by

---

20. John Dominic Crossan, *The Historical Jesus: The Life of a Mediterranean Jewish Peasant* (San Francisco: HarperCollins, 1991), xxvii–xxxiv, and see the appendices at the end of the volume, 427–66.

21. Ibid.

22. A few of the major studies used are as follows: Tom Carney, *The Shape of the Past: Models and Antiquity* (Lawrence, Kans.: Coronado Press, 1975); Gerhard Lenski and Jean Lenski, *Human Societies: An Introduction to Macrosociology*, 4th ed. (New York: McGraw-Hill, 1982); Gerhard Lenski, *Power and Privilege: A Theory of Social Stratification* (New York: McGraw–Hill, 1966); John Kautsky, *The Politics of Aristocratic Empires* (Chapel Hill: University of North Carolina Press, 1982).

more focused work in specific areas of agrarian societies and aristocratic empires, such as works in peasant studies, patronage, and the values of the Mediterranean world, such as honor and shame and the perception of limited goods.[23] At the next level of generality, these studies will be augmented by more specific historical studies of first-century Palestine using both ancient historians like Josephus and contemporary historians such as Horsley, Freyne, Ekkehard and Wolfgang Stegemann, and others. This study will also use the work of archaeologists to sketch as full a picture as possible of Jesus' world. To provide an adequate sketch of Jesus' world, it is important to use both larger models and more focused studies of Palestine in the first century.[24]

Finally, the search for the historical Jesus comes down to interpreting specific texts. All of the materials mentioned above will be used in the service of making sense of texts from the Gospels and construing them so that they can

23. A few key works here are as follows: K. C. Hanson and Douglas Oakman, *Palestine in the Time of Jesus* (Minneapolis: Fortress Press, 1998); Bruce J. Malina, *The New Testament World: Insights from Cultural Anthropology*, 3rd ed. (Louisville, Ky.: Westminster John Knox Press, 2001); Jerome Neyrey, ed., *The Social World of Luke-Acts: Models for Interpretation* (Peabody, Mass.: Hendrickson Publishers, 1991); John J. Pilch and Bruce Malina, eds., *Biblical Social Values and Their Meaning: A Handbook* (Peabody, Mass.: Hendrickson Publishers, 1993); Richard Rohrbaugh, ed., *The Social Sciences and New Testament Interpretation* (Peabody, Mass.: Hendrickson Publishers, 1996); James C. Scott, *The Moral Economy of the Peasant: Rebellion and Subsistence in Southeast Asia* (New Haven, Conn.: Yale University Press, 1976); Andrew Wallace-Hadrill, *Patronage in Ancient Society* (London: Routledge, 1990).

24. The two major studies on Galilee are Sean Freyne, *Galilee from Alexander the Great to Hadrian* (Notre Dame, Ind.: University of Notre Dame Press, 1980); and Richard A. Horsley, *Galilee: History, Politics, People* (Valley Forge, Pa.: Trinity Press International, 1995). Subsequently, each author produced a more readily accessible volume. They are Sean Freyne, *Galilee, Jesus and the Gospels: Literary Approaches amd Historical Investigations* (Philadelphia: Fortress Press, 1988); and Richard A. Horsley, *Archaeology, History and Society in Galilee: The Social Context of Jesus and the Rabbis* (Valley Forge, Pa.: Trinity Press International, 1996). More recently Ekkehard and Wolfgang Stegemann have produced a social history of the first century of Christianity entitled *The Jesus Movement: A Social History of Its First Century*, trans. O. C. Dean Jr. (Minneapolis: Fortress Press, 1999).

As noted above, Horsley has attempted to integrate archaeological information with his historical reconstructions. Recently, a collaborative effort between John Dominic Crossan and Jonathan L. Reed has produced an interesting volume entitled *Excavating Jesus: Beneath the Stones, Behind the Texts* (San Francisco: HarperSanFrancisco, 2001). Other works are as follows: Eric M. Meyers, ed., *Galilee Through the Centuries: Confluence of Cultures* (Winona Lake, Ind.: Eisenbrauns, 1999); Jonathan L. Reed, *Archaeology and the Galilean Jesus: A Re-examination of the Evidence* (Harrisburg, Pa.: Trinity Press International, 2000); Marianne Sawicki, *Crossing Galilee: Architectures of Contact in the Occupied Land of Jesus* (Harrisburg, Pa.: Trinity Press International, 2000).

contribute to the task of constructing a view of the work of the historical Jesus. The proof of the pudding is in the tasting, so the readers of this work will have to judge for themselves how successfully this project has been carried out. It is important to remember that the most we can hope for in an exercise like this is to make an arguable case. Certainty in matters of historical inquiry into the public activity of Jesus is not within our grasp. If this work stimulates conversation and curiosity, it will have made a modest contribution to the continuing preoccupation with Jesus of Nazareth.

3

Agrarian Societies and Aristocratic Empires

The Political and Social World of Palestine in the First Century

Jesus appeared as a public figure in Palestine during the 20s and early 30s of the first century. Luke describes the moment when Jesus appeared on the public scene in this manner: "In the fifteenth year of the reign of Tiberius Caesar, when Pontius Pilate was prefect of Judea, and Herod [Antipas] was tetrarch of Galilee, and his brother Philip was tetrarch of the region of Ituraea and Trachonitis, and Lysanius tetrarch of Abilene, during the high priesthood of Annas and Caiaphas, the word of God came to John" (Luke 3:1–2). In effect, Luke is describing a situation of colonial occupation, what Horsley has called an "imperial situation" maintained by a "politics of violence"[1] whose purpose was the subjection, pacification, and exploitation of the occupied land. To understand this more clearly, it will be useful to sketch the background of the situation that Luke describes so succinctly.

THE TWO FACES OF COLONIAL OCCUPATION: CLIENT KINGSHIP AND LOCAL ELITES

During his long reign (37 BCE to 4 BCE), Herod the Great had ruled both Galilee and Judea as one of Rome's client kings responsible for maintaining the Pax Romana in Palestine, a critical land bridge connecting Egypt and Syria. Herod succeeded by ruling through terror and exploitation. He taxed his subjects to near ruination in order to pay his assigned tribute to Rome, to maintain his own rule, and to support his numerous building projects, including the

---

1. See Richard Horsley, *Jesus and the Spiral of Violence: Popular Jewish Resistance in Roman Palestine* (San Francisco: Harper & Row, 1987), 3–19.

43

renovation and enlargement of the second temple.[2] To maintain order and the appearance of peace, he repressed all internal dissent by turning his kingdom into a brutal but effective police state. In his will, he had appealed to his patron, Caesar Augustus, to transfer his kingdom to Archelaus, his oldest son. The fact that Herod could not dispose of his kingdom as he wished indicates just how fully Rome was the power behind the Herodian throne. In this case, Augustus did not agree to Herod's request because he did not share his confidence in Archelaus. Rather than transfer Herod's extensive kingdom intact, he divided it, apportioning the larger and more prestigious portion, Judea, Idumea, and Samaria, to Archelaus while bestowing upon him the title of *ethnarch* (literally, ruler of a people) with the promise that, if he ruled well, he would receive the grander title of king (*basileus*). Augustus then placed Galilee and Perea under the rule of Herod Antipas who was given the title *tetrarch* (literally, ruler of one-fourth). Antipas would rule for more than forty years (3 BCE to 39 CE) before being deposed by Rome. Philip, who also received the title *tetrarch*, ruled the territories north and east of the Sea of Galilee, which included Batanea, Trachonitis, Auranitis, Gaulanitis, and Panias. He, too, enjoyed a long and stable rule (4 BCE to 34 CE). But as Augustus had anticipated, Archelaus, who had inherited his father's brutality but not his efficiency, did not fare so well and after ten tumultuous years (4 BCE to 6 CE), Augustus deposed him and sent him into exile.

Augustus then incorporated Judea and Samaria into the Roman province of Judea, which was, administratively speaking, a subprovince of the province of Syria. Judea was ruled by an internal priestly aristocracy centered in the temple in Jerusalem whose responsibility was to maintain order and deliver the tribute in timely fashion. These local elites were under the control of the prefect

2. The most recent study of Herod the Great is Peter Richardson, *Herod: King of the Jews and Friend of the Romans* (Columbia: University of South Carolina Press, 1996). The work of the Jewish historian Josephus is essential reading for anyone wanting to understand first-century Palestine. His works are available in the Loeb Classical Library (LCL). See Josephus, *The Jewish War*, books 1–3, trans. H. St. J. Thackeray (Cambridge, Mass.: Harvard University Press, 1976); *The Jewish War*, books 4–6, trans. H. St. J. Thackeray (Cambridge, Mass.: Harvard University Press, 1979); *Jewish Antiquities*, books 9–11, trans. Ralph Marcus (Cambridge, Mass.: Harvard University Press, 1978); *Jewish Antiquities*, books 12–14, trans. Ralph Marcus (Cambridge, Mass.: Harvard University Press, 1976); *Jewish Antiquities*, books 15–17, trans. Ralph Marcus and Allen Wikgren (Cambridge, Mass.: Harvard University Press, 1980); *Jewish Antiquities*, books 18–19, trans. L. H. Feldman (Cambridge, Mass.: Harvard University Press, 1981); *Jewish Antiquities*, book 20, trans. L. H. Feldman (Cambridge, Mass.: Harvard University Press, 1981). Other works include Josephus's *Vita*, his autobiography, and a polemical apologetic piece entitled *Against Apion*. Both are available in the LCL. For a detailed study of Herod Antipas, client king and ruler of Galilee, see Harold Hoehner, *Herod Antipas, A Contemporary of Jesus Christ* (Grand Rapids: Zondervan Publishing House, 1972).

of Judea, a Roman official drawn from the equestrian class. The best known prefect was Pontius Pilate, who held the post for ten critical years (26 CE to 36 CE), encompassing the years of Jesus' public activity as well as his show trial and crucifixion. The prefect of Judea was under the control of the legate (or governor) of Syria. During this same time span, Caiaphas ruled as high priest (18 CE to 36 CE) in the temple.

Historians have observed that Rome never developed an imperial bureaucracy adequate to meet the needs of its far-flung empire.[3] For this reason, Rome often ruled indirectly through local elites whose interests coincided with those of the empire. In the Palestine of Jesus' time, this meant that Roman occupation assumed two distinct forms: client kingship in Galilee and rule through local high priestly elites in Judea. This explains why two high priests, Annas and Caiaphas, appear in a list of political rulers cited by Luke. In the ancient world, religion was political, as the presence of the priestly figures indicates.[4]

This policy did not work well in Judea for a number of reasons. Martin Goodman has argued that Judea could be viewed as a case study in the failure of Roman colonial policy.[5] Rome usually worked with local landed aristocracies, that is, local ruling classes who controlled large tracts of land, dominated the peasant cultivators, and extracted the yield for their own purposes, leaving the peasants under their control with little more than a subsistence living. Since these local elites were already in a predatory relationship with their peasants, they were willing to add Rome's demands for tribute to the tribute they were already extracting. Ruling aristocrats often extracted multiple layers of tribute from the same peasant base.[6] But the high priestly aristocracy in Jerusalem was different. They were not a traditional landed aristocracy; rather, their power base resided in their control of the temple and its sacrificial system. This posed its own distinctive problem because the temple symbolized the refusal of Judeans to assimilate into the larger Greco-Roman world, a fact that differentiated the high priestly families from their counterparts elsewhere in the empire. These matters would be intensified during the pilgrimage

3. See Peter Garnsey and Richard Saller, *The Roman Empire: Economy, Society and Culture* (London: Duckworth, 1987), 20.

4. On political religion, see K. C. Hanson and Douglas E. Oakman, *Palestine in the Time of Jesus: Social Structures and Social Conflicts* (Minneapolis: Fortress Press, 1998), 131–59.

5. For a fuller discussion, see Martin Goodman, *The Ruling Class of Judaea: The Origins of the Jewish Revolt against Rome A.D. 66–70* (Cambridge: Cambridge University Press, 1987).

6. John Kautsky, *The Politics of Aristocratic Empires* (Chapel Hill: University of North Carolina Press, 1982), chaps. 5 and 6.

festivals that celebrated the liberating power of Yahweh to free a people from bondage. Yet these very festivals were presided over by a group of quisling high priests who had sold their birthright for a bowl of Roman pottage. To the degree that they maintained the temple system, the high priests marginalized themselves with Rome, and to the degree that they courted Rome's favor, they marginalized themselves with the peasants of the land whose tithes and offerings were supposed to be used to support the temple. The Romans were well aware of this situation but could devise no alternative to working with the high priestly caste.

Under Jonathan the Hasmonaean (152–143 BCE), the kingship and high priesthood had been consolidated into one office. When Herod the Great came to power (40–37 BCE), he attempted to duplicate this feat, but he lacked legitimacy so that, in spite of his efforts to circulate bogus genealogies proving his priestly lineage, he could never accomplish his goal. Having failed to consolidate the high priesthood into his own kingship, Herod responded by reducing the high priestly office to the status of a political appointment (*Ant.*, 15.39–41). Herod himself deposed high priests and disposed of them when they displeased him or posed a real or imaginary threat to his rule, and he appointed those he assumed would be more pliable and compatible with his goals. Herod's subjugation of the high priestly office to his control served his immediate, short-term political interests, but it initiated a process of eroding the authority of the office and degrading the importance of the high priest; both trends would undermine the high priest's status and stature during the period after Archelaus's departure when the Roman authorities themselves appointed the chief priest.

The high priestly houses responded to this challenge by working together to control the candidates available to hold the office and, as a consequence of their cooperation, four priestly houses provided nearly all of the high priests who occupied the office from the rise of Herod the Great (about 37 BCE) to the beginning of the first Jewish revolt in 66 CE. Of the twenty-five or twenty-eight high priests who served in the temple during this time, twenty-two came from just four houses, the house of Boethus, the house of Annas, the house of Phiabi, and the house of Kamith.[7] However, the people of Judea never accepted the legitimacy of these high priestly houses because they had been imported from the diaspora by Herod and could demonstrate no connection to a proper Zadokite lineage. Consequently, the occupants of the office were seen as interlopers without the pedigree proper for a high priest, a fact the community at Qumran never let them forget. Their legitimacy was a matter

7. Joachim Jeremias, *Jerusalem in the Time of Jesus*, trans F. H. and C. H. Cave (Philadelphia: Fortress Press, 1969), 191–98.

of no small importance. If they were illegitimate high priests, then the sacrifices they supervised were unacceptable to God, and if the sacrifices were unacceptable, then the benefits they conferred would be denied to the people. The sacrifices offered in the temple were intended, among other things, to secure the blessings of Yahweh on the land, to ensure timely rains and fruitful harvests. Without the sons of Zadok to oversee the sacrifices, the entire society was at risk.

If the priestly houses had been effective in addressing the problems facing the province of Judea, they might have attracted some modicum of popular support. But they ignored the widening gap between rich and poor exacerbated by the use of indebtedness to alienate peasants from their land and reduce them to the status of tenants or day laborers, and they ignored the increase of social tensions and hostility generated by the cycle of oppression and exploitation that they encouraged. Goodman argues that the aristocratic class in Jerusalem had saturated their need for luxury goods but could not purchase more land for their estates because, ideologically, the land belonged to peasant cultivators who had inherited their ancestral plots. Yet they still found a way to add peasant lands to their estates. They invested in loans to the poor at 20 percent interest rates (sometimes higher) with the clear intention of foreclosing on the debtors when they could not repay their loans. In this way, their excess wealth did procure more land while peasants entered into a spiral of increasing debt that left them with no choice but to forfeit their land and become debt slaves. Goodman's summary is pointed: "So Judaean society rotted from within because of the social imbalance caused by the excessive wealth attracted to Jerusalem during the Pax Romana."[8] Acknowledging these dynamics, G. M. E. de Ste. Croix has argued that the wealth of the ancient world was essentially built on "exploited unfree labor," a category that includes peasants but is not limited to them. This means, he concludes, that "the propertied classes derived their surplus not from wage labour but from unfree labour of various kinds from chattel slavery to serfdom and debt bondage."[9]

The pattern discerned in Judea then was common to the ancient world, and the high priests' blindness to the suffering it caused was equally widespread. A well-known lament from the Talmud captures the attitude of most people toward the priestly ruling houses:

8. Martin Goodman, "The First Jewish Revolt: Social Conflict and the Problem of Debt," *JJS* 33 (1982): 426 (see 419–26).

9. G. M. E. de Ste. Croix, *The Class Struggle in the Ancient Greek World from the Archaic Age to the Arab Conquests* (Ithaca, N.Y.: Cornell University Press, 1981), 39 and throughout.

Woe is me because of the house of Boethus,
    woe is me because of their staves.
Woe is me because of the house of [Annas],
    Woe is me because of their whisperings.
Woe is me because of the house of Kathros,
    woe is me because of their pens.
Woe is me because of the house of Ishmael ben Phiabi,
    Woe is me because of their fists.
For they are high priests, and their sons are treasurers, and
    their sons-in-law are temple overseers, and their servants
    beat the people with clubs.
                        (*Pesaḥ.* 57a; *Menaḥ.* 13:21)[10]

This indictment would seem to indicate that the peasants of the land, and no doubt many others, viewed the high priestly houses as part of the problem, not as part of the solution. If these laments reflect historical circumstances in the first century, they witness to the use of violence (staves, clubs, and fists), the employment of debt records and great tradition texts (pens), the control of important offices and temple functions (treasurers and overseers), and the use of rumor mongering and backstabbing (whisperings) to maintain their control of the province.

Horsley has argued that the high priestly families continually took the side of Rome when conflicts arose between Judeans and their Roman masters. This alliance would indicate that they were truly working on Rome's behalf in the interest of preserving their own power and privilege. The following two examples of significant protests document this pattern of collaboration and its results. When Vitellius, the legate of Syria, began a campaign against Aretas in Arabia by marching his army through Judea, he encountered mass demonstrations. The presence of the standards carried by the legions set off a great protest because they violated the aniconic provisions of the Torah. When popular protests threatened the instability of the region, leading Jews met with Vitellius and explained the offence he had created. Realizing how important it would be to keep his border provinces stable during his campaign, Vitellius withdrew his troops and proceeded by another way. Commenting on the incident, Horsley observes,

> Only when they [the high priests and Herodians] realized . . . the potential for disruption of the social order, with the resultant threat to their own position in the imperial system, did they begin to use their influence behind the scenes.[11]

10. Cited in Richard A. Horsley and John S. Hanson, *Bandits, Prophets and Messiahs: Popular Movements in the Time of Jesus* (New York: Winston Press/Seabury, 1985), 42.
11. Horsley, *Jesus and the Spiral of Violence*, 110, but see 90–120.

A similar pattern can be observed in the incident in which Gaius Caligula ordered that a statue of him be placed in the Holy of Holies in the temple in Jerusalem. The internal elites lamented the order but did nothing, while the peasants organized and rebelled against the sacrilege, an echo of which may be heard in Mark 13:14. The massive popular protests were prolonged, extending into the season for sowing the fields. Without sown fields and their subsequent crops, there would be no harvest and, therefore, no tribute. When the aristocracy realized that their economic house would be in disorder, they finally reacted and began to negotiate with Petronius, the legate of Syria, although it was the unexpected assassination of Caligula by his own palace guard that finally defused the crisis. Still, Horsley is right to observe that "the Jewish high priests and magistrates were in a compromised and somewhat helpless position, given their role in the imperial system."[12] If they were to align themselves with the protestors, they would jeopardize their role as collaborating elites and lose Caesar's confidence. If they acted as loyal servants of Caesar, they threatened to lose control of the very masses they were supposed to pacify. It was an unenviable position. It should be mentioned that these two examples are taken from events that occurred in the late 30s and 40s of the first century, after the crucifixion that occurred around 30–33 CE. Although they postdate the public activity of Jesus, they do disclose dynamics that were at work during the public activity of Jesus.

Since the power base of the high priestly families was located in the temple, the priestly houses focused on the health of the temple economy to the detriment of the wider economy of Judea, although the two were intertwined in important ways. The high priests used some of the wealth accumulated in the temple to supply loans to peasants, but, as Goodman notes, the "only logical reason to lend was thus the hope of winning the peasant's land by foreclosing on it when the debt was not paid off."[13] Every foreclosure served to heighten the tensions between ruling elites and peasant villagers, the rulers and the ruled. All of this means that the priestly rulers in Jerusalem would be sensitive to criticisms of the temple and priesthood, so sensitive that they would be willing to collaborate with the Romans to execute anyone bold enough to call into question the legitimacy of their rule. When Jesus entered Jerusalem, he was stepping into a volatile political arena.

In Jesus' time, Palestine was an example of what macrosociologists call an advanced agrarian society. This would be as true for the Roman Empire as it

---

12. Ibid., 112–13.

13. See Goodman, *The Ruling Class of Judea*, 57. See also Goodman, "The First Jewish Revolt," 417–27; and Douglas Oakman, "Jesus and Agrarian Palestine: The Factor of Debt," *SBLSP* 24 (1985): 57–73.

would for Herod Antipas's client kingdom and the province of Judea. In addition, it would be fair to characterize these societies as examples of aristocratic empires, a type of political system described by John Kautsky.[14] In order to set the stage on which Jesus appeared, it will be useful to sketch the characteristics of these social and political systems and apply them to Palestine.

SUPERSTRATIFICATION: "BETWEEN YOU AND US A GREAT CHASM HAS BEEN FIXED" (LUKE 16:26)

These remarks are intended to explain the diagram of the relationship between classes in agrarian societies. Agrarian societies are characterized by a great divide between the haves and the have-nots. In these societies, power is concentrated at the top in the hands of a very few. The ruling class comprises only about 1 to 2 percent of the population but controls the great bulk of wealth produced by the peasant base. Estimates place the collective wealth of ruling elites between one-half and two-thirds of the wealth produced by their societies. Ruling elites amass this wealth by controlling both the land on which it is produced and the peasants whose labor creates it. In agrarian societies, wealth is land, and whoever controls the land commands the wealth it produces. Since peasants live mostly in the villages, hamlets, and market towns of the countryside, elites must control this network of habitations if they are to rule the land. The issue is not ownership of the land but control of its yield and its cultivators. Ruling elites demonstrate their control by extracting tribute, taxes, and rents of various kinds from the peasants who live on the land. The act of extracting tribute, taxes, and rents reinforces the rulers' claims over both the land and its inhabitants; it is an act of domination that subordinates peasants to their will. In the Roman empire, tribute usually assumed two basic forms: the *tributum soli*, a land tax, and the *tributum capitis*, a poll tax. Taken together, the tribute enforced Rome's claim to rule the land and the bodies of those who worked the land. David Fiensy spells out the significance of these two forms of tribute.

Just as all land was considered as belonging to the Roman Empire, and thus, subject to taxation as a kind of rent, so also did one's body belong to Rome.[15]

14. See Kautsky, *The Politics of Aristocratic Empires*; Gerhard and Jean Lenski, *Human Societies: An Introduction to Macrosociology*, 4th ed. (New York: McGraw-Hill Book Company, 1982), 169–217; Gerhard Lenski, *Power and Privilege: A Theory of Social Stratification* (New York: McGraw-Hill, 1966), 189–296.

15. Mireille Corbier, "City, Territory and Taxation," in John Rich and Andrew Wallace-Hadrill, eds., *City and Country in the Ancient World* (London: Routledge, 1991), 217. See also David Fiensy, *The Social History of Palestine in the Herodian Period: The Land is Mine* (Lewiston, N.Y.: Edwin Mellen Press, 1991), 99–101.

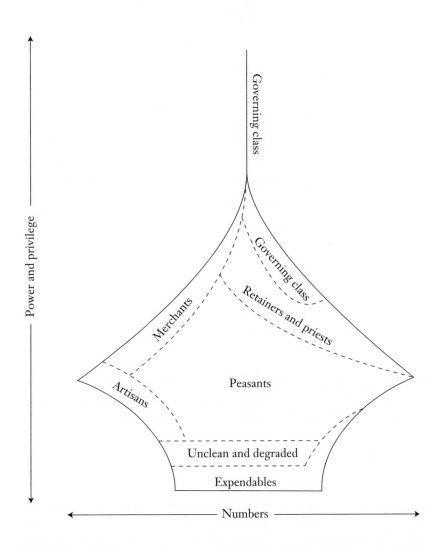

Figure 1 A graphic representation of the relationship among classes in agrarian societies.*

Commenting on the necessity of taking a census, the Emperor Claudius explained that its purpose was "to make our resources known."[16] Note the use of "our," an example of the mind-set that reflects the proprietary theory of the state, that is, the ruler assuming that the land he controls is his to assess and dispose of as he pleases.

Of course, Rome was not the only political power extracting tribute. In Galilee, Herod Antipas collected tribute to support his rule, and in Judea the high priests collected tribute (called tithes and offerings) to support the temple as well as Roman rule. Rome assessed its tribute and then left Herod and the high priests free to exploit the people of the land to whatever degree they could enforce, a pattern often found in aristocratic empires and colonial powers. In addition to Herodian and Roman tribute, the peasants of Galilee were subjected to demands made by the temple in Jerusalem for tithes and offerings, even though they were not within the political jurisdiction of Judea. This made for a triple burden of tribute and taxation. Douglas Oakman identifies three levels of tribute taking:

1. The old aristocracy (priests and elders, centered in Jerusalem)
2. The new Herodian aristocracy (centered in Sepphoris and Tiberius)
3. The Roman overlords[17]

For peasants, tribute taking was, in Oakman's words, "brutal compulsion and oppression." Josephus recounts rulers traveling to the threshing floors to claim their share of the peasants' harvest (*Ant.*, 20.181, 206).

Yet it is typical for peasants to ask not "how much was taken" but rather "how much is left."[18] Oakman has compiled the following list of the demands placed on the subsistence harvest, the "how much is left": 1) subsistence food supply; 2) seed for planting next crop; 3) funds reserved for barter and other needs; 4) the ceremonial fund to cover participation in the life of the village; 5) the fund to cover extractions for tribute, taxes, rents, and other debts.[19] If they gauge that they have been left with enough to ensure their subsistence for another year, peasants will not complain—at least openly.[20] Fiensy has calcu-

---

16. Corbier, "City, Territory and Taxation," 213–14.

17. Douglas Oakman, *Jesus and the Economic Questions of His Day* (Lewiston, N.Y.: Edwin Mellen Press, 1986), 65. Horsley (*Galilee: History, Politics, People* [Valley Forge, Pa.: Trinity Press International, 1995], 59) makes the same point, and Fiensy, (*Social History of Palestine*, 99–104) concurs that tribute/taxes must have been a burden since they were extracted from a harvest that left barely enough for subsistence.

18. James C. Scott, *The Moral Economy of the Peasant: Rebellion and Subsistence in Southeast Asia* (New Haven, Conn.: Yale University Press, 1976), 7.

19. Oakman, *Jesus and Economic Questions*, 49–57.

20. For an extended discussion of peasants' attitudes, see Scott, *The Moral Economy of the Peasant*, 7.

lated the tribute taken from peasants in Palestine. Rome took about 12 percent as a land tax, a denarius head tax on each member of the household, and a wave offering about 1/40th of the harvest, for a grand total of 15 percent. Add to this the 20 percent of the harvest set aside for sowing the next crop, and the peasant household is left with 65 percent of their subsistence crop, 55 percent if they tithe to the temple and 45 percent if they pay a second tithe.[21] Although there is some debate about the amount of tribute and taxes to which peasants were subjected, the usual estimates run from 20 to 35 percent.[22] If we remember that the rulers appropriated the so-called surplus from each harvest, leaving peasants with nothing more than a subsistence living from which the tribute was deducted, the true burden of these demands becomes evident.

It is also clear that peasants had the most flexibility where their obligations to the temple were concerned. In addition, their seed planting fund could be raided to cover unexpected costs but that would mean that the family would have to borrow to plant their next crop, a grim prospect since it placed the peasant family on a slippery slope that led to the loss of their land and eventual debt slavery. Scott has sketched what happens when peasants lose their moral claim to a subsistence living. In Judea and Galilee, this would entail losing the claim that Yahweh has distributed the land so that each person has a guaranteed subsistence. First, peasants lose their land, crossing a threshold that has provided some minimum security. The second threshold occurs "when subsistence guarantees within dependence (=tenancy or day laborers) collapse."[23] Peasants will fight most ferociously as they approach each one of these thresholds because they know how devastating the consequences will be.

In Jesus' time, the peasants of the villages and towns of Galilee were under increasing financial pressure, owing to the building of Tiberius and the rebuilding of Sepphoris. These two cities were situated so as to place all the villages of Galilee within easy reach of the tribute collectors.[24] As Horsley notes, "once Tiberius was built, there was, within a day's walk of every village in Lower Galilee, a city in which lived their rulers and tax collectors,"[25] and yet the hamlets, villages, and towns of Galilee did not form a traditional

---

21. Fiensy, *Social History of Palestine*, 103.

22. See discussions in Marcus Borg, *Conflict, Holiness and Politics in the Teaching of Jesus*, rev. ed. (Harrisburg, Pa.: Trinity Press International, 1998), 47–48; E. P. Sanders, *Judaism: Practice and Belief, 63 BCE–66 CE* (Philadelphia: Trinity Press International, 1992), 146–69; Sean Freyne, *Galilee from Alexander the Great to Hadrian* (Notre Dame, Ind.: University of Notre Dame Press, 1980), 281–87; Horsley, *Galilee*, 137–44.

23. Scott, *Moral Economy of the Peasant*, chap. 2.

24. For a discussion of the urbanization of Galilee, see Freyne, *Galilee*, 121–34, and Horsley, *Galilee*, 159–81.

25. Horsley, *Galilee*, 178.

hinterland for Sepphoris and Tiberius as other rural settlements did in other areas of the empire. This means that the hamlets, villages, and towns of Galilee, however remote they might seem, could not escape the effects of urbanization. Lower Galilee was densely populated with cities as large as Sepphoris and Tiberius and as small as Capernahum. As Andrew Overman has noted, "there was no bucolic separation of the countryside from the city."[26] Yet, in spite of the general truth of his statement, there appears to have been minimal contact between urban centers and villages in Galilee. Contacts primarily concerned tribute collection. For this task, the importance of the cities can hardly be over-stated since tribute demands were made to the rulers in the cities who would then exploit the countryside to collect the amount assigned. The basic unit for tribute collection was the city.[27] This situation reinforces the idea that cities are basically parasitic. As Corbier observes,

> Yet, cities could only live by siphoning off the resources of the coun-try, and this did not only take the form of rents. They derived profit from the collection of taxes and its inequalities, and they also imposed more or less exceptional levies such as requisitions of grain.[28]

The peasantry of Galilee could not, in all likelihood, meet all three layers of demands for tribute. Since they were unable to avoid Herodian and Roman tribute, they were forced to withhold their tithes from the temple in order to survive. The temple responded by condemning the peasants of the land, declaring them to be perpetually indebted and unclean. Oppenheimer notes that there are two notions surrounding the phrase 'am ha-aretz (the people of the land), the 'am ha-aretz le mitzvot and the 'am ha-aretz la-torah, the first sig-nifying people who failed to tithe their produce and the second identifying those who did not know the Torah.[29] These reprobates could not receive the benefits of the temple and its sacrifices unless and until they were "paid up." The inability to pay tithes meant the denial of the benefits that accrued to those who supported the temple's sacrifices, no small matter to a peasant fam-ily hoping for a good harvest. It is possible that the Galilean peasants did pay their offerings (amounting to about 2–3 percent of their harvest) but avoided paying the tithes they could not afford. If so, this expedient would not have been well received by the temple authorities.

26. J. Andrew Overman, "Who Were the First Urban Christians? Urbanization in the First Century," *SBLSP* (1988): 165–66.

27. Corbier, "City, Territory and Taxation," 211–39, see 231.

28. Ibid., 234.

29. A'haron Oppenheimer, *The 'Am Ha-aretz: A Study in the Social History of the Jew-ish People in the Hellenistic-Roman Period* (Leiden: E. J. Brill, 1977), 12.

In an advanced agrarian society, the ruler, guided by what Lenski calls "the proprietary theory of the state,"[30] treats all the lands he controls as his personal estate to confiscate and disperse as he deems fit. This explains why Caesar Augustus could redistribute the lands controlled by Herod the Great. Herod held them at the pleasure of his Roman patron, but the land ultimately was Caesar's to redistribute as he intended. In this way, a ruler could punish those elites who opposed his rule and reward his supporters. When Herod the Great came to power, he executed a number of nobles who were still loyal to the Hasmonaean house and redistributed their lands to aristocrats loyal to him. The group called "Herodians" in the Gospels probably refers to this political faction of aristocrats loyal to the house of Herod and dependent on Herodian rule and patronage. The ruler usually stands in a patron-client relation with other elites, dispensing patronage in the form of lands and estates or political appointments while expecting personal loyalty and support of his policies in return. When patron-client relations involve the members of the ruling class, they are usually called patron-protégé relations to avoid applying the demeaning term, client, to a member of the aristocracy. The high priests of the province of Judea were clients of Rome, and they ruled by Rome's dispensation. The same arrangement obtained in Galilee where Herod Antipas continued in his role as a "friend" (read client or protégé) of Caesar's. It was common to use the language of "friendship" to mask the harsher and more demeaning elements of patron-client relations.

These patron-client networks would replicate themselves throughout the ruling class and beyond. Typically, members of the ruling class would view themselves as protégés of the ruler, but the ruling class was composed of networks of patron-protégé relations, often in political competition with each other. Party or factional politics in the Roman empire was, in large part, the politics of patron-client or patron-protégé networks. It was one way that elites participated in the political process. Members of the ruling class would also enlist clients from the lower classes, especially the retainer class, offering them benefits in return for their support, loyalty, and services rendered. Of course, loyalties are subject to change depending on the fortunes of the elite patron, and since loyalties are based on personal relationships, the coalitions formed are fragile and ever changing. The purpose of patron-client relations is to exercise power over others. In this sense, it reflects the core values of agrarian elites. The poor enter into patron-client relationships because they afford peasants an opportunity to secure something more than a subsistence living.

Rulers in agrarian societies usually come to power through the use of force as the outcome of intense power struggles. For this reason, they favor traditional

30. Lenski, *Power and Privilege*, 214–19.

forms of legitimation, especially the use of temples and cults, to justify their rule and declare their divine right to rule. This need may explain why Herod Antipas allowed the temple to press its claim for tithes and offerings on the peasants of Galilee. Support of the temple helped to legitimate his rule and blunt the endless power struggle to claim the ultimate prize in agrarian societies, the right to rule.

Kautsky has used the term "superstratification" to describe the great divide characteristic of aristocratic empires in which the few have almost everything and the many have almost nothing. Both Galilee and Judea in Jesus' day reflected this situation and the tensions that it generated.

RETAINERS AND BUREAUCRATS: BETWEEN THE HAVES AND THE HAVE-NOTS

Agrarian societies and aristocratic empires face a common problem. If 2 percent of the population is trying to control 98 percent, then the control ratio is 1:49. This creates an unmanageable situation. To counter this problem, ruling elites enlist the services of a retainer class, comprising about 5 to 7 percent of the population, thereby reducing the control ratio to something between 1:11 and 1:14, and establishing a much more manageable political and military situation.

Retainers are used primarily to staff bureaucracies and the military.[31] All agrarian societies require some bureaucracies in the following areas: 1) ecclesiastical bureaucracies, or temples and cults (hierarchies of priests and temple functionaries); 2) economic bureaucracies, or collection of tribute and direct and indirect taxation (hierarchies of tribute, tax and toll collectors and their hirelings); 3) judicial bureaucracies for codification of the few laws that exist in agrarian societies (use of scribes, judges, and those who apply the laws or decrees); 4) military bureaucracies, or standing armed forces and their chains of command; 5) administrative bureaucracies, or centralized structures that attempt to coordinate the work of all the others. It is important not to think of bureaucrats and retainers as an ancient middle class. Retainers belonged to the have-nots and usually lived in a patron-client relationship with an elite, largely or completely dependent on their patrons.[32] However, Tom Carney has observed that everyone in the bureaucratic apparatus had power compared

31. A full description of bureaucratic empires can be found in Tom Carney, *The Shape of the Past: Models and Antiquity* (Lawrence, Kans.: Coronado Press, 1975); and S. N. Eisenstadt, *The Political System of Empires* (New York: Free Press, 1963).

32. For an extensive discussion of the stratification of agrarian societies, see Ekkehard W. Stegemann and Wolfgang Stegemann, *The Jesus Movement: A Social History of Its First Century*, trans. O. C. Dean Jr. (Minneapolis: Fortress Press, 1999), 67–95.

with those outside of it. But like so many other aspects of life in agrarian societies under colonial occupation, the life of retainers could be described in the same way: "This was a power-ridden, fear-dominated society."[33]

Bureaucracies pose a potential threat to rulers because the ruler has to endow each bureaucracy with enough authority and power to perform its job and fulfill its purpose. When they do their jobs, bureaucrats will naturally attempt to institutionalize their perquisites and make their positions hereditary. The ruler will counter these moves by appointing members of the ruling class to oversee each of the bureaucracies and sometimes even their major divisions. Bureaucracies were staffed by three levels of retainers and elites: 1) the lowest level of bureaucrats were the *illiterati* such as jailers and porters; 2) the middle level consisted of *literati*, which included scribes, lawyers, and accountants; and 3) the highest level contained the *dignitates*, the possessors of titles, who often came from the aristocracy. At every level, the bureaucracy was organized around patron-client relations, and appointments were usually the result of patronage and power struggles, not rationalized criteria for service.[34]

As Kautsky notes, the bureaucracies established by the ruler were replicated in the great households of the ruling elites. Just as the empire required elaborated bureaucracies to perpetuate itself so the ruling houses required their own internal bureaucracies to maintain the generation and flow of wealth necessary to fuel the constant conflicts of intraclass politics. The more elaborated the bureaucracies, the more prestigious the household.[35] Jesus' parables provide a number of glimpses into these bureaucracies and the retainers who staffed them (e.g., Matt. 18:23–35; 25:14–30; Luke 16:1–8a).

In Galilee, Herod Antipas's bureaucrats were concentrated at Sepphoris and Tiberius. The temple likewise was run by a bureaucracy that included priests, Levites, and numerous officials associated with the daily activities of the temple. The lament concerning the four high priestly houses (cited above) indicates that the elites controlled the offices of temple treasurer and overseer.

CITIES, TOWNS, AND COUNTRYSIDE: THE POLITICAL GEOGRAPHY OF AGRARIAN SOCIETIES

In agrarian societies, the families that constituted the ruling class, along with many of their retainers, were concentrated in cities while peasants lived in

---

33. Carney, *Shape of the Past*, 52, 60.

34. For a description of bureaucracies, see Carney, *Shape of the Past*, 47–82; the three-fold hierarchy, 52.

35. See the discussion in Kautsky, *The Politics of Aristocratic Empires*, 190–94.

hamlets, towns, and villages of various sizes. Oakman has suggested the following schema:

Type of Habitation	Population Range
hamlet	10s
village	100s
town	1,000s
city	10,000s[36]

Appelbaum uses the phrase "nucleated village"[37] to describe the first two types
of habitation on Oakman's list. In a similar effort, Ben-David reckons the population of a hamlet around 50, a village between 400 and 600, a country town
(similar to market town) between 600 and 7,500, and a large city from 10,000
to 60,000 inhabitants.[38] Hamlets, villages, and towns were distinguished from
cities by their lack or scarcity of public buildings, a city wall, and a lack of a
street plan. Owing to the considerable upheavals during the Hellenistic period
in Palestine, peasants had abandoned the small farms on which they once lived
and moved into villages for protection. The basic unit of housing in the village was the courtyard house, which usually consisted of four houses built
around a central courtyard. Throughout this period of change, the household
remained the smallest unit of peasant social life. The courtyard arrangement
provided peasant families with an extended social space and relations. For the
purpose of sabbath observance, courtyard units connected by a common alley
could function as a single social unit.[39] Beyond these arrangements, peasants
belonged to their village, and if they traveled beyond their village and its
immediate neighboring villages, they would journey to a local market town.

Scott has suggested that "the market area" was the largest geographical and
social unit of peasant life, not the peasant village. Klausner believes that there
was a market day on Friday before sabbath, "the day of assembly," and regular market days on Mondays and Thursdays.[40] Market days included more
than economic transactions in the marketplace. Market towns attracted wandering philosophers and sages willing to debate, entertainers of various kinds

36. Douglas Oakman shared this schema at a meeting of the Context Group. It has
not, to my knowledge, yet been published. Used by permission.
37. Shimon Appelbaum, "Judaea as a Roman Province: The Countryside as a Political and Economic Factor," *ANRW* 2, no. 8 (1977): 361–79.
38. Cited in Fiensy, *The Social History of Palestine*, 138.
39. For an excellent discussion of "The Peasant Household and Village," see Fiensy,
The Social History of Palestine, 120–45.
40. Joseph Klausner, "The Economy of Judea in the Period of the Second Temple,"
in Michael Avi-Yonah, ed., *The World History of the Jewish People*, vol. 7, *The Herodian
Period* (New Brunswick, N.J.: Rutgers University Press,), 198.

(jugglers, storytellers, and other carnival types), and places to gather and share the gossip or news of the day. The market town was one place where ideas and news could be communicated, something like the mass-media center of the first century. It also afforded a wandering rabbi like Jesus an opportunity to tell parables or debate the meaning of Torah in honor challenges.

If the Gospel materials are accurate on this matter, it is clear that Jesus avoided the two major cities in Galilee, Sepphoris and Tiberius, and concentrated his work in the countryside where the great bulk of the population lived. Peasants constitute about 70–80 percent of the population, living in rural habitats along with the rural artisans who shared village life with them. Sean Freyne contends that the geography of Galilee favors the isolation of hamlets and villages from the influence of major urban centers.

This means that geographically the interior of Galilee was particularly suited to a peasant style of life with people living together in close ties of kinship in relatively small and isolated settlements.[41] Most peasants would travel as far as the nearest market town during their lifetime but not much farther away from home, unless they were conscripted to serve in the military, usually as auxiliary troops, or in the case of Galileans loyal to the temple, went on pilgrimage to Jerusalem.

Ruling elites tended to leave peasant villages alone as long as they paid their tribute, taxes, and rents. Villages were ruled by village elders who handled matters according to local customs and local forms of the little tradition that guided and governed rural life. The villages of Galilee provided places where the "little tradition" of Israel's past was nurtured in part because the history of Galilee conspired with its geography to produce an environment hospitable to the development of a little tradition. Horsley emphasizes this point:

> [T]he Galileans lived directly under foreign imperial administrators without a native (priestly) aristocracy. . . . Their own popular Israelite tradition, moreover, may have been all the more self-consciously cultivated as a way of maintaining their own identity over against the foreign culture of the imperial administrators.[42]

The "great tradition" that emanated from Jerusalem was focused on the Torah as interpreted by the oral Torah of the Pharisees or the readings of other groups like the Sadducees and Essenes. Their great traditions offered readings of the Torah in the service of the priestly and ruling elites, as its emphases on purity and tithing suggest. In the villages, peasants kept alive the prophetic traditions associated with Elijah and Elisha and nurtured their own cultural traditions as

41. Freyne, *Galilee*, 16.
42. Horsley, *Galilee*, 148–49.

best they could. Horsley is confident that it is highly likely, from what we know of agrarian societies under foreign rulers, that Israelite traditions continued to be cultivated independently in the popular oral traditions of Galilee.[43]

Rulers usually attempt to impose their great tradition on the villages they control, but the little tradition is remarkably resilient, able to absorb the great tradition of the rulers and adapt it to more local purposes. This study will suggest that Jesus articulated a reading of the Torah congruent with the little tradition of the villages and hamlets of Galilee, whose inhabitants supported his vision and work.[44]

Adapting Richard Fox's "urban anthropology," Freyne has suggested that cities in first-century Palestine served one of two functions, either an "orthogenetic function" of "codifying, conserving and constructing society's traditions" or a "heterogenetic function" as centers of "technical, economic and cultural change."[45] In the time of Jesus, Jerusalem served an "orthogenetic function" as the repository of the temple and the Torah. It is reputed that the scroll of the Torah from which all other copies were made was located in the temple, although this claim may reflect an ideal masking the varieties of versions of the Torah that were then extant. Clearly, Jerusalem was the place where the meaning of the Torah was debated by the Pharisees and other political factions. It is also quite possible that Torah, at this time, was itself a fluid concept, not yet a clearly delimited authoritative collection of writings but something more like a proto-Torah, a Torah in the making. Even though the oral Torah provided for an innovative updating of the text, it was presented as simply making explicit what was already contained within the Torah. The four major pilgrimage festivals preserved the great traditions by rehearsing them through ritual and liturgy. One of the purposes of pilgrimage was to bring Judeans and Galileans from the margins to the center of power where they could renew their ties to the temple and its sacrificial system.

By contrast, in Galilee the cities of Sepphoris and Tiberius served a heterogenetic function. In these cities, so Freyne has argued, "a new kind of Galilean Jew"[46] would emerge, a person who was both a Judean and a partic-

43. Horsley, *Galilee*, 33.

44. For a description of the great and little traditions and how they operate, see James C. Scott, "Protest and Profanation: Agrarian Revolt and the Little Tradition," *Theory and Society* 2 (1977): 1–38, 211–46.

45. Richard Fox, *Urban Anthropology: Cities in their Cultural Setting* (Englewood Cliffs, N.J.: Prentice-Hall, 1977), 10–11. See also Sean Freyne, "Urban-Rural Relations in First-Century Galilee: Some Suggestions from the Literary Sources," in Lee I. Levine, ed., *The Galilee in Late Antiquity* (New York: Jewish Theological Seminary of America, 1992), 75–91.

46. See Freyne, *Galilee*, 71.

ipant in the Hellenistic world, a figure who "differed both from the older priestly aristocracy and the peasant people alike."[47] Antipas himself attempted to model this new role. He constructed the city of Tiberius over the site of a graveyard in violation of the Torah, and when he built his palace, he filled it with images of animals in violation of the aniconic provisions of the Torah. He organized Tiberius on the model of the Greek *polis* with its magistrates (*archōn*), ten leading men (*prōtoi*), council of citizens (*boulē*), and popular assembly (*dēmos*).[48] The events leading up to the first Jewish revolt reveal the political orientation of both cities. The aristocracy of Sepphoris pursued a clear pro-Roman policy, a decision that generated suspicion and hostility among the villagers of Galilee. Freyne even speaks of the hatred of the Galileans toward Sepphoris and Tiberius and their hope to destroy them.[49]

Beyond their orthogenetic or heterogenetic functions, cities can also be classified by their social, political, and religious roles. Of the many roles that Fox surveys in his work, two apply to first-century Jerusalem, which could be seen as both a "regal-ritual" center and an "administrative city."[50] The primary function of a regal-ritual city is to produce an "image of an ordered state"[51] that reinforces the symbolic world of its subjects. Such a city is a "theater state" in which the "ideology, core values and symbols"[52] of the ruling class are replicated and disseminated to the whole population. In the first century, Jerusalem's role as a regal-ritual city was fundamentally compromised by its subjection to Roman rulers. To the degree that the high priestly elites in Jerusalem used the festivals to reinforce the symbolic world of Judeans by celebrating the liberation from bondage in Egypt and by remembering the God who led the people to freedom in the land of promise, they alienated Jerusalem from its Roman rulers. The prefect of Judea wanted Jerusalem to project an "image of an ordered state" in line with Roman rule and policies. The conflict between these two agendas was irreconcilable. The political theater of the festivals could not be held on the same stage as the political theater of Roman occupation and colonial rule. This may explain why the pilgrimage festivals were often seed beds of discontent.

Its role as an administrative city was no less riddled with conflict. The high priestly families and their aristocratic supporters, including no doubt some Sadducees as well as elders, demanded tithes to support the temple and the

---

47. Ibid., 133.
48. See Josephus, *Life*, 271, 278, 294; *War*, 2.618, 639, 641.
49. See Freyne, *Galilee*, 122–34.
50. Fox, *Urban Anthropology*, chaps. 3, 4.
51. Ibid., 53, see 41–54.
52. Ibid.

holy city. The Torah contains basically three key references to tithes. The oldest reference (Deut. 14:22–29 [D]) refers to the yield of grain, wine, and oil. The tithe is to be brought to a central sanctuary and shared as a sacred meal with the priests and used to support the Levites who had no land. In the third and sixth years, the tithe is to be stored in towns to support the Levites as well as resident aliens, orphans, and widows. Those who live too far away from a central sanctuary are permitted to convert their harvest into money and spend the money at the site of a central sanctuary. The priestly materials (Num. 18:21–32; Lev. 27:30–33 [P]) emphasize the support of the Levites, who, in turn, provide a tithe of their support to the priests. It is quite likely that these three passages provide different descriptions of the same system, but when the Torah was edited during the exile, its priestly tradents determined that the Torah required double tithes, not just one. The first tithe (P materials) was given to support the Levites and priests who staffed the temple in Jerusalem, and the Deuteronomic materials (D) required that a second tithe be spent in Jerusalem. When combined with the other offerings required by the Torah, the temple demanded tithes and offerings adding up to about 23 percent of a peasant's harvest.

This demand came on top of the tribute collected by Herod Antipas to underwrite his rule in Galilee and to cover the tribute demanded by Rome. When these demands were added together, they placed every peasant household, already existing at a subsistence level, in the 20 to 35 percent tribute bracket, possibly even higher. The demand was literally unbearable. Peasants could not survive if they paid all of their tribute, tithes, offerings, and rents. They were unable to avoid Roman and Herodian tribute, since it was collected by force, but they could avoid paying their tithes to the temple, since the temple was reduced to using persuasion, not coercion, to collect its tithes and offerings. Galilean peasants were loyal to the temple in Jerusalem as indicated by the numerous references in ancient sources to Galileans making pilgrimage to Jerusalem. But they could not pay what they did not have, so they may have paid their offerings but could not pay their tithes. The result was predictable. The temple authorities vilified the peasants and condemned them for not supporting the temple.

From the point of view of the high priests and other temple authorities, the peasants of Galilee were unclean and indebted. They interpreted peasant noncompliance as an expression of rebellion against the temple rather than an action dictated by survival needs. For these reasons the issue of debt and forgiveness of debt will figure in Jesus' public activity. At this point, it is enough to note that considerable tension existed between Jerusalem and Galilee, especially between the temple authorities and the peasants of Galilee, but unlike the Essenes at Qumran who judged the priests illegitimate and their sacrifices invalid, the peasants' concern was located elsewhere, in the burden of tribute to which they were subjected.

All of this means that the relationship between Galilee and Jerusalem, in its role as an administrative city (on behalf of the temple), was contentious and predatory in a manner typical of cities in agrarian societies. There is, however, debate about the relationship between the cities of Galilee and their surrounding villages. Some scholars believe that a mutually beneficial relationship existed between city and village. This fairly recent proposal seemed to be supported by the discovery that pottery made at Kefer Hananiah was evidently sold throughout Lower Galilee, Upper Galilee, and the Golan. The determination that the pottery found at so many diverse sites came from a single village was made based on the analysis of the composition of the clay in the area around the village. This fact convinced Douglas Edwards and David Adan-Bayewitz that the small village served as a center of pottery production and distribution. Edwards went so far as to conclude that "a reciprocal market relationship between city and village existed even on the boundaries of the cities since Kefer Hananiah lies on the perimeter of several urban areas."[53] While it is impressive to learn that one small village supplied pottery to large portions of Galilee, it is stretching the evidence to the breaking point to suggest that this fact witnesses to the presence of a capitalistic market economy in first-century Galilee. For several reasons, this conclusion goes beyond the evidence. First, peasants usually turn to trades and handicrafts to augment their resources only when they are finding it difficult to survive on the basis of their agricultural production alone, not because they are driven by entrepreneurial motives and ambitions. As James C. Scott has observed, peasants turn to "secondary subsistence resources . . . trades such as basketry, pottery, and weaving for local markets" as a source of "subsistence insurance,"[54] often brought on by the presence of colonial occupation or a monetizing economy, both of which conditions were operative in Galilee. So the presence of pottery making does not suggest an entrepreneurial enterprise so much as it suggests that peasants were reverting to secondary subsistence activities, perhaps because of the pressures for greater tribute introduced by Roman overlords and reinforced by their Herodian client rulers. Second, when peasants do develop a promising resource, it is usually appropriated by elites who garner its profits for themselves. Garnsey and Saller, for instance, mention in passing the takeover of the Italian pottery industry and its exploitation of laborers for increased profit.[55] But the issue is not the likely fate of a particular local craft project; it was the orientation of the Roman

---

53. Douglas Edwards, "First-century Urban/Rural Relations in Lower Galilee: Exploring the Archaeological and Literary Evidence," *SBLSP* (1988): 174.

54. Scott, *The Moral Economy of the Peasant*, 61–62.

55. Peter Garnsey and Richard Saller, *The Roman Empire: Economy, Society and Culture* (London: Duckworth, 1987), 52.

Empire as a whole. To use Garnsey's and Saller's characterization, "this was exploitation, and in the aggregate exceeded anything witnessed previously in the Mediterranean world."[56] Within this larger pattern of exploitation, cities played a crucial role, a "fundamentally exploitive role" as the tribute collector. As A. H. M. Jones noted in his study of cities in the Eastern Empire,

> The new cities served no useful economic function, for the larger vil-
> lages supplied such manufactured goods as the villagers required, and
> the trade of the countryside was conducted at village markets. The
> only effect of the foundation of cities was the creation of a wealthy
> landlord class which gradually stamped out peasant proprietorship.[57]

No peasant village within the shadow of Sepphoris and Tiberius would be allowed to develop a lucrative cottage industry producing pottery and selling it throughout Galilee.

Yet Edwards and Adan-Bayewitz imagine that the city offered numerous benefits to its surrounding villages that represented "a sophisticated market that addressed a large buying public" seeking consumer goods to meet their needs and desires, something like an ancient mall. Keith Hopkins lists a variety of goods and services that he imagines would be available to peasants fortunate enough to live near a Galilean city, such as "law, protection, peace, rituals, ceremonies and medical advice, even surgery. Towns gave independent peasants and free tenants opportunity to buy extra food and services, necessities and luxuries (tools, pots, clothes, seeds and pastries)."[58]

To peasants living at the edge of destitution, or at the very best, just above subsistence, the list of goods and services is irrelevant. In the economies of the first century, there were no markets of peasant consumers.[59] The only market was provided by the elite class since they were the only class with what we would call "discretionary income." Peasants would have no resources to purchase either necessities or luxuries. In spite of all this, Edwards insists that the city

56. Ibid., 56.

57. A. H. M. Jones, *Cities of the Eastern Roman Provinces*, 2nd ed. (Oxford: Oxford University Press, 1971, original ed., 1937), 294.

58. Keith Hopkins, "Economic Growth and Towns in Classical Antiquity" in Philip Abrams and E. A. Wrigley, eds., *Towns in Societies: Essays in Economic History and Historical Sociology* (Cambridge: Cambridge University Press, 1975), 75.

59. Since so much depends on the nature of the first-century economy, see the following works for a fuller description. The classic description is found in Karl Polanyi, Conrad Arensberg, Harry Pearson, eds., *Trade and Market in the Early Empires: Economies in History and Theory* (Glencoe, Ill.: Free Press, 1957). For a brief overview of the issues, see Douglas Oakman, "The Ancient Economy in the Bible," *BTB* 21 (1991): 34–39. See also M. I. Finley, *The Ancient Economy*, 2nd ed. (London: Hogarth, 1985). See also Stegemann and Stegemann, *The Jesus Movement*, 15–52.

was in an administrative, not exploitive, relationship with its peasant villages that included keeping legal documents and records, collecting taxes, and offering a judicial system for adjudicating disputes. He does admit to having a more difficult time delineating the role of the villages in this mutually beneficial exchange. As he confesses, "the exact nature of the village's participation remains clouded."[60] The difficulty with this argument is that it makes a distinction without a difference. An administrative relationship between city and village is an exploitive relationship as his own examples testify. What he euphemistically calls "legal records" are most likely to be debt records, and collecting taxes and tribute only reinforces the power of the rulers over their peasant villagers. How could this function possibly be seen as mutually beneficial when taking tribute reduces the peasantry to abject poverty? The law courts would serve the interests of elites who formulated the very laws and decrees that it would be adjudicating. How could this possibly work for the benefit of peasant villagers?

Jesus' advice to reconcile with a brother or sister rather than to resort to legal action reflects the peasants' distrust of law courts (Matt. 5:23–26; cf. 1 Cor. 6:1–11). The introduction of the *prozbul* suggests why law works in the interests of the rulers rather than the poor. The Torah included sabbatical and jubilee provisions designed to break the cycle of poverty and the accumulation of land in the hands of a ruling class (Lev. 25; Deut. 15:1–18). This meant that debts would be canceled each sabbatical year, a provision that affected peasants' ability to secure loans to plant their crops. The rulers simply refused to issue loans to peasants that they knew would never be repaid. To address this dilemma, Hillel "ordained the prozbul on account of the order of the world."

> That he saw people, that they held back from lending to one another and transgressed what is written in the Torah.
>> He arose and ordained the prozbul.
>> And this is the formula of the prozbul: "I give to you, so-and-so and so-and-so, the judges in such-and-such place, every debt which I have, that I may collect it whenever I like," and the judges seal below, or the witnesses.[61]

The economic interests of the elite determined the course of events leading up to the formulation of the prozbul. This is exactly the situation anticipated and condemned in Deut. 15:9–10.

> Be careful that you do not entertain a mean thought, thinking, "The seventh year, the year of remission, is near," and therefore view your

---

60. Edwards, "First Century Urban/Rural Relations," 178–79.
61. Cited in Jacob Neusner, *The Rabbinic Traditions about the Pharisees before 70*, part 1, *The Masters* (Leiden: E. J. Brill, 1971), 217–20.

needy neighbor with hostility and give nothing; your neighbor might
cry to the LORD against you, and you would incur guilt.

For peasants, the introduction of the prozbul meant that debt would be perpetual, and the elites were free to press the use of debt instruments to alienate
peasants from their land. Appelbaum recognizes that "such a grave modifica-
tion of a fundamental Jewish principle must have been the result of a situation
in which the pressure for loans was extreme."[62] Well intentioned though it may
have been, the use of the prozbul served the interests of the ruling class at
the expense of peasant villagers and showcases the way the court system (in
this case, not the Roman law courts but the Torah courts) could be coopted to
serve the interests of the rulers. In spite of its seemingly neutral language, the
prozbul violates the justice provisions of the Torah. To the argument that the
city offers protection to the peasant villages they control, it could be countered
that the urban elites are the very predators from whom the villagers need protection! To expect urban aristocrats to protect peasant villagers is like asking
foxes to guard the chicken coop, as the brief history of the prozbul indicates.

The reason that the role of the village remains "clouded" is that the activity of the village is shrouded in its hidden transcripts and facade of compliance
with oppressive rulers. It is all a part of what James C. Scott calls "domination
and the arts of resistance," or "the weapons of the weak."[63] This is why peasants generally tended to avoid cities and turn their villages or market areas into
self-sufficient enclaves. We will return to these themes later in this study (see
chapters 6 and 8).

Perhaps the most basic flaw in the position advocated by Edwards and others is that it confuses the means of production with the relations of production. Archaeologists have made a convincing case that the village of Kefer
Hananiah made pottery that was widely distributed through Lower Galilee
and the Golan, perhaps Upper Galilee as well. But who controlled the production and who benefitted from the production of pottery? Given the usual
relationships between elites and peasants in advanced agrarian societies, it is
most likely that the peasants developed the craft and then were subjected to a
hostile takeover when their pottery business proved profitable. The villagers
would not have realized many benefits from their labor, any more than they
realized profits from their toil in their fields and orchards. The great bulk of

---

62. Shimon Applebaum, "Judaea as a Roman Province: The Countryside as a Political and Economic Factor," *ANRW* 2, no. 8 (1977): 370.

63. For a discussion of hidden transcripts see James C. Scott, *Domination and the
Arts of Resistance: Hidden Transcripts* (New Haven, Conn.: Yale University Press, 1990),
and *Weapons of the Weak: Everyday Forms of Peasant Resistance* (New Haven, Conn.: Yale
University Press, 1985). See also chapters 6 and 8 of this study.

what they produced was expropriated by their rulers, whether the produce of their fields or the products of their kilns. It is more likely that the peasants of Kefer Hananiah initially turned to pottery making because their agricultural subsistence was threatened, perhaps because Rome was increasing its demands for tribute or continued to monetize the economy. When their craft project succeeded, the Herodians and Romans were on the scene to exploit the new development. They mobilized the peasants and turned the craft venture into a small industry. This scenario is far more likely and less anachronistic than the capitalist, entrepreneurial model championed by Edwards. It also accords with the patterns observed by James C. Scott in his study of "the moral economy of the peasant."

Martin Millett has warned that what we call archaeological evidence is nothing more than "the accidental by product of human activity" so that "the information it communicates is latent, passive and static." This means that it must be "articulated through interpretive models imposed by the observer, whether or not these are made explicit."[64] The danger when these implicit models are not made explicit is that they will assume the guise of unbiased and objective description while they actually "echo our contemporary views of the world."[65] Garnsey and Saller would add that "archaeology cannot uncover 'economic structure' or the 'social mode of production'" even though its results are enlisted to support anachronistic frames of refrence.[66] This seems to be the situation with Edwards's study. He has imported a capitalistic view of a market economy and retrojected it onto first-century Galilee.[67] The picture of an active market economy squares neither with the way the Roman Empire functioned nor the way advanced agrarian societies work. It is hard for us to imagine how much power the rulers had over the ruled, and how little the peasant villagers could do about it. The power relations were asymmetrical in the extreme.

SUMMARY

Jesus conducted his public work in what we now call an advanced agrarian society and would have been familiar with its social, political, and economic dynamics. He was born in a village (whether Bethlehem or Nazareth is uncertain), and

64. Martin Millett, "Roman Towns and Their Territories: An Archaeological Perspective," in John Rich and Andrew Wallace-Hadrill, eds., *City and Country in the Ancient World* (London: Routledge, 1991), 169.

65. Ibid.

66. Garnsey and Saller, *The Roman Empire*, 46.

67. For an introductory discussion of the ancient economy, see Douglas Oakman, "The Ancient Economy in the Bible," *BTB* 21 (1991): 34–39.

he was raised in Galilean village life where his father Joseph was a *tektōn*, sometimes translated as carpenter. I prefer to translate the term as "handyman." He was skilled at fixing things and making some of the rudimentary tools required for peasant life. There in Nazareth, at the village assemblies (synagogue as a gathering) Jesus learned the northern Israelite traditions and became familiar with some versions of the little tradition on which the peasant villagers relied for guidance and wisdom as well as a source of inspiration for resistance to Herodian client kingship and Roman colonial rule.[68] It is very likely that he learned to read and argue Torah in the local synagogue gathering. This was important, for it would enable Jesus to develop his own prophetic voice yet remain rooted in the common ethos and corporate experience of his people. As John Meier notes, "For all the differences among various groups of Jews, the narratives, laws and prophecies of their sacred texts gave them a corporate memory and a common ethos."[69] When Jesus appeared on the public stage, he was already able to debate Torah, the most basic skill needed to become a public figure. Parables like the friend at midnight (Luke 11:5–8) reveal a knowledge of peasant life and customs, while parables like the unforgiving servant (Matt. 18:23–35) and the talents (Matt. 25:14–30) convey us into the world of bureaucrats and retainers.[70] It is clear from his teaching and parables that Jesus was familiar with advanced agrarian societies.

It is also true that Jesus showed relatively little interest in Rome but focused his attention on internal elites like Herod and the Herodians or the high priests. Even then, Jesus interacted with their proxies and retainers like the Pharisees or their scribes, rather than confronting the elites directly. One possible reason that Jesus focused on internal elites and virtually ignored the Roman colonial presence was the fact that Jewish leaders were honor bound to follow the Torah, and prophets from Amos to Jeremiah had used the appeal to Torah as leverage to launch their prophetic critiques of abusive ruling elites and institutions like the temple. Rome had no counterpart to the Torah, at least not one that would resonate in Galilee and Judea.[71]

---

68. For a fuller discussion, see Horsley, *Jesus and the Spiral of Violence*, chaps. 6–9.

69. John Meier, *A Marginal Jew: Rethinking the Historical Jesus*, vol. 1, *The Roots of the Problem and the Person* (New York: Doubleday, 1991). Meier's volume contains an extensive discussion of the issues related to Jesus' birth and roots.

70. A fuller discussion of these parables can be found in William R. Herzog II, *Parables as Subversive Speech: Jesus as Pedagogue of the Oppressed* (Louisville, Ky.: Westminster John Knox Press, 1994), chaps. 8, 9, 11.

71. For a summary of Roman imperial ideology, see Warren Carter, *Matthew and Empire: Initial Explorations* (Harrisburg, Pa.: Trinity Press International, 2001), chaps. 1, 2.

This chapter has sketched what it meant to live in an advanced agrarian society struggling with Roman colonial occupation. It will be helpful to keep this world in mind as this study progresses because it proposes that Jesus was a contextual theologian who understood his setting. The next chapters will test this hypothesis.

4

"And he taught in their synagogues being honored by all."

(Luke 4:15)

How did Jesus become a public figure in Galilee? What means did he use to get the attention of the people who eventually gathered around him in large crowds or followed him in small bands? How did he emerge from the obscurity of a backwater village to gain public recognition as a traditional healer, an exorcist, a teacher, a reputational leader, a broker of God's covenant, and a prophet? What social systems and institutions did he use, and how did they serve his purposes? What was his message, and why was it called "good news"? These are some of the questions that we will address in a preliminary way in this chapter. Before we can answer them, we need to examine the traditional picture of Jesus in Galilee and explain why it may not be as reliable as we once believed.

THE TRADITIONAL SCENARIO

At first glance, the Gospels seem to provide a straightforward account of the beginnings of Jesus' public activity. Jesus entered the synagogues of Galilee and argued Torah with the Pharisees who opposed him (Luke 6:7). This opposition is often characterized as a conflict between Judaism, represented by the Pharisees, and Christianity, represented by Jesus, even though this is clearly an anachronistic reading of the texts. The Gospel writers do say that Jesus "taught in their synagogues" (Luke 4:15; Matt. 13:54), "went to the synagogue as was his custom" (Luke 4:16), healed in the synagogue and argued with the "ruler of the synagogue" (Luke 13:10–17), and even exorcized in the synagogue (Mark 1:23–28). The Gospels also record the presence of scribes (presumably scribal Pharisees) and Pharisees who pursue Jesus to argue with him in the synagogues, houses, towns, and fields of Galilee (see, for example, Mark

2:1–12; 2:13–17; 3:22–27; Matt. 12:1–8; 12:9–14). The "scribes who came down from Jerusalem" (Mark 3:22) accuse Jesus of being in collusion with Beelzebul (Mark 3:19b–30), and Jesus accuses the Pharisees of being "hypocrites" and worse (Mark 7:1–16; Matt. 23:1–36). The overall picture is one of conflict, argument, and, at times, heated debate.

THREE PROBLEMS

1. Synagogues, Houses, and Village Squares

There are three immediate problems with this scenario. The first is that, to date, archaeologists have not found a single synagogue in Galilee that dates to the first century. The well-known synagogue at Capernahum, for example, is a good deal later (second to fourth century, perhaps later), and the identification of assembly hall structures with synagogues in places like Masada and the Herodium remains in doubt. The same holds true for the supposition that there was a synagogue on the temple mount. All of this means that, according to the current state of research, there is no evidence to indicate that Jesus ever saw a synagogue building in Galilee.[1] This suggests that when the Gospel writers speak of a synagogue, they are quite likely referring to a meeting rather than a meeting place, a gathered community rather than a building (the sole exception in the Gospels seems to be Luke 7:5).

But where would such meetings take place? Even a community has to find some place to gather. There are at least two possibilities. The first is that *synagōgē* referred to a house in which the community met. In this case, the house would not have been devoted exclusively to synagogue meetings but would have served as a residence for a family in the synagogue, perhaps in some cases, the figure called the "ruler of the synagogue." If this were the case, the house church may have grown out of the model of the house synagogue. Howard Kee summarizes the current state of affairs when he concludes,

> What seems most plausible, therefore, is the conclusion indicated by
> a convergence of archaeological and literary studies of both Jewish and
> Christian materials: Jews and Christians in the Galilee in the pre-70

1. For a fuller discussion of these matters, see Lee I. Levine, ed., *The Galilee in Late Antiquity* (New York: Jewish Theological Seminary of America, 1992). In particular, see the essays by Howard Clark Kee, "Early Christianity in Galilee"; Lee I. Levine, "The Sage and the Synagogue in Late Antiquity: The Evidence of the Galilee"; and Gideon Foerster, "The Ancient Synagogues of the Galilee." See also Joseph Gutman, ed., *The Synagogue: Studies in Origins, Archaeology and Architecture* (New York: Jewish Theological Seminary of America, 1975).

period met in homes or small public halls for study of Scriptures, worship and instruction.[2]

This would suggest that in the Gospels the scenes set in houses may not be as different from the scenes set in synagogues as previously believed. The two settings may be, in some situations, more closely related than we realized. For example, Luke depicts a scene in which Simon the Pharisee invites Jesus to recline at table with him (7:36–50). If, as Kenneth Bailey has proposed, the meal in the house of a Pharisee was a public occasion in which the villagers were invited to attend and listen to the conversation around the table even if they were not invited to recline at table, then it is possible that Simon's house is also the village synagogue.[3] This would explain, in part, the public character of the meal and the debates that follow. It is an informal synagogue session, not just a private meal in a private home. The problem with this reading is that archaeologists have not been able to document the transformation of private space into public space before the mid to late second century. However, the reading proposed here does not assume the transformation of private into public space but the use of space simultaneously for domestic (family) and public (synagogue) activity.

The second option is that synagogue referred to a village gathering in a public square or at the village gate, a position developed in detail by S. B. Honig.[4] Most likely, peasant villages in Galilee were governed by a council of elders who held court, so to speak, twice a week to adjudicate disputes and deal with other community issues. If these were either synagogue gatherings or the precursors of such meetings, then the meetings of the synagogue could well have grown out of public gatherings that dealt with the social and political matters of daily life. It is possible that these public gatherings were correlated with market days (most likely on Mondays and Thursdays). As the study of Torah and prayer came to prominence in these gatherings, they may have been either moved to sabbath days or expanded to include sabbath days. Given the nature of ancient life, politics and religion were not viewed as separate and independent domains of life but were part of a larger whole, so the proposal is not far-fetched. Honig suggests that the marketplace (or *agora*) might have served as the place where these gatherings occurred. In smaller villages and towns, the group would meet

2. Kee, "Early Christianity in Galilee," 12.

3. Kenneth E. Bailey, *Through Peasant Eyes: More Lucan Parables, Their Culture and Style* (Grand Rapids: Wm. B. Eerdmans Publishing Co., 1980), 1–21. Bailey does not consider the scene as set in a synagogue house but in the house of a prominent Pharisee in a village of Galilee.

4. S. B. Honig, "The Ancient City-Square: The Forerunner of the Synagogue," in *ANRW* 2.19.1 (1979): 448–76.

at the village gate or some comparable space, perhaps in a courtyard. In either setting, the people would read the sections of Torah being read in the temple so that "the city square was the locale parallel to the temple service."[5] Smaller villages without an *agora* might gather less often, perhaps only on sabbath, to conduct village business and study Torah. Richard Horsley is convinced that the origin of the synagogue lies in these village assemblies.[6]

By the first century, the household, the village, and the market area were the primary forms of social life, and the village assemblies may have become the primary means for maintaining social cohesion and relieving the stresses and strains caused by the increasing exploitation of Galilean villagers. Yet even under the colonial rule of Rome and Herodian oversight, local villages were usually left to their own devices as long as they paid their tribute, taxes, and rents and met their other obligations in a timely manner. So these assemblies may have provided a place for peasants to maintain what little autonomy they had left and to nurture their forms of the "little tradition." This would include not only hearing the Torah read aloud in the assembly but listening either to a local rabbi or an itinerant teacher comment on it. Perhaps the villagers discussed the Scripture among themselves, much as the peasants in the fishing village of Solentiname on Lake Nicaragua reflected on the Gospel lectionary readings with their priest, Ernesto Cardenal, during the waning years of the Somoza regime.[7] The Gospels portray Jesus speaking to such gatherings (Mark 1:21–28; 6:1–6a; Matt. 12:9–14; Luke 4:16–30), and it is certainly possible that he taught on such occasions. Insofar as the synagogue gatherings (village assemblies) were one of the important means of maintaining local forms of the "little tradition" and the Israelite traditions of the villagers, they became focal points for encouraging resistance through the use of what James C. Scott calls "the weapons of the weak."[8]

2. Pharisees in Galilee?

At the same time, village assemblies were also centers of conflict as the stories of healing on the sabbath indicate. This leads to a second problem with the traditional scenario. In the Gospels, the Pharisees appear more often than not

5. Honig, "The Ancient City-Square," 468.

6. See Richard A. Horsley, *Galilee: History, Politics, People* (Valley Forge, Pa.: Trinity Press International, 1995), 227–30.

7. For a verbatim of the peasants' reflections on the Gospel lection, see Ernesto Cardenal, ed., *The Gospel in Solentiname*, 5 vols. (Maryknoll, N.Y.: Orbis Books, 1982). Solentiname is a fishing village on Lake Nicaragua. The verbatims were recorded during the dark days of the Somoza regime.

8. For a fuller account, see James C. Scott, *Weapons of the Weak: Everyday Forms of Peasant Resistance* (New Haven, Conn.: Yale University Press, 1985).

as Jesus' adversaries, yet their very presence in Galilee poses a problem that needs to be addressed. According to the Jewish historian Josephus, the Pharisees were located primarily in Jerusalem, while the Gospels portray the Pharisees as active in Galilee. It is true that Josephus depicts Pharisees being sent from Jerusalem to Galilee to implement decisions made in Jerusalem, as when, during the early stages of the First Jewish Revolt, they form part of a deputation sent to Galilee to depose Josephus from his position of military leadership.[9] But this mission may be nothing more than the exception that proves the rule. This discrepancy between Josephus and the Gospels has led Horsley to conclude that the Pharisees were not in Galilee at all. He believes that the

> governance and cohesion of village and town communities were provided by local assemblies (and courts) operating more or less democratically with certain officials such as the *archisynagōgēs* (ruler of the synagogue) and *hyperētēs* (attendant) mentioned in the synoptic Gospel tradition responsible for supervising communal finances, aid to the poor, public works and religious matters.[10]

In spite of the fact that both Honig and Horsley trace the origin of the synagogue to public gatherings or village assemblies, they disagree on whether Pharisees were present in Galilee. Honig thinks they were; Horsley does not.

Who then were the Pharisees and why might they have been either present or absent from Galilee? Jacob Neusner[11] has proposed that the Pharisees were, by the first century, a table companionship group dedicated to maintaining their own strict reading of the Torah, which required "keeping everywhere the laws of ritual purity that normally apply only in the Jerusalem temple."[12] This meant that Pharisees and their households attempted to eat every meal in a state of ritual purity equal to that of the priests in the temple. Every Pharisee needed to be as holy and ritually clean as the priests in the temple, so "the Temple altar in Jerusalem would be replicated at the tables of all Israel."[13] It was a way of fulfilling the promise in Exod. 19:6, "You shall be to me a kingdom of priests and a holy nation." The tables of Galilee and Judea became the battlefields where Jesus and the Pharisees argued the meaning of Torah. In this environment, it is easy to see why Jesus' table companionship with toll collectors and sinners was so offensive (Mark 2:15–17 and pars.; see chap. 9 for a fuller discussion).

9. See Josephus, *Life*, 195–98.
10. Horsley, *Galilee*, 232.
11. Jacob Neusner, *From Politics to Piety: The Emergence of Pharisaic Judaism*, 2nd ed. (New York: KTAV, 1979).
12. Ibid., 67.
13. Ibid., 146.

But the Pharisees were more than a table companionship group; they were a political faction as well. Although Neusner believes that by the first century, the Pharisees had retreated from active political involvement in the life of Judea and Galilee, Anthony Saldarini is convinced that they remained an active political interest group seeking to ally themselves with powerful patrons through whose influence they could promote their agenda for all Israel.[14] Their political influence would wax or wane depending on their connections with powerful members of the ruling class who were willing to forward their agenda and the fortunes of those sponsors. If we take Neusner's view of the Pharisees, they resemble an "introversionist sect" (to use Bryan Wilson's typology of sect types),[15] whereas they look more like a "reformist sect" when seen through Saldarini's eyes, although it should be added that the Pharisees do not resemble a sect in important ways and may not be best described as a sect. The Pharisees were devoted to promoting a political agenda based on the purity codes of the Torah in order to transform all Israel into a holy people as ritually pure as the priestly caste performing sacred duties in the temple in Jerusalem.

Neusner believes that the three issues over which Jesus and the Pharisees came into conflict, namely, "sabbath observance, ritual purity and tithing," were the right issues, but this still leaves unanswered the question whether the Pharisees clashed with Jesus in Galilee. It is clear that the Pharisees would need to be based in Jerusalem in order to develop and maintain advantageous contacts with powerful political patrons. Josephus appears to be correct in placing the Pharisees in Jerusalem. Are there circumstances which might explain how they might also appear in Galilee? There are indeed such circumstances related to the relationship between the center and the periphery. The peasants of Galilee posed a problem for the temple in Jerusalem. The temple represented the center of Jewish life, and Galilee was on the periphery. Jerusalem was the center from which varied forms of the great tradition of the elites were promulgated through the work of their retainers. The great tradition, associated with the oral Torah of the Pharisees or what the Gospels call "the tradition of the elders," offered a "social construction of reality,"[16] an interpretation

---

14. See Anthony J. Saldarini, *Pharisees, Scribes and Sadducees in Palestinian Society* (Grand Rapids: Wm. B. Eerdmans Publishing Co., 2001, original, 1988).

15. See Bryan Wilson, *Magic and the Millennium: A Sociological Study of Religious Movements of Protest among Tribal and Third-World Peoples* (London: Heinemann, 1973), 16–26.

16. The phrase is taken from the title of a study by Peter Berger and Thomas Luckmann, *The Social Construction of Reality: A Treatise in the Sociology of Knowledge* (Garden City, N.Y.: Doubleday/Anchor Books, 1967). The phrase emphasizes that human society is a human construction.

of the world that justified and legitimated the existing political, social, and economic order. The Pharisaic faction in Jerusalem was in competition and conflict with other factions, such as the Sadducees and the Essenes, over who would control the meaning of the great tradition or whose version of the great tradition would be accepted as normative, a struggle that had considerable political and economic consequences. But there is a problem in the relationship between the center and the periphery. Normally, social control is greatest and most effective at the center while it tends to become weaker and less effective at the periphery. How then can the groups at the center impose their versions of the great tradition on the peasants at the periphery?

One way to maintain control is through the use of pilgrimage, which brings the folks from the periphery to the center, but an equally useful tactic is to encourage messengers to travel between the center and the periphery. This brings figures from the center to the periphery. These messengers serve as rule enforcers, interpreting the meaning of the great tradition and specifying its meaning for those at the edges of the social order, including not least of all the necessity for tithes and tribute. It is possible to view the Pharisees who appear in the Gospels as serving this role. This would explain their presence in Galilee even though they were, for political reasons, centered in Jerusalem while, at the same time, it would make sense of phrases like "the scribes who came down from Jerusalem" (Mark 3:22). Part of their program of control was to travel to areas peripheral to Jerusalem in order to enforce their reading of the Torah and to maintain their network of local sympathizers and synagogue leaders. In this role, the Pharisees were working as retainers of powerful ruling elites centered in the temple in Jerusalem, especially the high priestly houses and the lay aristocrats or "elders." Since one of the most important tasks of ruling elites is to transfer some version of their reading of the great tradition to the peasant villages and villagers, these travels served an important purpose.

As Paulo Freire noted long ago,[17] oppression works most efficiently when the oppressed have internalized the world as seen through the eyes of the oppressor. In this social cosmology, the oppressed see themselves as objects in their oppressor's world and, therefore, without power. This social construction comes to the oppressed, buttressed by forms of religious legitimization, as an unchangeable reality that explains the deprivation of the poor and the abundance of the rich. To use Freire's language, this view of the world needs to be "deposited" in the minds and souls of the oppressed for systems of domination

---

17. See Paulo Freire, *Pedagogy of the Oppressed*, trans. Myra Ramos (New York: Seabury, 1973, original, 1968). For an application of Freire to Jesus' public activity, see William R. Herzog II, *Parables as Subversive Speech: Jesus as Pedagogue of the Oppressed* (Louisville, Ky.: Westminster John Knox Press, 1994).

to work effectively. So the work of the Pharisees and their scribes fulfills an important function.

In turn, peasants would resist this act of domination because they know it does not serve their interests, and they will work all the harder to maintain their native forms of the "little tradition" through their synagogue gatherings and their interpretations of the Torah. Since peasants do not have enough power to resist openly the imposition of the great tradition, they must find ways to undermine and erode its influence, to achieve, in the apt phrase of James C. Scott, a "negotiated subordination." Of course, the stronger and more unitary the great tradition is, the more influence it will wield over peasant life. In the first century, three factors tended to weaken the power of the "great tradition" reading of Torah that came from Jerusalem. First, the temple in Jerusalem was under a political jurisdiction different from the peasants of Galilee, who were under the rule of Herod Antipas. While Antipas evidently allowed the temple to press its claims for tithes and offerings, he had to balance his own need to exploit his peasant base with the temple's demands for tithes. The conflict weakened the effectiveness of temple demands. Second, the internecine struggle between political factions like the Pharisees, Sadducees, Essenes, and high priests over the meaning and application of the Torah meant that Jerusalem would not speak with a single voice. Any such conflicts afforded the peasants some maneuvering room, perhaps even the opportunity to set contrasting positions against each other. Third, the Torah contained its own critique. The prophetic strands of the Torah provided a powerful witness to the justice of the reign of God (or the covenant community envisioned by God at Sinai) that did not fit comfortably with the patterns of exploitation and oppression so common in first-century Galilee. The Torah may have called for tithes and offerings, but it also called for a sabbatical and jubilee pattern of debt cancellation, redistribution of land, and freedom from debt servitude. How could one appeal to the Torah for support of tithes and ignore the call for justice found in the sabbatical-jubilee traditions?

If these factors, among others, had the effect of weakening the great tradition, there would be all the more reason for the Pharisees to send their moral entrepreneurs, rule creators, and rule enforcers to the periphery to strengthen the control of their readings of the Torah over the lives of the peasants whose behavior it purported to prescribe and proscribe.[18] In short, there were good

---

18. The language of moral entrepreneurs, rule enforcers, and so on comes from Erdwin H. Pfuhl Jr., *The Deviance Process* (New York: D. Van Nostrand Co., 1980). For an application of this perspective to Matthew's Jesus, see Bruce J. Malina and Jerome Neyrey, *Calling Jesus Names: The Social Value of Labels in Matthew* (Sonoma, Calif.: Polebridge Press, 1988).

reasons why the Pharisees would have been centered in Jerusalem but could still be present in Galilee. No doubt, the Pharisees had their local sympathizers in Galilee and collaborated with them. These figures may have included those who were attendants (*hyperetēs*) or rulers of the synagogue (*archisynagōgos*) although this must remain a matter of speculation.

3. Jesus and the Pharisees

The third problem is the anachronistic reading of Jesus' conflicts with the Pharisees as a religious quarrel in which Jesus is replacing the law (read Torah) with a Christian theology of grace and discipleship. It is possible to read many of the traditions in the Gospels through this lens. When this happens, interpreters assume that the Gospels are not disclosing the historical Jesus but the Jesus of the early church and that the texts reveal the theological disputes of the early church with the synagogue. This view of the Gospels appears to be one enduring legacy of form criticism. However, if the context sketched to this point has anything to commend it, it does indicate that it is possible to glimpse the historical Jesus in conflict with the Pharisees and their scribes over issues of importance to the peasants of Galilee and Judea. This means that materials previously dismissed as useless in the search for the historical Jesus may be more helpful than we have been willing to admit.

To summarize the ground covered so far, we have examined three problems that face any effort to construct or reconstruct the public life of the historical Jesus. We will suppose that, unless archaeological evidence changes the picture, there were no synagogue buildings in first-century Galilee. A "synagogue" referred to a meeting that most likely occurred either in a house or in the marketplace or village gate. The location may even have changed during inclement weather or at different times of the year. Although the Pharisees were centered in Jerusalem, they had reason enough to travel to Galilee to maintain their networks of agents and supporters. In this role, either they or their proxies could very well have entered into conflict with Jesus over the interpretation of the Torah. This means that Jesus' conflicts with the Pharisees are not to be understood as a Christian theologian (Jesus) fighting against a legalistic Judaism (Pharisees) but are better understood as arguments about the application of Torah for Galilean villagers and its implications for the meaning of a covenant community.

THE ART OF PUBLIC DEBATE

But how were such arguments conducted? Most societies have characteristic ways of disputing and arguing in public forums (for example, televised debates between candidates or radio talk shows), and first-century Palestine was no exception. One major cultural form used for conducting public disputes was "the honor challenge and riposte."[19] Palestine in the first century was an "agonistic" society (from the Greek *agon*, which means contest) in which social contests for acquiring honor were daily occurrences. Such a contest began with a public challenge through a provocative word or action. The person challenged had to decide whether to respond. Since honor challenges were conducted between parties who were more or less social equals, the person challenged could ignore the challenge, that is, reinforce the social distance between the challenger and himself by snubbing him. If the one challenged accepted the provocation, then he was bound to respond with a riposte. The original challenger then would respond, and the two would engage in debate until one of them emerged as a winner. These challenges were highly visible contests held in public, often crowded spaces, and the crowd usually decided who won and who lost. What was at stake? Honor primarily, but to gain honor is also to gain political leverage because the actions and words of an honorable man are treated with respect and carry weight. The greater one's honor, the more political power and social prestige one could accrue. These debates may quite possibly reveal a clash between the guardians of the great tradition and the defender of the little tradition. The purpose of these confrontations was to acquire honor by shaming one's opponents and discrediting the norms they represented as a step toward dislodging them, thereby gaining public recognition and political leverage. These challenges were viewed as zero sum games, so the winner prevailed at the expense of the loser.

Since Jesus was a rural artisan from a peasant family living in an undistinguished village (John 1:46, "Can anything good come out of Nazareth?"), he entered adulthood without a good deal of ascribed honor.[20] He was not related

---

19. For a fuller discussion of the honor/shame riposte (or challenge), see Bruce J. Malina, *The New Testament World: Insights from Cultural Anthropology*, 3rd ed. rev. and exp. (Louisville, Ky.: Westminster John Knox Press, 2001), 32–36; Bruce J. Malina and Richard L. Rohrbaugh, *Social-Science Commentary on the Synoptic Gospels* (Minneapolis: Fortress Press, 1992), 41–42; Bruce J. Malina and Jerome H. Neyrey, "Honor and Shame in Luke-Acts: Pivotal Values of the Mediterranean World," in Jerome H. Neyrey, ed., *The Social World of Luke-Acts: Models for Interpretation* (Peabody, Mass.: Hendrickson Publishers, 1991), 46–52. The form will be called by a number of names, the honor/shame riposte, the honor challenge and riposte, but all designations refer to the same basic social form.

20. I am assuming that the birth narratives in the Gospels of Matthew and Luke are later attempts to claim ascribed honor for Jesus. In the traditions surrounding Jesus' public ministry, he seems to deny royal Davidic lineage. See Mark 12:35–37a; Matt. 22:41–46; Luke 20:41–44. But the meaning of this passage has been debated, and some argue that Jesus is actually claiming Davidic lineage.

to kings, nor did he come from a priestly family, nor was he born into a noble household. The genealogies in Matthew and Luke may reflect the efforts of the early church to raise the honor level of Jesus by associating him with King David, or they may show that Jesus was profoundly related to the people of God known as Israel, but even these birth narratives depict Jesus as born into a peasant family. If Jesus were to achieve the status of an honorable man worthy of public recognition, that is, become a force to be reckoned with, it is most likely that he earned such recognition, at least initially, through his skill in public debate and through his reputation as a healer and exorcist, activities that he could have pursued in market towns when crowds were present. The peasants returning home would have something to talk about, and Jesus would gain ascribed honor and public notice. He acquired honor because the crowds in Galilee recognized him as a truthful interpreter of the Torah and a renewer of the covenantal community of Israel. Steeped in Galilean versions of the little tradition, or the Israelite traditions of Galilean villagers, he argued Torah with the representatives of the great tradition and challenged their interpretive hegemony as well as the prerogatives claimed by the temple. Jesus gained his public stature (he was called rabbi and prophet) one honor challenge at a time, one healing at a time, one exorcism at a time, and one parable at a time.

REPUTATIONAL OR CHARISMATIC FIGURE?

In this context, it is important to note the kind of public figure Jesus became. In spite of a good deal of discussion about Jesus as a charismatic leader,[21] it is unlikely that this adequately characterizes his type of leadership. Bruce Malina has argued that Jesus is an example of a "reputational" leader rather than a "charismatic" leader.[22] Charismatic leaders stand out from the people they lead as extraordinary figures, whereas reputational leaders gain the support of their followers because they embody the values of the group they are leading. More to the point, reputational leaders are able to question and even dislodge important norms and values that are shared by the larger society. As Malina says,

> This authority derives from the successful criticism and dislocation of the higher-order norms which legitimate the authority prevailing in a given society. This authority emerges from a person's effective ability

21. See, for example, Martin Hengel, *The Charismatic Leader and His Followers* (New York: Crossroad, 1981).

22. Bruce Malina, "Jesus as Charismatic Leader?" *BTB* 14 (1984): 55–62, reprinted as "Was Jesus a Charismatic Leader?" in Bruce Malina, *The Social World of Jesus and the Gospels* (New York: Routledge, 1996), 123–42.

to convince members of a given society to recognize no longer some
higher-order norm as binding.[23]

In the case of first-century Galilee, Jesus can be seen dislodging support for
the temple through his prophetic reading of the Torah. In the process, he also
undermined the great-tradition reading of the Torah and argued for a little-
tradition reading of its covenant themes. To the extent that Jesus subverted
higher-order norms like Torah obedience, as interpreted by the Pharisees,
support of the temple's sacrificial system, and the need to send tithes to the
temple, he posed a serious threat to the leaders in Jerusalem whose base of
power resided in the temple and was buttressed by their control over the interpretation of the Torah.

"WHAT IS THIS? A NEW TEACHING— WITH AUTHORITY!" (MARK 1:27)

Let's take a look at a passage that begins to put these pieces together. It is the
story of the healing of a paralytic (Mark 2:1–12 and parallels Matt. 9:1–8; Luke
5:17–26). Most scholars cite two basic reasons to support their belief that this
passage reflects the influence of the early church and, therefore, does not reflect
the concerns of the historical Jesus. First, they argue that the text is a composite that combines a healing story with a controversy dialogue inserted into it.
This controversy dialogue must have been created by the early church, so the
argument runs, as a way of interpreting the significance and application of the
healing story for the life of the church. The story can be divided as follows:

2:1–5a	healing story (primary story)
2:5b–10	controversy (secondary insertion)
2:11–12	healing story (primary story)

In this view, the repetition of the phrase "he said to the paralytic" (2:5a, 10b)
stitches the two parts of the story together to make a complete whole. Second,
those who contend that the story in its present form reflects the concerns of
the early church assume that the issue of the "forgiveness of sins" was not an
issue for the historical Jesus and hence the text must be seen ipso facto as a creation of the early church reflecting its emerging theological concerns.[24] Its

23. Ibid., 129.
24. For a fuller statement of this position, see Arland Hultgren, *Jesus and His Adversaries: The Form and Function of the Conflict Stories in the Synoptic Gospels* (Minneapolis:
Augsburg, 1979).

current, composite form strongly argues that it traces to the early church, not to Jesus. This view is bolstered by the fact that the theme of the forgiveness of sins is part of the controversy but absent from the account of the healing and, therefore, must trace to a later editorial hand. The introduction of the theme, the forgiveness of sins, is a later overlay. Obviously, if Jesus is found to be arguing issues that reflect the theological concerns of the early church but not the concerns of the peasantry of Palestine, then this healing controversy does fit a situation and time subsequent to the time of Jesus. But is this the case? Does the argument over the forgiveness of sins simply not resonate with the setting of Palestine in the 20s and 30s of the first century? Before we can answer these questions we must take a closer look at the story as a whole.

The incident can be read as an example of an honor challenge and riposte. It is important to remember, as we read this text and others, that the Gospels do not supply verbatim accounts of honor challenges and ripostes. They present these confrontations in highly condensed form, shaped by the needs of oral transmission and the limits of memory, as well as the interests of the early church. The most we can hope for is a glimpse of the dynamics and the conflicts so portrayed as well as the issues that animated them.

There are, in fact, two challenges in this text. The first is a positive honor challenge initiated by the men who carry the paralytic to Jesus. By bringing him to Jesus, they are declaring their conviction that Jesus can do something for him, but this is a challenge to Jesus' honor as a traditional healer and prophet. The fact that they see Jesus as a prophetic healer may indicate the persistent influence of the Elijah/Elisha traditions in Galilee that portray the great prophets as healers of Israel. For whatever reasons, they put Jesus on the spot. He has been in a house (*en oikō*), a reference our ears should pick up. Is this a house synagogue in which Jesus is teaching Torah? Or is it just a private home? Or is it a reference to a house church? The text says that he is "speaking the word to them" (*elalei autois ton logon*), not preaching the word. The reference to the "word" (*ton logon*) can mean "the gospel," but it could as easily refer to the word of the Torah and, as we shall see, the two may not be as far apart as commonly thought. When the paralytic is lowered before him, Jesus looks at the man and declares, "My child, your sins are forgiven." Fernando Belo has noted that the phrase could equally well be translated "My child, your debt is discharged."[25] With this statement, Jesus is both responding to the challenge initiated by the paralytic's friends and initiating a challenge of his own. This is the second challenge in the text.

25. Fernando Belo, *A Materialist Reading of the Gospel of Mark*, trans. Matthew J. O'Donnell (Maryknoll, N.Y.: Orbis Books, 1981), 108.

Jesus has responded to the paralytic like a traditional healer. When anthropologists study healing and healers, they distinguish between illness and disease.[26] Disease is a physical malady; illness represents the social repercussions of disease. Whatever paralyzed the man on the pallet was a disease. Its social consequences (illness) involved isolation and dependence on others, perhaps even begging to survive. His social bonds were disrupted and broken, and he was in danger of becoming an outcast. So Malina and Rohrbaugh note,

> Illness in antiquity was a social as well as a physical phenomenon. A person with a disease or deformity was socially as well as physically abnormal. Healing therefore required reestablishing relationships as well as restoring physical health.[27]

Similarly, the paralyzed man was not only afflicted with a physical ailment (disease), but he was also viewed as an example of God's judgment who should be shunned (illness). Disease was widely considered to be a judgment of God (cf. John 9:2), so when Jesus announces God's forgiveness of sin or cancellation of debt, he is addressing the issue of illness. N. T. Wright is correct when he suggests,

> The effect of these cures, therefore, was not merely to bring physical healing; . . . but to reconstitute those healed as members of the people of Israel's God. . . . The vindication for which Israel looked to her god was being brought forward into the present, close up, in the case of these individuals.[28]

All of this reflects on the work of Jesus as a broker of God's healing and forgiveness of debt.

At first glance, the scribes' reaction seems odd. They accuse Jesus of blasphemy, because only God can forgive sins. But Jesus has used the passive voice in speaking to the paralytic. When Jesus says, "Your sins are forgiven," he means, "God has forgiven your sins." The use of the divine passive (a verb in the passive voice, e.g., "are forgiven") was a common way of speaking indirectly and respectfully about God's activity. It is important to note that Jesus was not saying, "I forgive your sins." Rather, his words were spoken like a pious Jewish teacher. Why then do the scribes accuse him of such a serious crime? Some argue that blasphemy was punishable by death. Whether it was or not,

26. For a full discussion, see John J. Pilch, *Healing in the New Testament: Insights from Medical and Mediterranean Anthropology* (Minneapolis: Fortress Press, 2000). For a broad discussion of Jesus as healer, see Graham Twelftree, *Jesus the Miracle Worker: A Historical and Theological Study* (Downers Grove, Ill.: InterVarsity Press, 1999).

27. Malina and Rohrbaugh, *Social-Science Commentary on the Synoptic Gospels*, 363.

28. N. T. Wright, *Jesus and the Victory of God* (Minneapolis: Fortress Press, 1996), 192.

it was a serious charge. The most probable answer is that the scribes are representing the temple and protecting its interests. From their point of view, the only place people can go to have sins forgiven (or debt discharged) is the temple, and the only people authorized to forgive sins on God's behalf, the only true brokers, are the priests. The scribes viewed Yahweh's relation to Israel in patron-client terms. Yahweh was the patron God of Israel, and the people were God's clients. The only brokers authorized to mediate God's blessings were the priests in the temple. They alone could decide who was indebted and who was not.[29]

As noted earlier, as long as this system was in place, the peasants of Galilee were effectively shut out of the temple system because they could not afford to pay their double tithes and other obligations. This left them perpetually indebted to Yahweh and the temple, unable to discharge their obligations and claim the advantages of the sacrifices offered there. When Jesus announced the forgiveness of sins to the paralytic, he was claiming that God was acting through him as broker to discharge debt even though it meant bypassing the temple system. Through this healing, Jesus demonstrated that God was reconstituting the covenant community of Israel, including the outcasts like the paralytic who is now addressed in kinship terms as a member of the family ("my child"). All of this occurs outside the temple and sacrificial system. If Jesus proclaimed this new order as the reign of God, it is little wonder that the peasants of Galilee and the assorted outcasts and castaways who wandered its paths and trails called this "good news." It was good news rooted in Jesus' reading of the Torah and his application of its covenant themes. The good news was the good news version of the Torah as interpreted by Jesus. If this were the case, then "gospel" may refer to Jesus' reading of the Torah even though it became the early church's word to describe his particular proclamation (Mark 1:14–15).

The scribes perceived the seriousness of the threat. This is why they escalate the conflict by "questioning in their hearts" or, as Matthew says, "said among themselves" (9:3). The scribes evidently believe that Jesus is too far below them socially to respond to his challenge in a direct manner. Yet they cannot let his remarks pass in silence, lest their silence be construed as consent. So they choose to speak among themselves, just loud enough to be heard by the group gathered in the house or house synagogue. It is an example of shaming by snubbing and negative labeling. They stigmatize him as a blasphemer, a serious form of name calling. The assumption of most eavesdroppers would be that the scribes are honorable and, as a consequence, their

---

29. For a fuller discussion, see Bruce Malina, "Patron and Client: The Analogy Behind Synoptic Theology," in Malina, *The Social World of Jesus and the Gospels*, 143–75.

judgments carry weight. This may be why the scribes themselves seem to believe that their campaign of murmuring among themselves to stigmatize Jesus will work. Their words are not really intended for Jesus but are designed for the ears of the people gathered in the house since the crowd decides who wins the honor challenge and riposte. Having been identified as a blasphemer, Jesus cannot allow such an affront to his honor and threat to his political standing to pass without a response, but neither can he defend himself against such a slander. To defend yourself is to admit defeat. In this kind of engagement, a strong offence is the best defense.

So Jesus escalates the challenge by posing a forced choice, "Which is easier to say?" Of course, the scribes find neither choice particularly to their liking. They cannot concede that his initial remark to the paralytic is acceptable but neither do they want to concede a healing, for a healing would demonstrate that God was working through Jesus as a broker of God's restorative power, a prerogative previously reserved for the temple and its priests. At this point, Jesus utters a "son of man" saying (Mark 2:10). The phrase "son of man [*ho huios tou anthrōpou*]," has a long and complex history but usually carries one of four meanings: 1) It can refer to the mysterious figure of Dan. 7:13–14 and function as a christological title (Mark 14:62); 2) it can serve as a circumlocution for "I" (Matt. 16:13; cf. Mark 8:27); 3) it can refer to an ordinary mortal (see Yahweh's address to Ezekiel as "son of man," Ezek. 2:1; 3:1; 4:1; 5:1, and throughout); 4) it can refer to a vocation with the meaning "someone like me" (Mark 2:10; 2:28). For the purposes of this reading, we will take the last two meanings as our guides. If we take the third meaning as our starting point, Jesus may be declaring that he, as an ordinary human being (lay person) who is not a member of the priestly caste, has been given the authority to broker God's forgiveness of sins; or taking the fourth option, it can mean that Jesus is claiming the role of broker not only for himself but for those who follow him and emulate him, thereby becoming "one like me." In either case, the saying fits the context of the conflict and intensifies it. Malina has argued that Jesus recruited a faction as part of his public project. Small-group formation usually occurs because a leader perceives a problem and recruits a group to assist him in addressing that problem. In Malina's words, "group formation is always rooted in the solution to some problem. It is a truism in small group research that small groups emerge because some person becomes aware of a need for change."[30] It is already clear that Jesus had diagnosed a problem in Galilee and Judea and may well have recruited a faction or group to address that problem. The shift of

---

30. Bruce Malina, "Social-Scientific Methods in Historical Jesus Research," in Wolfgang Stegemann, Bruce Malina, and Gerd Theissen, eds., *The Social Setting of Jesus and the Gospels* (Minneapolis: Fortress Press, 2002), 11.

focus from Jesus to his group may be captured in the so-called mission discourse or sending out of the disciples (Mark 6:6b–13 pars. Matt. 10:1, 7–11, 14; Luke 9:1–6; see also Luke 10:1–12).

Up to this point, the debate has been an argument that leaves the state of the paralytic in limbo. Is he forgiven or not? Is his debt discharged, or is he still in debt? Is he part of the people of Israel or just another broken body giving testimony to Yahweh's judgment? It really is a "he said, they said" situation. This is where the healing enters the picture. When Jesus commands the paralytic ("I say to you"), he is not claiming the miracle for himself but demanding that the paralytic manifest the forgiveness that God has already offered him. Jesus speaks with the authority of a broker who represents his patron and is, therefore, certain of his ground. The "I" is not a personal "I" but a prophetic "I," as when a prophet says, "Thus says the Lord, I. . . ." The crowd is clear about what has happened, for Mark says that "they were all amazed and glorified God" (2:12). If the church had been shaping this account for christological purposes, it would most likely have emphasized that the crowd glorified Jesus.

The healing poses interesting questions for historical Jesus research. As noted earlier in chapter 1, the consensus among Jesus scholars that Jesus healed and exorcized dissolves when any particular healing or exorcism is discussed.[31] Add to this the fact that the ancients saw disease differently from the way we do and did not have our knowledge of medicine. All that we can say is that the man was confined to his pallet until Jesus brokered God's forgiveness, which changed his life. He could rise and walk. The healing vouches for Jesus as a reliable and powerful broker of Yahweh's forgiveness of sin and cancellation of debt. After the man rises and takes his pallet with him as he leaves the house, Jesus is no longer just a disputant. He is a force to be reckoned with, a shamanistic figure and broker who mediates power. He is a public, political presence who cannot be ignored or snubbed in the hope that he will wither and go away. The healing is, therefore, a necessary part of the incident, not just an add-on, but how Jesus healed and just exactly what the man's malady was can no longer be known.

The clear implication of all this is that the controversy does not stand by itself. It would not make sense if it were extracted from the story. If the text is composite, then the controversy was composed to fit into the healing story. But it is equally possible to read the whole encounter as a unified incident that reveals the conflicts that energized Jesus' public work in the early decades of the first century. The issue of forgiveness is about how God through his

31. For a full discussion of this issue, see John Meier, *A Marginal Jew*, vol. 2, see part 3.

broker Jesus is liberating peasants from their indebtedness to the temple, free-ing them from their debt servitude to become the people of the covenant God once again. The healing reinforces that agenda. In addition, it could be said that many of the healings have symbolic resonances, and this one is no excep-tion. Paralyzed by a burden of debt that crippled their lives, many peasants may well have seen in this healing a symbol of their own condition and God's liberating response to it. In this context, the wider implications of the healing were felt by the crowd as well as by the healed man.

When Jesus entered the synagogue meeting at Capernahum and exorcized a demoniac (Mark 1:21–28), the people were amazed at his teaching because "he taught them as one who had authority, and not as the scribes" (1:22). Put in the terms we have been discussing, Jesus taught them a prophetic form of the little tradition that carried authority for the people of the land, whereas the scribes taught a version of the great tradition that came across as an impo-sition on the peasants of Galilee and, therefore, without authority. The same theme appears again after the exorcism when the people exclaim, "What is this? A new teaching—with authority! He commands even the unclean spir-its, and they obey him" (1:27). At first glance, it might seem odd to identify an exorcism with "a new teaching," but if the reference is to Jesus' announcement that God is discharging debt and forgiving sin without the permission of the temple and its priests, the connection makes sense. This new action of God is reclaiming those who have been paralyzed and possessed as a step toward restoring them to their local communities. It is an act of gathering in the lost and of reconstituting Israel as the people of God, a theme found in Jesus' para-bles (see Luke 15:3–7, 8–10, 11–32). The very people forgotten and cast away now become the focal point of God's patronal love and care.

HEALING AS A POLITICAL CHALLENGE

Another synagogue healing underscores many of the same themes. In Luke 13:10–17, Jesus heals a woman who "was bent over and could not fully straighten herself" (v. 11). The episode brings together the themes of teach-ing and healing, much as the exorcism in the synagogue at Capernahum brought together the themes of teaching and exorcism (Mark 1:21–28). The central conflict in the synagogue is portrayed as an honor challenge and riposte, except that in this case, Jesus initiates the challenge. While in the role of a teacher, perhaps commenting on the meaning of the Torah text, Jesus sees the bent woman and calls out, "Woman, you are loosed from your weakness" (v. 12). As if that were not enough, he approaches her and lays hands on her, and she straightens up and stands erect. When Jesus calls to her, he uses the divine passive ("you are loosed"), indicating that her healing comes from God, and when he lays hands on her, he does so as a broker of the healing and liberating power of God that he has already announced. But the challenge is no less pointed because of that.

The episode breaks into two distinct parts:

13:10–13   healing
13:14–17   controversy

The first portion of the text is a classic healing story and could stand on its own. If it did, it would tell how Jesus healed a bent woman and responded to the needs of one person. But this healing also sends a social and political challenge, and the ruler of the synagogue responds to the provocation by citing Torah, in this case, the creation accounts in Genesis. It is no longer possible to know exactly who the ruler of the synagogue was, but he was most likely a prominent local official, probably with Pharisaic leanings. For him and for others, the status of the sabbath was no small matter. After the destruction of the temple in 586 BCE, the Judean people lost their sacred space, but they still had access to sacred time, so keeping the sabbath became a way of both retaining their identity as strangers in a strange land and reaffirming the order of creation. By implication, the ruler is portraying Jesus as an agent of chaos who is undoing the created order and challenging the God who established it. Indeed, with this healing, Jesus has challenged the way Torah was being interpreted. From the point of view of the ruler of the synagogue, the woman did not have a life-threatening disease, so she could have been healed on any other day of the week when work could be done. By invoking the Torah, he plainly means to discredit Jesus for violating its sacred guidance. The Torah is honorable, but Jesus is not, for he has ignored its way of keeping the sabbath. Note also that the ruler has addressed himself to the people in the synagogue, not to Jesus. He evidently hopes to retain their loyalty by invoking the Torah against a Torah breaker. It is a powerful and savvy response.

Jesus cannot defend himself. If he becomes defensive, he has lost the battle. Instead, he must go on the offensive, and this is exactly what he does by branding the ruler and his supporters as "hypocrites" (*hypokritai*) who keep the sabbath provision to rest but keep it selectively. It violates the sabbath to heal the woman, but it does not violate the sabbath to loose an ox or an ass from its tether and lead it to water. Why does the Torah (in a great tradition reading) care for the needs of an ox and an ass but ignore the pain of a bent woman? Why does it render animals visible and a broken woman invisible? For this argument to work, Jesus would have to cite a provision that is common knowledge, a provision on which everyone agrees, so he chooses the loosing (untying) and watering of animals on sabbath. Then, in rabbinic fashion, he argues from the lesser to the greater, from animals to the woman. In making the comparison, Jesus parallels the loosing (*luei*) of the animals with the loosing of the woman from bondage to Satan (*luthēnai*). If the lesser "loosing" is permitted, then why not a greater "loosing" that demonstrates the power of God to liberate his people from Satan's grip. The significance of this healing only deepens when Jesus describes the woman as a "daughter of Abraham." Once again, healing serves to reconstitute the people of God, including the broken outcasts, as a covenant community, the children of Abraham.

The language of "binding" and "loosing" carries other overtones. The task of an interpreter of the Torah was either to bind people to a particular reading of a text or to loose them from it. In this context, the healing reproduces the social function of figures like the ruler of the synagogue, except for the fact that, in this case, Jesus is loosing the members of the synagogue from a reading of Torah that overlooks the pain of the bent and broken members of the community. As he liberates the woman from Satan's grasp, so he frees the members of the synagogue from the grip of the ruler of the synagogue. The physical act of healing parallels the political act of breaking the bonds of the great tradition over the people. The sabbath will never be the same.

Why call the ruler and his supporters "hypocrites"? The standard definition of a hypocrite is someone who says one thing and does another. But this description fits neither the Pharisees nor the ruler of the synagogue. They not only seek to impose a great-tradition reading of Torah on the villagers, but they live the very provisions of Torah that they want others to obey, so they are clearly not hypocrites in our sense of the word. The word *hypokritai* (hypocrites) is a term drawn from the theater, meaning "stage actor" or "role player." By extension, the word came to mean a pretender or a dissembler. By using the term to describe the ruler of the synagogue, Jesus may be suggesting that, in the guise of teaching Torah, the ruler was pretending to broker God's instruction to the people while he actually served a corrupt temple system that oppressed the very people it was supposed to protect. Under the guise of calling the people back to keeping the sabbath (v. 14b), he was actually attempting to reinforce the authority of a great-tradition version of the Torah, whatever the cost to the bent woman now freed from her weakness.

A good portion of the onlookers in the synagogue judged that Jesus had prevailed over his adversaries. As Luke puts it, "all his adversaries were put to shame," and the people honored "all the glorious things done by him" (v. 17). It is possible to read the final comment as a glorification of Jesus and hence the christological reflection of the early church. But read in context of Jesus' public activity, the comment can refer to Jesus' healing of the woman and his stout defense of his actions in the political challenge and debate that followed his healing. Both could count as "glorious things." Note that the healed woman "praised God," not Jesus (v. 13) and that the people in the synagogue had a great deal to be glad about. It would make as much sense to note the covenant renewal echoes of "glorious things" (*endoxois*) as its christological implications. The word appears in Exod. 34:10 (LXX) in the context of Yahweh renewing his covenant with Israel after her apostasy, but this single usage is too small a foundation on which to build the case that Jesus was fulfilling a similar role in Galilee. We have argued that Jesus' actions can be viewed in this light but on the basis of other materials.

HOW WILL YOU UNDERSTAND ALL THE PARABLES?

In the discussions of the healing of the paralytic (Mark 2:1–12) and the healing of the bent woman in the synagogue (Luke 13:10–17), this chapter has argued that Jesus used the cultural form known as the honor challenge and riposte as a means of gaining political visibility and recognition as a public figure. It has suggested that the most likely social setting for these contests was the synagogue, understood as a gathering in the public square of a market town, the village gate of a smaller town or hamlet, or perhaps even in a household that doubled as a synagogue. Up to this point, we have focused on Jesus as a debater arguing the meaning of the Torah and as a healer announcing that God is once again liberating his people from debt servitude by forgiving sins. But Jesus had another weapon in his arsenal. He was a storyteller or parabler and was adept at using parables in a variety of ways. Long ago, Joachim Jeremias argued that Jesus used the parables as weapons of controversy.[32] This meant that parables spoken to the disciples in the Gospels may originally have been told to Jesus' adversaries. To use the language we have been developing, they may have been part of the honor challenges in which Jesus was involved.

Earlier, this chapter mentioned the incident in which Jesus was invited to recline at table in the house of Simon the Pharisee (Luke 7:36–50). If a household could double as the place where the synagogue gathered, then Simon's house may be the location where villagers gather to study Torah and discuss village issues. Kenneth Bailey has argued that the meal held in Simon's house was a public occasion. Although not everyone was invited to recline at table with the supposedly honored guest, everyone was invited to sit around the wall of the *triclinium* (dining room) and listen to the Pharisees discuss Torah with their visitor. The public character of this meal may reflect the fact that it is a

---

32. Joachim Jeremias, *The Parables of Jesus*, 6th ed., trans. S. H. Hooke (New York: Charles Scribner's Sons, 1963).

synagogue gathering, and Simon the Pharisee may be acting as something like
the ruler of the synagogue. He is surely the host of the meal.

The encounter is framed as a complex of honor challenges and ripostes
although, in this case, the initial challenge is not easy to find. The passage in
its current form can be divided into six sections which, taken together, provide
a complicated pattern of challenges and ripostes.

v. 36	the setting at table in Simon's house
vv. 37–38	the woman's inexplicable actions
v. 39	Simon's censure (challenge)
vv. 40–43	Jesus' parable as riposte
vv. 44–46	the woman's actions explained
vv. 47–50	the consequence: another challenge and riposte

Because the passage in its current form uses a flashback, it may help to put the
events in chronological order.

1. Challenge 1 (vv. 36, 44–46): Jesus is invited to recline at table but is insulted
   when he enters the house.
2. Riposte 1 (vv. 37–38): The woman sees the lack of hospitality and acts out
   a hospitable welcome.
3. Challenge 2 (v. 39): Simon censures Jesus for allowing the woman to touch
   him.
4. Riposte 2 (vv. 40–42): Jesus tells a parable to Simon.
5. Challenge 3 (vv. 44–48): Jesus exposes Simon's inhospitality and the
   woman's hospitality and the consequences for the woman.
6. Riposte 3 (v. 49): The Pharisees question Jesus' presumption to forgive
   sins.
7. Challenge 4 (v. 50): Jesus honors the woman as a model of trust (faith).

It may help to walk through this complex encounter. Note that Bailey has a
detailed discussion of this text that is very useful.[33] When a guest was invited
to recline at table, he was usually greeted with characteristic ceremonies of
hospitality. The host would greet his guest with a kiss of peace, wash his feet
(or have his wife or servants wash his feet), and, if the guest were prominent
enough, anoint his head with oil. In this instance, Simon invites Jesus to
recline at table with him but denies him these rituals of hospitality. It is hard
to read this snub as anything other than a severe insult. Of course, Simon and
his Pharisaic friends are not the only ones who witness this breach of hospitality. Everyone gathered around the walls to listen to the conversation would
see it as well.

33. Bailey, *Through Peasant Eyes*, 1–21.

When the woman "who was a sinner" either hears of Simon's behavior through the town's effective rumor mill or witnesses it because she is one of the villagers sitting around the outside wall, she responds by washing Jesus' feet with her tears, drying them with her hair, kissing his feet, and anointing Jesus with a flask of ointment. Every one of her actions reverses one of the insults that Simon has inflicted on Jesus. She is identified as a sinner, a designation that most likely means she did not keep Torah according to the tradition of the elders; it does not mean that she was a prostitute, as has been assumed so often in discussions of this text. Like most of the peasants in Galilee, she is consid-ered unclean because she does not keep the purity codes of the Torah in the Pharisaic way (this means that she was, from Simon's point of view, a sinner). She does, however, violate both gender and social boundaries in her outra-geous actions. Remember that Jesus is reclined at table, his feet stretched out behind him. The woman can easily reach his feet even though she is seated along the wall. In her desire to offer hospitality to Jesus, she does touch him without his permission, and she lets down her hair to dry his feet, "an intimate gesture that a peasant woman is expected to enact only in the presence of her husband."[34] Kissing Jesus' feet also represents a shocking act.

Simon has seen enough to utter a challenge. He evidently fails to connect the woman's actions with his own rudeness toward his guest, so that he fails to perceive her behavior as a riposte that counters his own shameless lack of hos-pitality. Instead, he issues a challenge to Jesus, once again spoken softly but loud enough to be heard by those in the room. It is interesting that Simon attacks Jesus' status as a prophet, but not a surprising move in light of Jesus' prophetic critique of the Torah. By undermining his claim to be a prophet, Simon perhaps hopes to neutralize his reading of the Torah. Simon is specifi-cally concerned about the woman touching Jesus. From his point of view, the very touch of a sinner can render one unclean so that, as soon as the sinful woman touches Jesus, he becomes unclean (if he were not already). If Jesus had a prophetic bone in his body, he would understand this. Clearly, he neither knows nor perhaps even cares about who touches him and what consequences he will suffer.

Exhibiting the sensitive ears of an honorable man, Jesus hears the challenge and responds. He takes charge and goes on the attack: "Simon, I have some-thing to say to you." In his response, Simon calls Jesus "teacher," quite possi-bly in a sarcastic or mocking tone. Let the unclean prophet instruct the well-versed Pharisee if he dares! Jesus tells a simple story, but the parable

34. Ibid., 9.

changes the nature of the debate. It is hardly a profound riddle and much more like commonplace wisdom or common sense. Perhaps it is even a piece of folk wisdom or a little-tradition way of viewing the world but, in the hands of a subversive pedagogue, it serves an important purpose, for the point of the parable is not its profundity. Its purpose is to shift the conversation from the question of purity to the matter of debt. In this light, the parable produces a sea change in the conversation. The woman is a condemned unclean sinner when judged by the purity codes but when seen through the debt codes, she is a forgiven woman and more! Perhaps sensing a trap, Simon replies tentatively to Jesus' question about which of the two debtors will love the creditor more, "the one I suppose to whom he forgave more" (v. 43).

If the parable has set the scene, the woman is now placed on center stage. "Simon, do you see this woman?" Good question, because he does not really see the woman. He sees only a sinner. Jesus then places the woman's actions in the perspective of hospitality, Simon's lack of hospitality, and the woman's abundance of hospitality. On this ledger, Simon is a debtor and the woman the creditor. Jesus then makes the astounding remark "Therefore, I tell you, her many sins are forgiven because she loved much" (v. 47). If this text were being edited to suit the needs of Christian theology, it would read the reverse: the woman loved because she was forgiven, but Jesus reverses the order here. His remark honors the woman's care for hospitality and her desire to annul the insults that Simon had directed at Jesus. Her actions lead to forgiveness. By contrast, the phrase "the one who is forgiven little, loves little" is an apt description of Simon. Notice that Jesus has spoken of God's forgiveness by using the passive construction (are forgiven) to indicate divine activity. He is not arrogating to himself what belongs to God. But the Pharisees around the table accuse Jesus of claiming to forgive sins: "Who does he think he is, who even forgives sin?" (v. 49). They make the same mistake as the scribes in Capernahum (Mark 2:1–12) because they think of the priests in the temple as the only brokers who can forgive sin, but Jesus has staked a claim to the role of God's broker. Once again, Jesus has challenged the monopoly of the temple and its priesthood in the (synagogue?) house of Simon the Pharisee.

It is notable that the woman is not named, even though Simon is, and she says not a word, although her actions speak louder than words. Yet she embodies the virtue of hospitality for which her ancestors in the faith, Abraham and Sarah, were renowned (Gen. 18:1–33). She is, therefore, a daughter of Abraham and Sarah as surely as the bent woman in the synagogue. When Jesus says, "Your trust has saved you, go in peace," he acknowledges that she, too, is being gathered into the people of God and need live no longer stigmatized as a sinner.

FACTION FORMATION:
JESUS BECOMES A MOVEMENT

As the accounts of the popular prophets like Theudas and the Egyptian indicate (for details see chapter 5), public figures often gathered around themselves
a band of followers, sometimes quite large in number if Josephus's figures are
accurate. Although Jesus does not fit this pattern common to the popular
prophets, he did begin to gather about him a faction of followers who accompanied him on his travels, although the group was relatively small. The Gospel
traditions stylize the number at twelve for symbolic and theological purposes
(Mark 3:13–19a; Matt. 10:1–4; Luke 6:12–16). Luke suggests that there were
women among the core group of his followers (Luke 8:1–3). In all likelihood,
this group of followers formed a fictive kinship group, much to the confusion
and chagrin of Jesus' own family (Mark 3:19b–21, 31–35; Matt. 12:46–50; Luke
8:19–21). Malina and Rohrbaugh discuss faction formation in these terms:

> A faction is a type of coalition formed around a central person who
> recruits followers and maintains the loyalty of a core group. Factions
> share a common goal though membership beyond the core group is
> often indistinct and fluid. . . . Rivalry with other factions is basic; hence
> hostile competition for honor, truth (an ideological justification) and
> resources is always present.[35]

In such a group, the leader is responsible for maintaining the honor of the
group, and the group members must maintain the honor of their central
leader. That Jesus and his disciples were seen as members of a faction can be
inferred from the way Jesus' opponents complain to the disciples about his
behavior (Mark 2:15–17) and the way Jesus defends the behavior of his followers (Mark 2:18–20; 2:23–28; 7:5). These references and others witness to
a level of conflict between Jesus' faction and other coalitions and political
interest groups. One obvious example of this sharp conflict is found in the
Beelzebul controversy (Mark 3:22–27; Matt. 12:22–30; Luke 11:14–15,
17–23). Within the group, Peter names Jesus' significance as the central leader
(Mark 8:27–29; Matt. 16:13–16; Luke 9:18–20) while Jesus renames key members of the group. Peter becomes "rocky" (*Petros*), and James and John "the
sons of thunder" (*boanērges*). As Malina and Rohrbaugh note, since thunder
was a symbol for the voice of God, "this nickname would mean 'Echoers of
the voice of God.'"[36]

35. Malina and Rohrbaugh, *Social-Science Commentary on the Synoptic Gospels*,
198–99.
36. Ibid., 198.

In time, Jesus would not only recruit followers, that is, disciples (*mathētai*) who were willing to learn about the little-tradition versions of the reign of God, but he would also encourage and empower them to conduct their own public work (Mark 6:6b–13, 30–31; Matt. 10:1, 5–15; Luke 9:1–6, 10a). This would be in keeping with Jesus' use of the phrase "son of man," as we learned earlier in this chapter. Jesus was identifying these disciples as "one like me" and, therefore, able to continue the public work begun by Jesus because they share a common vocation. The figure of a prophet surrounded by his followers would echo a familiar theme in Galilee where Elijah, and especially Elisha, were surrounded by a group called "the sons of the prophets" (see 1 Kings 20:35; 2 Kings 2:3, 5, 7, 15; 4:1, 38; 5:22; 9:1), evidently a prophetic conventicle of some kind. The association of Jesus and the disciples with Elisha and the sons of the prophets is strengthened by the fact that the calling stories in Mark (1:16–20; 2:13–15) seem to be influenced by and modeled on the call of Elisha by Elijah (1 Kings 19:19–21) as the following comparison indicates.[37]

Call of Elisha (1 Kings 19:19–21)	*Call of the Disciples (Mark 1:16–20; 2:13–17)*		
1. setting the scene 19:19a	1. setting the scene 1:16	1:19	2:13
2. the call 19:19b	2. the call 1:17	1:20a	2:14
3. the response 19:20	3. the response 1:18	1:20b	2:15
4. final meal 19:21a	4. omitted		festive meal 2:16–17
5. departure 19:21b	5. departure 1:20c		

The traditions reflect some diversity. After Elijah casts his mantle over Elisha, he asks for an opportunity to bid farewell to his family (19:20a), which Elijah grants (19:20b). This leads to a final meal or farewell scene depicted in 19:21a, b. In the Gospel traditions, Jesus' call is so immediate and sudden that it allows no time for farewell rituals. However, the theme of the meal associated with the call receives an unusual twist in the call of Levi because his call leads to a festive meal with Jesus, toll collectors, and sinners. It might be possible to see this as Levi's farewell to his work as a toll collector and to his association with other local toll collectors and sinners, but the presence of Jesus at the table is

---

37. For a discussion of the relationship between call narratives, see Ferdinand Hahn, "Pre-Easter Discipleship," in Ferdinand Hahn et al., *The Beginnings of the Church in the New Testament* (Minneapolis: Augsburg Publishing House, 1970), 14–18.

a reminder that Levi's new work will continue to involve the outcasts and the rejected in Israel. One reason why the farewell scene is omitted from the call of the disciples may be found in one of Jesus' sayings about discipleship.

> Another said, "I will follow you, Lord; but let me first say farewell to those at my home." Jesus said to him, "No one who puts his hand to the plow and looks back is fit for the reign of God." (Q, Luke 9:61–62; see also 9:59–60)

Other scholars have suggested that the omission of the farewell scene reflects the eschatological urgency of the call to follow Jesus. In light of the coming advent of the reign of God, all human ties must be considered secondary.

For the purpose of this chapter, the point to be made is that as Jesus began to come to local prominence as a debater, a teacher, a healer, and an exorcist, and as he came to be seen as a prophetic figure in continuity with the little traditions of the Galilean villagers, he began to gather a small core of followers who would continue his public work and analysis of oppression and exploitation in Galilee and Judea. As Malina has already made clear, Jesus would have formed a faction to address some clearly perceived problem. It is quite possible that this core group was supported by a network of supporters in the villages and countryside of Galilee and perhaps Judea as well. This much is implied in Jesus' response to Peter, who protests that he has left everything to follow Jesus: "Truly, I tell you, there is no one who has left home or brothers or sisters or mother or father or children or lands . . . who will not receive a hundredfold now in this time, houses and children and lands with persecutions, and in the age to come eternal life" (Mark 10:29–30; Matt. 19:29; Luke 18:29–30).

As is the case with factions, "membership beyond the core group is often indistinct and fluid." This is evident in the way the Gospels reflect the presence of a distinct core group of disciples (whether twelve or a larger group) and the indistinct crowds (*ochloi*). There appears to be nothing in between. Mark 4:10 speaks of "those who were about him with the twelve," indicating that Jesus may have had a core group larger than the twelve, as Luke 8:1–3 and the presence of the women at the tomb also suggest. The crowds do not seem to remain with Jesus as the followers of the popular prophets shadowed their leaders. Crowds simply form wherever Jesus stays to teach and heal. Every now and then a figure emerges out of the crowd and approaches Jesus, usually as a supplicant. These figures provide a glimpse of the kinds of people who inhabited the crowds and give a sense of identity to the crowds that gathered around Jesus (see Mark 5:21–43; 8:22–26; 10:46–52 and others). The presence of the crowds would seem to indicate the growing awareness of Jesus as a prophetic figure and his increasing prominence in Galilee.

SUMMARY

This chapter has suggested that Jesus became a public figure by engaging in honor challenges, often in the context of the synagogues (village gatherings) of Galilee, and by his healings, exorcisms, and subversive teaching. These synagogues were more like public forums than buildings, and they afforded villagers opportunities to hear the Torah read and to comment on it and discuss its meaning for their setting. It appears that Jesus challenged the authorities who controlled the synagogue by offering a reading of the Torah different from the version being advanced from Jerusalem with its emphasis on purity and tithes. In its place, Jesus introduced a prophetic reading of Torah that conveyed a strong critique of the temple and its priests. This can be read as a clash between Jesus' form of the little tradition and a particular reading of the great tradition promulgated from Jerusalem in the interests of the temple, the high priestly families, and their retainers. But Jesus did more than argue the meaning of Torah; he healed and exorcized, thereby restoring men and women to the covenant community as sons and daughters of Abraham. His public work was a form of covenant renewal for the villagers of Galilee as he assumed the role of broker of God's renewing work. When he announced that God was forgiving sins or canceling debt, Jesus implicitly criticized the temple and the version of the Torah sponsored by the high priestly houses in Jerusalem and promulgated by their Pharisaic retainers. In short, he made powerful enemies.

At some point, Jesus did gather a group of followers (called disciples) forming a faction, a type of coalition, that propagated Jesus' prophetic reading of Torah and his critique of the temple. No longer an isolate individual and lone voice crying in the wilderness, he became a public, political figure. At stake was the nature of the covenant and the character of the covenant God, so it would be fair to say that Jesus was also a contextual theologian.

The next chapter will examine Jesus' debates over the meaning of Torah.

5

"A prophet mighty in word and deed"

(Luke 24:19)

JESUS AS A PROPHET

It is quite likely that Jesus was called a prophet in his lifetime. Jesus is often called a prophet or assumed to be a prophet in materials seeking to make other, more christological points. Members of Herod Antipas's court think he is like "one of the prophets of old" (Mark 6:15; cf. Luke 9:8). As a dishonored guest in the house of Simon the Pharisee, his host condemns him for letting a woman touch him by muttering, "If this man were a prophet, he would have known what sort of woman this is who is touching him" (Luke 7:39). Simon assumes that Jesus is popularly held to be a prophet but questions the validity of that appellation. When he enters Jerusalem, he is greeted as "the prophet from Nazareth of Galilee" (Matt. 21:11). When Jesus is in Jerusalem, the authorities are forced to take precautions in plotting his arrest because "they feared the crowd [who] held him to be a prophet" (Matt. 21:46). In a formulaic fragment used by Luke in the Emmaus narrative, Jesus is called "a prophet mighty in word and deed" (Luke 24:19b), an evident testimony to the church's continuing view that Jesus was a prophetic figure of some magnitude. The Gospel of John also bears witness to the designation of Jesus as a prophet (John 4:19; 7:52; 9:17). In none of the passages cited, with the exception of John 7:52, is it the point that Jesus was a prophet; it is assumed as part of a larger narrative purpose. Therefore, even though the materials are later, they all take for granted that Jesus was popularly acclaimed as a prophet or called a prophet by his opponents. N. T. Wright also cites a cogent reason why it is likely that these materials provide a glimpse of the historical Jesus when he notes that

> the early church is highly unlikely to have invented many sayings . . .
> which call Jesus a prophet. It might have seemed risky theologically to
> refer to him in this way; it might have appeared that he was simply
> being put on a level with all the other prophets.[1]

Even though the identification of Jesus as a prophet may have inspired christological developments, such as the typological connection of Jesus with
Moses and Elijah, it did not become a major christological theme in the theology of the early church.

The title "prophet" is not without a certain ambivalence. When Jesus was
rejected at Nazareth, he interpreted the event by noting that "prophets are not
without honor, except in their own hometown and among their own kin, and
in their own house" (Mark 6:4; cf. Matt. 13:57; Luke 4:24). Where prophets
are concerned, familiarity breeds contempt, at least for the kind of prophet
Jesus was. Prophets are ambiguous figures who will be evaluated in a variety
of ways by their contemporaries. They foment division and invite debate.
Prophets can shift the balance of power in a given situation, and if they do,
they will be evaluated according to the political position of the observer. Jesus'
comments about John the baptizer are germane to this point. Jesus calls John
both "a prophet" and "more than a prophet" (Q: Luke 7:26 par. Matt. 11:9).
His description of John associates his prophetic activity with "the wilderness,"
a location antithetically opposed to a "royal palace or court" (Luke 7:25), thus
implying an adversarial relationship between ruling powers and the prophet
John. The contrast between wilderness and royal court also establishes a symbolic geography focused on the center and the periphery. Gerd Theissen has
argued this case in some detail.[2] He takes the "shaken reed" to be a popular
characterization, perhaps even a mocking reference or "a title of ridicule" that
accuses Antipas of bending with every wind and whim of Roman rule in order
to maintain his own position. If this is true, then Jesus' saying contrasts "the
cleverly adaptive politician" and "the uncompromising prophet proclaiming
his message."[3] Herod represents the "Hellenistic power elite" and John "the
common people" who resent the intrusion of foreign customs into the Herodian court at Tiberius. To the degree that Jesus is identifying with John, he is
locating himself with prophets who live on the margins and yet address rulers
who reside at the center of power.

1. N. T. Wright, *Jesus and the Victory of God* (Minneapolis: Fortress Press, 1996),
162.

2. Gerd Theissen, *The Gospels in Context: Social and Political History in the Synoptic
Tradition*, trans. Linda Maloney (Minneapolis: Fortress Press, 1991), 26–42.

3. Ibid., 38, 41.

TYPES OF PROPHETS IN THE SECOND TEMPLE ERA

In his study of John the Baptist, Robert Webb has proposed a useful typology for identifying the kinds of prophets active from the Hasmonaean era (167–63 BCE) to the destruction of the temple (70 CE). He classifies these prophetic figures into three types: clerical, sapiential, and popular.[4]

Clerical Prophets

The clerical prophet is essentially a priest performing prophetic functions. For Josephus, the paradigmatic example of the clerical prophet is John Hyrcanus (135–104 BCE), who, in his person, combined the offices of prophet, priest, and king (*War* 1.68–69; *Ant.* 13.299–300). His prophetic gift enabled him to predict the future. On one occasion, he foresaw that neither of his sons would succeed him (*War* 1.68–69; *Ant.* 13.299–300, 322); on another, he predicted his sons' military victory over Cyzicenus (*Ant.* 13.282–83). Webb places Josephus himself in this category, based on his prophecy that Vespasian would become emperor (*War* 3.400–402) and his own claim to have received revelatory dreams (*War* 3.351–54). If John Hyrcanus and Josephus are typical examples of clerical prophets, then it can be inferred that these prophets come from the ruling class or priestly elites. They receive or interpret revelatory dreams, hear the divine voice through which God communicates with human beings, and can therefore predict the future.

Sapiential Prophets

Sapiential prophets belong to retainer groups or political factions who emphasize the need for purity in order to acquire the wisdom needed to interpret sacred texts. Webb organizes sapiential prophets according to the groups to which they belong. In Josephus's works, he finds two types of sapiential prophets, those belonging to the Essenes and those who are Pharisees. Judas the Essene, for example, predicted the murder of Antigonus at the hand of his brother, Aristobulus I (*War* 1.78–80; *Ant.* 13.311–13), and another Essene named Menahem predicted Herod the Great's rise to power and the disastrous consequences it would have for the Sanhedrin. In similar fashion, Simon the Essene foresaw that Archelaus's rule was coming to an end (*Ant.* 17.345–47).

---

4. Robert L. Webb, *John the Baptizer and Prophet: A Socio-Historical Study*, JSNT Supplemental Series 62 (Sheffield: Sheffield Academic Press, 1991), 307–48.

The Pharisees, also known for their ability to read God's plans, served as a retainer group or political interest group deeply involved in court intrigues. When Herod the Great was called to appear before the Sanhedrin to defend his execution of the social bandit Hezekias, Samaias (or Pollion as he is also called) predicted Herod's accession to the throne and its ominous threat to that body. He was right on both counts (*Ant.* 14.172–76; 15.3–4). Josephus also recounts a later court intrigue in which the Pharisees attempted to depose Herod and promote Pheroras as Herod's successor, but their prophecies proved to be bogus, and the plot failed (*Ant.* 17.41–45).

As these examples indicate, sapiential prophets come from the retainer class, perhaps as intellectuals or sages whose counsel is valued because of their reputed ability to predict the future. The sole exception is Samaias (Pollion), who appears as a member of the Sanhedrin and therefore most likely belongs to the ruling class, although he could be functioning in a scribal role in the Sanhedrin without being one of its power brokers. This combined emphasis on purity, wisdom, and study of sacred texts fits a larger pattern identified by Rebecca Gray:

> Josephus . . . believed that God controlled history in a direct and com-
> prehensive way and that events on earth unfolded in accordance with
> the divine plan. Predicting the future, then, depended on gaining
> insight into God's character, purposes and intentions. Scripture . . .
> had been written by God or . . . by prophets inspired by God and con-
> tained a record of God's actions in the past and his plans for the
> future.[5]

What better way to learn God's seemingly inscrutable purpose than through purification that prepared human beings to investigate the sacred books in which such mysteries were encoded, just waiting to be revealed to the inquirer who had "eyes to see." The political advantages accruing to any group who claimed to be able to see the future are obvious.

Popular Prophets

In many ways, the most interesting group of prophetic figures from the first century are the popular prophets. Webb divides the popular prophets into two subcategories: "leadership popular prophets" and "solitary popular prophets."[6] These same figures have been studied elsewhere, where they are called "sign

---

5. Rebecca Gray, *Prophetic Figures in Late Second Temple Jewish Palestine: The Evidence from Josephus* (New York: Oxford University Press, 1993), 110.
    6. Ibid., 333–42.

prophets."[7] Horsley and Hanson, who call them "popular prophets," subdivide them into "oracular prophets" and "action prophets."[8]

The differences in terminology cannot obscure the fact that these popular prophets shared two traits in common. First, they all gathered large bands of followers around them, and second, they promised to perform some kind of dramatic action. During Pilate's time as prefect (26–36 CE), an unnamed Samaritan gathered a considerable following and attempted to lead them up Mount Gerizim, where he promised to unearth the "sacred vessels" buried where "Moses had deposited them" (*Ant.* 18.85–87). Pilate dispatched both cavalry and infantry who fought a "pitched battle" before dispersing the group and executing their leaders. A few years later, during the procuratorship of Fadus (44–46 CE), a figure named Theudas inspired a group of disciples to follow him to the Jordan River, where he promised to part the waters. Before he could perform his mighty act, armed forces dispersed his group, captured and decapitated him, and then sent his head to Jerusalem to be displayed as a means of discouraging others from following his lead (*Ant.* 20.97–98). A few years later, during Felix's procuratorship (52–60 CE), an Egyptian is purported to have gathered thirty thousand followers. He led them first into the wilderness and then returned out of the desert to congregate on the Mount of Olives, where he promised that the walls of the city would crumble at his command so that he and his followers could enter the city in a triumphal entry, after which he would establish himself as king (*War* 2.261–63; *Ant.* 20.169–72). Other figures are mentioned throughout Josephus's works (*War* 2.258–69; 6.285; 6.286, 288; 6.300–309; *Ant.* 20.167–68), indicating that the popular prophets were an enduring phenomenon during this period.

In some ways, the most interesting figure is a solitary oracular prophet, Jesus, son of Ananias, who appeared in the temple during its waning days and began to proclaim an oracle of doom. His oracle is interesting because he claims to have heard the divine voice, the very means by which Hyrcanus had earlier predicted the future. Josephus describes him as follows:

> There came to the feast . . . one Jesus, son of Ananias, a rude peasant, who, standing in the temple, suddenly began to cry out, "a voice from the east, a voice from the west, a voice from the four winds; a voice against Jerusalem and the sanctuary, a voice against the bridegroom and the bride, a voice against all the people." (*War* 6.301)

---

7. P. W. Barnett, "The Jewish Sign Prophets—AD 40–70: Their Intention and Origin," *NTS* 27 (1980): 679–97.

8. Richard A. Horsley and John S. Hanson, *Bandits, Prophets and Messiahs: Popular Movements at the Time of Jesus* (New York: Winston Press, 1985), 135–89.

In spite of punishments by the authorities, he continued his litany of judgment until he was killed by a siege ball during the city's dying days.

The popular prophets share some commonalities that distinguish them from the clerical and sapiential prophets. With the possible exception of the Egyptian and the Samaritan, they were all from the peasant class, and it seems probable, given their manner of operation, that the Samaritan and the Egyptian were also peasant figures. Unlike the clerical and sapiential prophets, the popular prophets were not involved in issues of political succession, the fate of rulers, and court intrigues. Nor were they literate like the sapiential prophets, whose authority was directly tied to their ability to interpret sacred texts. They relied instead on appeals to popular memory and signs, which may explain the confusing conglomeration of events described by Josephus. Perhaps their actions give us an insight into the character and concerns of some forms of the little tradition circulating in the villages and hamlets of Galilee and Judea. When they led their followers into the wilderness, these popular prophets were either reliving the exodus led by Moses or reenacting the conquest led by Joshua. Their actions suggest that the motifs of exodus and conquest may have coalesced in the popular imagination into a general scenario of redemption.

It is also possible that they were reflecting the view of Hosea that the time in the wilderness had been a time of prophetic visions (Hos. 12:9–10). In either case, the appeal to the past for help in solving a present dilemma is entirely in keeping with the time orientation of peasants in agrarian societies,[9] and it suggests a word of caution in speaking about the beliefs of these prophets as "eschatological." The popular prophets and their followers were looking for "signs of redemption" so close at hand that they were virtually part of the present, not the future. The Egyptian and his group evidently imagined that, when they reached the Mount of Olives, he would speak the word, and the walls of Jerusalem would come tumbling down. Their hope was so vivid that it seemed as much an accomplished fact as the story of Joshua before the walls of Jericho, and they made themselves characters in this enacted prophetic drama by adapting a familiar script. Like Theudas, who promised to part the waters of the Jordan, these prophets were bringing the imagined past into present experience. They did not propose to do anything new or unprecedented.

Peasants in the Mediterranean area are typically oriented to the present rather than the past or the future. The present time orientation of the peasant included a time horizon shaped by the cycles of nature, agricultural tasks such

9. For a fuller description of time orientation, see Bruce Malina, "Christ and Time: Swiss or Mediterranean," *CBQ* 51 (1989): 1–31. Reprinted in Bruce Malina, *The Social World of Jesus and the Gospels* (London: Routledge, 1996), 179–214. References are to the reprinted article.

as tilling the land, and other rituals that marked the return of important events, such as Passover and the other great pilgrimage festivals. This sense of the present, or what anthropologists call "experienced time," took into account the antecedent processes being worked out in the present and the consequences that flowed from them.[10] It was a notion of time as cyclical and rooted in the processes of nature, a view that reflected the basic operations and conditions of peasant life. Beyond this present time frame, all past events and future possibilities existed in "imaginary time."[11] In other words, peasants had no sense of historical or linear time. They existed in an extended present beyond whose realm all past events and future possibilities blended together just beyond the time horizons oriented to the events and recurring activities of their lives. This means that Moses and Joshua were not so much inhabitants of a distant historical past (as they would be for us) as they were figures looming on the time horizon separating present from past. They were as close to hand as the temple's periodic celebrations of God's mighty acts made clear. Since time is cyclical, what has happened is a clue to what is happening. This allowed the popular prophets to draw on the memory of God's great acts, located just beyond the time horizon of the present, in order to address the ever-pressing questions of survival.

Malina also observes that peasants act in the present to ensure their continued survival, often reflecting an integrated temporal perspective that views the proximate results being sought "continuous with the present, yet with no personal control over the realization of outcomes."[12] This awareness of their political impotence may have led these popular prophets to repose their confidence in God alone. Gray notes quite accurately, "One thing, however, is reasonably certain: the sign prophets believed that the deliverance they expected and announced would be wrought miraculously by God."[13] Only God was powerful enough to deal with Roman colonial rule and the local collaborating elites. The peasant prophets were no fools; they knew that they were relatively powerless and politically vulnerable. It was enough for the sign prophets to lead their followers to sacred sites where God had acted—to the Jordan, to Mount Gerizim, the Mount of Olives, or the Temple Mount itself. They evidently believed that showing up at the site was adequate to inspire God to act again and trigger a repeat performance.

Since we only know about these popular prophets from a few unsympathetic portrayals of them by their adversaries, it is not easy to discern

10. Ibid., see diagram on 208.
11. Ibid., 192–93.
12. Ibid., see chart, 186.
13. Gray, *Prophetic Figures*, 138.

what motivated them. Josephus, in his characterization of these figures, is unrelentingly critical although he does supply some clues for understanding them. For example, he accuses the anonymous group under Felix of "fostering revolutionary changes" (*War* 2.259), promising to perform "unmistakable marvels and signs" (*Ant.* 20.168; see 20.167–68), or providing "tokens of their deliverance" (*War* 2.259; see also 6.285). Under Festus, an unnamed popular prophet, whom Josephus labels an imposter, promised his followers "salvation and rest from their troubles." The majority of the popular prophets seemed to have tapped into a deep well of discontent. After all, the promise of deliverance or redemption implies oppression and misery, just as the desire to uncover the "sacred vessels" hidden by Moses on Mount Gerizim suggests discontent with the temple in Jerusalem and accuses it of profaning sacred vessels (cf. Mark 11:16). The effort to repeat the mighty acts associated with the exodus and the conquest implies a people held in bondage. In this framework, the story of the unnamed Egyptian is laden with irony. Now it is the Egyptian who leads the exodus from the burdensome oppression of the temple state and Roman colonial presence. As Webb notes of the movements of the popular prophets, "the entire orientation of the strategy and ideology of these prophetic movements indicates that their primary goal was deliverance," a factor that strongly implies a "widespread sense of oppression and dissatisfaction among the peasantry."[14] Horsley and Hanson note that Elijah and Elisha combined the activities of judge and prophet "in communicating Yahweh's redemptive action, his protection of his people against foreign invasion and domination."[15] These concerns were shared by the sign prophets. In her work, Gray has culled out six characteristics of the popular prophets which can be summarized as follows:

1. They led reasonably large movements, large enough to capture the attention of Rome, the Herods, and the high priests.
2. They were peasant movements.
3. The leaders presented themselves as prophets, especially in the mode of the great prophets of the past, Moses and Joshua.
4. They often led their followers on a journey to sacred sites or symbolic landscapes, such as the wilderness, the Jordan River, Mount Gerizim, or the temple mount.
5. They believed and announced that God would redeem them in a dramatic fashion.
6. The prophets viewed the signs they promised to perform as a prelude to this mighty act of God.[16]

14. Webb, *John the Baptizer*, 342.
15. Horsley and Hanson, *Bandits, Prophets and Messiahs*, 139.
16. Gray, *Prophetic Figures*, 113, 133–43.

The presence of these movements from the turn of the eras through the First Revolt (66–73 CE) indicates that Galilee, Judea, and Samaria were not only under duress but, through these movements, were beginning to express the symptoms of that stress.

In their political context and operating out of a time orientation different from our own, the popular prophets and their movements make sense. They were acting to increase the possibility of their survival, a factor made increasingly difficult by the multiple layers of ruling classes (Roman, Herodian, and priestly) with which they had to cope and contend. Their movements were symbolic appeals to the God who dwelt beyond the present time horizon of their lives to act to ensure their survival, just as God had acted in the past. They were not so much driven by a vision of a future as by confidence in the past, the past that had antecedently shaped their present and could continue to influence its forthcoming course.[17] All that was needed was a leader like Moses or Joshua and a people oppressed by their rulers.

The sign prophets mentioned in Josephus mostly operated after the time of Jesus and John, although they are roughly contemporaneous figures. This section has examined them because the social and political conditions they addressed are much the same as those prevailing at the time of Jesus. While it is evident that Jesus was neither a clerical prophet nor a sapiential prophet, as Webb has defined them, he does seem, in some ways, to belong in the tradition of the popular prophets. There are obvious differences between them, however. The sign prophets gathered relatively large followings, whereas Jesus called a few disciples (Mark 1:16–20 pars. Matt. 4:18–22; Mark 2:13–17 pars. Matt. 9:9–13; Luke 5:27–32) and may have been accompanied by an itinerant group including women (cf. Luke 8:1–3).[18] He attracted crowds in the villages and countryside of Galilee, but he did not attempt to lead a large multitude around with him. He was probably accompanied by a band of pilgrims on his journey to Jerusalem, but this is a far cry from the journeys of the sign prophets and their followers (Mark 11:8–10 pars. Matt. 21:8–9; Luke 19:37–38). Clearly, Jesus was well received by the common people, villagers, peasants, rural artisans, and the more destitute as well. If he had not been popular with the masses (*ochlos* =crowd), he would not have been tried and executed by Jerusalem elites and their Roman rulers. Like the popular prophets, Jesus does seem to have claimed to be a prophet, or at least he identified with prophets

17. Malina, "Christ and Time," 209, for relationship of antecedent and forthcoming to the present.

18. For a general discussion of the issue, see Ben Witherington III, *Women in the Ministry of Jesus* (Cambridge: Cambridge University Press, 1984); see 116–18 for a discussion of Luke 8:1–3.

at the time of his rejection at Nazareth (Mark 6:1–6a; cf. Luke 4:16–30). Similarly, in his answer to John's inquiry, Jesus virtually identifies himself as a prophet (Q: Luke 7:18–23 par. Matt. 11:2–6). Like the sign prophets, Jesus did announce God's impending action in the present, the coming of the reign of God, but he does not seem to have associated this coming kingdom with spectacular signs he promised to perform. However, in light of the actions of the sign prophets, it is possible to view the feeding in the wilderness as a sign (Mark 6:30–44; 8:1–10 and pars).[19] Jesus may also have viewed his exorcisms as signs of God's imminent rule (Q: Luke 11:20 par. Matt. 12:28). Jesus was wiser than the sign prophets and more subtle. With the possible exceptions of the entry into Jerusalem (Mark 11:1–10 pars. Matt. 21:1–9; Luke 19:28–40) and the incident in the temple (Mark 11:15–17 pars. Matt. 21:12–13; Luke 19:45–46), he did not announce deadlines or concoct public events that challenged the hegemony of the temple or the power of Rome. Such frontal confrontations always ended in the death and destruction of those who encouraged them.

Indeed, in Jesus' teachings, "signs" are not viewed in a positive manner. Following the feeding of the four thousand in Mark 8:1–10, the Pharisees come seeking "a sign from heaven" and in his reply Jesus refuses to give a sign, saying, "No sign shall be given to this generation" (8:12). The Q tradition contains a variation of this comment to the effect that "no sign shall be given to it except the sign of Jonah" (Q: Luke 11:29 par. Matt. 12:39; 16:4). But what is the sign of Jonah? Morna Hooker has proposed that Jonah's preaching is the sign. This is implied in Luke's words in Q 11:30, "for as Jonah became a sign to the people of Nineveh." Presumably, the prophet's preaching provided the people of Nineveh with a sign of God's judgment and renewal. If Jonah's preaching is the sign, it would be in keeping with Jesus' avoidance of "signs and wonders" such as those trumpeted by the popular prophets. It is even possible that Jesus' reference to the "something greater than Jonah [that] is here" (11:32) is a cloaked allusion to his proclamation that the reign of God is at hand. Yet while the popular prophets offered to perform signs as a way of recruiting followers, Jesus refused to perform signs on request. Whatever approach we take, it is clear that Jesus' attitude toward signs sets him apart from the popular prophets sometimes called "sign prophets."

But it is a far cry from admitting this to asserting, with Gray, that "John and Jesus, I hope it will be agreed, were definitely apolitical by my definition."[20] Her definition of apolitical is indebted to Sanders, "not involving a plan to liberate

19. It is possible to view the feedings as other than so-called nature miracles. They are modeled on the provision of manna in the wilderness and may admit to a more social reading.

20. Gray, *Prophetic Figures*, 140.

and restore Israel by defeating the Romans and establishing an autonomous government."[21] To limit the definition of political in this manner overlooks most of the means of political involvement available to nonelites.[22] It solves nothing to define the political in a manner inaccessible to Jesus and others of his peasant class, and then conclude on the basis of that definition that Jesus was apolitical. The only thing such a definition really proves is that Jesus was neither an elite nor involved in the power games of the politically dominant ruling class and, therefore, was neither a clerical nor a sapiential prophet. Finally, it needs to be said that Sanders's definition assumes a modern Western view of linear time, future planning, and political action that one could not reasonably expect to find in the world of ancient Palestine. Its absence does not indicate that actors like Jesus were apolitical; more likely, it indicates that they acted politically in ways that we have not been trained to see.

The phenomenon of the sign prophets in their various manifestations raises the larger question of their relationship to the tradition of prophecy in Israel. It is time to turn to this matter.

THE PROPHETIC TRADITION IN ISRAEL

Any attempt to speak about the role of prophecy in the traditions of Israel must account for the perspectives of the Deuteronomic history (Deuteronomy through 2 Kings), which portrays Moses as the quintessential prophet and the model for all future prophets,[23] because he assumed the mediating role between Yahweh and the people at Sinai. Moses may have been, to use Webb's categories, the prototypical sapiential prophet. In large measure this means that "the chief function of the prophet is . . . to promulgate the law, preach its observance after the manner of Moses and transmit it to posterity."[24] The prophet is also called to warn the people of the consequences of their failure

---

21. E. P. Sanders, *Jesus and Judaism*, 296, quoted in Gray, *Prophetic Figures*, 138.

22. See, for example, the work of James C. Scott: *The Moral Economy of the Peasant* (1976); *Weapons of the Weak* (1985); *Domination and the Arts of Resistance* (1990). (See note 34, chap. 1, and note 23, chap. 2).

23. Much of this section is indebted to Joseph Blenkinsopp, *Sage, Priest, Prophet: Intellectual Leadership in Ancient Israel* (Louisville, Ky.: Westminster John Knox Press, 1995), 115–65.

24. Ibid., 120. Blenkinsopp also observes that the prophet interprets the fall of the divided kingdom as the judgment of Yahweh and therefore justifies the course of events while articulating a theodicy that justifies the ways of God to the people: "The prophetic task is therefore to proclaim the law, to predict the consequences of ignoring or contravening it and, by so doing, to exonerate the Deity of responsibility for bringing about these disasters" (ibid., 121).

to observe the covenant. This responsibility was passed on from generation to generation, from Joshua and the judges through Samuel to the prophets of the monarchic period, culminating in Jeremiah, the last of the prophets in this great succession.[25] It is important to note that the prophet does not undermine or subvert the Torah but appeals to it and upholds its traditions of justice and judgment. The Torah then is one expression of the covenant between Yahweh and his people, and insofar as the prophet appeals to the covenant revealed at Sinai, he is also appealing to the Torah.

The prophet is also a political figure, and prophets were visibly involved in the politics of the premonarchic era and throughout the period of the monarchy as well. Samuel's call involved a prophetic denunciation of the house of Eli, and the fact that his words did not "fall to the ground" but came to pass marked Samuel as a "trustworthy prophet" (1 Sam 3:1–21). Twice, Nathan the prophet mediated the word of the Lord to David. After David revealed his plans to build a temple for Yahweh, Nathan informed him that he would not be the one to do the job (2 Sam. 7:1–17), and the very same Nathan confronted David with his sin after he had taken Bathsheba and ordered her husband, Uriah the Hittite, killed (2 Sam. 11–12). Gad, who is referred to as "the prophet Gad, David's seer" (2 Sam. 24:11), brings the word of Yahweh's judgment on David for conducting a census (2 Sam. 24:1–25). At a later time, Elijah and Elisha are similarly involved in the power politics of the Northern Kingdom. Elijah was a constant thorn in the side of Ahab and Jezebel (1 Kgs. 17–22). Elisha "anointed Jehu to be king in place of Ahab's son Jehoram"[26] (2 Kgs. 9:1–13).

In their public role as political brokers, prophets could come into conflict with each other. For example, when Ahab consulted his court prophets, Zedekiah and his colleagues all predicted victory in battle against Ramoth-gilead, but Micaiah alone announced Ahab's defeat (1 Kgs. 22:1–40). Jeremiah locked horns with Hananiah over the fate of Jerusalem, Jeremiah prophesying its destruction and Hananiah, its escape from capture (Jer. 28). Grabbe has noted that the difference between true and false prophets may be in the eye of the beholder. Of Ahab's court prophets, including Micaiah, he notes that "all the prophets speak in the name of Yhwh," and it was "quite normal for omens to be tested against each other."[27] The same could be said of Jeremiah and Hananiah. Numerous passages bear witness to the presence of intraprophetic conflict in ancient Israel and Judah (Ezek. 13; Hos. 4:4–6; 9:7–9; Mic. 3:5–8; Zech. 7:7–14; 13:2–6).

25. Ibid., 120–22.
26. Lester L. Grabbe, *Priests, Prophets, Diviners, Sages: A Socio-Historical Study of Religious Specialists in Ancient Israel* (Valley Forge, Pa.: Trinity Press International, 1995), 71.
27. Ibid., 72.

In his study of the role of the prophets, Blenkinsopp has proposed a framework for understanding the distinctive development of prophecy in ancient Israel.[28] Beginning in the eighth century, he argues, a new kind of intellectual leadership emerged in Israel. It was embodied in the work of Amos, Hosea, Isaiah, and Micah, all of whom came from a privileged class yet managed to fashion a tradition of social protest and intellectual dissent that lasted for two hundred years. Their protest can be understood in the context of the emergence of the monarchy and its effects on the peasantry and the clan or tribal systems already in place. As the state increasingly encroached on the rights, resources, and eventually the land of its peasant base, it coopted the religion of Yahweh and impressed its prophets to serve its own ends by legitimating the newly emerging state policies. The court prophets obeyed their rulers, but the four prophets mentioned here did not. They witnessed the collateral damage caused by the state system and denounced its abuses. They shared a common vision and advocacy.

They spoke or wrote on behalf of the socially and economically disadvantaged, the victims of the gradual and inexorable undermining by the state of the cohesion and ethos of a more or less egalitarian system based on the kinship network.[29] Though they themselves were social and intellectual insiders, they advocated for outsiders. Indeed, their genius was the way they used their social position as leverage. "What is clear is that all four belonged to the very small minority of the population that was literate and educated, and it was from that socially privileged position that their protest was launched."[30] The social, economic, and political conditions that the great prophets faced would have been familiar to Jesus. In the first century CE as well as in the eighth century BCE, peasants were being alienated from their land, and ruling elites were redistributing wealth to an indigenous ruling class while creating bureaucracies to mediate their power and manage their domination. Priests and prophets were collaborating with the emerging rulers, thereby legitimating this juggernaut of change and justifying the ways it trampled and destroyed the traditional clan system and network of tribal loyalties.

The process of state control moved more smoothly in the Southern Kingdom of Judah than in the Northern Kingdom of Israel. The antimonarchic tradition expressed so clearly in 1 Sam. 8:10–18 (cf. also Deut. 17:14–20) continued to influence the course of events in Israel. There, the conflict between "tribal ethos and state system" created "chronic political instability" and a tradition of "resistance . . . to the apparatus of state control."[31] The more

28. Blenkinsopp, *Sage, Priest, Prophet*, 147–54.
29. Ibid., 147.
30. Ibid., 154.
31. Ibid., 139.

unstable and uncertain the state's control, the more maneuvering room for the prophets. Many of the Elijah and Elisha traditions reflect this political situation as, for instance, in the story of Naboth's vineyard (1 Kgs. 21:1–29). It is helpful to remember that the Galilee of Jesus' day represented one portion of the former Northern Kingdom, a connection that Horsley notes carefully in his study of "the roots of Galilean independence."[32] Although the intervening history of rule by Hellenistic empires, Hasmonaean rulers, Herodian tyranny, and Roman hegemony must be factored into the history of Galilee, its roots remain entwined with the history of the Northern Kingdom and the aftermath of its fall.

It is tempting, but would be misguided, to place Jesus in the tradition of Amos, Hosea, Isaiah, and Micah and to view him as an extension of them, because he does share some commonalities with them. In spite of the similarities, Jesus was not born into a socially or politically privileged elite. He may have known how to read Torah, but he was not an intellectual in the same way his illustrious prophetic ancestors were. Nor did he have their leverage either in the court of Herod Antipas or the temple courtyard in Jerusalem. He was more an outsider than an insider and, in this respect, is closer to the popular prophets mentioned by Josephus. Jesus came from the margins of his society, not its centers of power; recent efforts to turn Jesus into an urban sophisticate show how bankrupt such an approach can be.[33] Nowhere do the Gospel traditions depict a privileged Jesus using his social status and prominent position on behalf of the poor and the outcast. He emerges from the village life of Galilee, a representative of the little tradition, not an exponent of the great tradition. Like the great prophets, Jesus does argue Torah and appeal to the covenant traditions of Israel's past,[34] as they reflect the interests of village life and peasant existence, and he not only brings good news of Yahweh's redemption but a word of judgment as well.

JESUS, A PROPHET "MIGHTY IN WORD AND DEED" (LUKE 24:19)

Jesus was an odd combination of prophetic types. First, he argues Torah, and he understands the role of Torah in the life of the common people as well as

32. Horsley, *Galilee*, 19–33.

33. See, for example, R. A. Batey, *Jesus and the Forgotten City: New Light on Sepphoris and the Urban World of Jesus* (Grand Rapids: Baker Book House, 1991); Shirley Jackson Case, "Jesus and Sepphoris," *JBL* 45 (1926): 14–22; Thomas W. Longstaff, "Nazareth and Sepphoris: Insights into Christian Origins," *ATR* Supp Series 11 (1990): 8–15; Stuart S. Miller, "Sepphoris, the Well Remembered City," *BA* 55 (1992): 74–83.

34. This point is also emphasized by N. T. Wright, who also views Jesus as a prophet (*Jesus and the Victory of God*, 147–474).

the purposes it has served for the ruling elites. Like a prophet in the mold of the Deuteronomic tradition, Jesus continues the work of the prophet Moses, because he uses Torah to disclose the will of God and to define the justice of God. In addition, he warns those who abuse the Torah by turning it into an instrument of oppression. Jesus neither opposes the Torah nor obliterates it, but attacks a reading of the Torah promulgated by the Jerusalem elites to justify their oppression of "the people of the land." His ability to argue Torah and apply it to the lives of his hearers may explain why, at least in part, Jesus may have been called "rabbi." Rabbi was not an official title but a mark of recognition and respect, an honorific designation or an honorable way to address one who "[taught] the way of God in accordance with truth" (Mark 12:14).

But Jesus does more than argue Torah. He brings his own distinctive message to his work, although this proclamation is neither discontinuous with the history of his people nor a denial of previous traditions. To use Malina's language, Jesus' teachings are the forthcoming result of antecedent tradition focused on the present questions of survival. In his study of cross-cultural parallels to prophecy in Israel, Grabbe identifies a key quality of Nuer prophets that made their work both memorable and durable. It resided, he suggested, in "their ability to enunciate a coherent set of ideas which helped the members of contemporary Nuer society comprehend their own time and situation."[35] This sounds as though the Nuer prophets were dealing with abstractions, but it can equally well mean that the prophets developed a critique of their society that illumined the larger processes affecting the lives of the people. This is what I have already argued with regard to the parables. Put Jesus in the role of a peasant prophet, and he is a "pedagogue of the oppressed."[36] However, it is in this role that Jesus most resembles the oracular prophets of the great tradition. Like Amos, Hosea, Isaiah, and Micah, Jesus the prophet interpreted what was happening to the people of Galilee who were being increasingly squeezed by colonial domination and internal exploitation. He taught them to read their distressing situation not as God's will but as a consequence of the violation of God's covenant. Yet, as already noted, Jesus did not share the social privilege and political leverage of the great prophets of the past. He did not launch an advocacy campaign from a prominent position in court and society.

This is why Jesus must also be seen as a popular prophet who performed signs as part of his public work, in this case, healings and exorcisms. Having little ascribed honor, Jesus had to contend for acquired honor in public debate (honor/shame ripostes) and perform signs that evoked donations of honor

35. Grabbe, *Priests, Prophets, Diviners, Sages*, 95.
36. See William R. Herzog II, *Parables as Subversive Speech: Jesus as Pedagogue of the Oppressed* (Louisville, Ky.: Westminster John Knox Press, 1994), 16–29.

from the crowds. These signs were primarily healings and exorcisms, but they were never done for mere effect; they were part of a larger conflicted context and political strategy. Healings and exorcisms are about power: who channels God's power; who mediates God's power; and on whose behalf it is exercised. Any claim to mediate God's covenant love (healings) or liberating power (exorcisms) was inherently a challenge to those who, in their own estimation, held a monopoly on that power through temple and Torah. To call Jesus "a prophet mighty in word and deed" (Luke 24:19) is to claim for him a powerful role as the broker of God's patronal power. However, in his role as popular prophet, Jesus resembles Elijah and Elisha more than the sign prophets mentioned by Josephus, with the exception that, unlike Elijah and Elisha, he is not involved in the politics of the court and the shifting of dynasties. Jesus seems a less overtly political figure than either of his predecessors, but, like them, he is associated with mighty deeds. At this point, it would be tempting to use Scott Hill's portrayal of "local heroes" to build a bridge between Elijah and Elisha, on the one hand, and Jesus of Nazareth, on the other. Local heroes are, first of all, "holy" figures, that is, they are deemed to be holy "in conjunction with shifting balances in social forces," and in the midst of those shifting forces, they are seen "as having privileged access to power (generally meaning God) beyond the reach of other people."[37] They are venerated figures in their village and its surrounding environs, although they rarely attain national prominence. In their local domain, they are liminal, even numinous figures.

> Beyond the realm defined by "conventional wisdom," however, there always lies an area of unrealized alliances, untapped power, unexpressed yearnings, and untold truth, and it is there that the prophets establish themselves. There are always flaws and oversights in the official explanations of where power and truth lie, and identifying these areas gives local heroes a following that separates them from leaders merely filling an established role.[38]

Quite obviously, when such figures attract the attention of power brokers, they are labeled in negative ways, a tactic that actually serves to increase their power and expand their popular following. Still, it is in their relationship to their origins that their power resides. "By serving as a projection of a community's identity, local heroes allow that community to express power that has lain dormant."[39] In this respect, the local hero resembles the reputational leader.

---

37. Scott D. Hill, "The Local Hero in Palestine in Comparative Perspective," in Robert B. Coote, ed., *Elijah and Elisha in Socio-Literary Perspective* (Atlanta: Scholars Press, 1992), 39.
38. Ibid., 45.
39. Ibid., 48.

It may seem useful to view Jesus as a type of "local hero," but to do so poses other problems. He was not venerated in his home town and country. To the contrary, he met stiff opposition when he did return to his own village (Mark 6:1–6a; Matt. 15:53–58; cf. Luke 4:16–30). Although, in at least one instance, Jesus was sought out to adjudicate conflicts (Luke 12:13ff.), he never became the focus of local shrines after his death, nor, for that matter, did Jesus gain ascribed honor through his family or kinship ties.[40] Like local heroes, he was itinerant, but in the framework being proposed here, itinerancy actually enables local heroes to remain disentangled from the bickering and petty affairs of their village while providing the opportunity to expand their influence over a larger territory.[41] This does not seem to reflect the reasons that Jesus became an itinerant. Jesus did expose the "tension between periphery and center, prophet and priest, popular and traditional, old and new" (Mark 2:21–22), and in his identification with Galilee, he stood "consciously or unconsciously, at a key point of tension between the center and the periphery of power . . . where the fulcrum must be placed to achieve a new balance."[42] The figure of the local hero does provide some useful insights for illuminating Jesus' role as a popular prophet, but it must be used with caution.

In his role both as a popular and oracular prophet, Jesus exhibited the fundamental characteristic common to all prophets. Grabbe summarizes it succinctly: "The prophet is a mediator who claims to receive messages direct from a divinity, by various means, and communicates these messages to recipients."[43] The prophet may receive those messages by various means, "vision, audition, 'angel,' the 'spirit' or 'hand' of Yhwh, even a dream,"[44] and likewise can communicate that message through word or deed, including signs and bizarre symbolic actions. So Jesus greets the returning disciples with the significance of their mission by saying, "I saw Satan fall like lightning from heaven" (Luke 10:18). Clearly, this saying assumes that Jesus has a privileged view into the spirit world and can therefore interpret events around him through this lens. For this reason, prophets and miracle workers begin to

---

40. Ibid.
41. Ibid., 51.
42. Ibid., 52. Compare the role of the local hero with the figure Peter Brown calls "the holy man in Late Antiquity" ("The Rise and Function of the Holy Man in Late Antiquity," *JRS* 61 [1971]: 80–101). Brown sees the holy man of the fifth and sixth centuries acting as village patron and mediator between the village and the larger world as well as settling disputes within the village. He was a "hinge man" who could "place his *dynamis*, his know-how and (let us not forget) his culture and values at the disposal of the villagers." Though some of the similarities are intriguing, the holy man of late antiquity does not provide a good analogy to Jesus' public work.
43. Grabbe, *Priests, Prophets, Diviners, Sages*, 107, 116.
44. Ibid., 116.

overlap. As the prophet draws upon insights gleaned through his vision or audition, so the miracle worker draws upon the power of that numinous realm to heal and exorcize.

> Many prophets have the reputation of an ability to call on God's power to accomplish supernatural deeds: to perform signs and wonders, to benefit friends or to harm enemies, to see into the spirit world and even into the future.[45]

Jesus adds to this general description a distinctive perspective when he rejoices in the Holy Spirit and thanks "the Lord of heaven and earth" who has "hidden these things from the wise and understanding and revealed them to babes" (Q: Luke 10:21–24 par. Matt. 11:25–27; 13:16–17). Evidently, the little tradition extends into the spirit world. Prophets, righteous men, and kings longed to see what Jesus' followers see and to hear what they hear, but they have neither eyes to see nor ears to hear. In other words, Jesus' teachings and actions were all part of his prophetic identity. They need not, indeed they cannot, be separated.

This discussion of Jesus' prophetic role has studiously avoided the use of the words "charismatic" and "charisma," although Blenkensopp does devote attention to Weber's discussion of charisma "as a way of encapsulating the irreducibly personal and nonascriptive element" in the prophet and the prophetic vocation.[46] To this extent, the notion of charisma may be helpful, but not much further. First-century Palestine was a dyadic society rooted in the values of honor and shame.[47] Leaders gained honor not by standing apart from their people but by embodying their values; a charismatic figure would most likely be viewed as a deviant unable to inspire others to follow. For this reason, Malina argues that Jesus was a "reputational" leader rather than a charismatic leader.[48] At the very heart of a reputational leader is his or her ability to dislodge the norms and values that have guided a particular society. Malina notes, "In sum, reputational authority unseats the higher-order norms which stabilize and fix custom and thus calls existing custom into question."[49] This activ-

45. Ibid., 117.
46. Blenkinsopp, *Sage, Priest, Prophet*, 115–19.
47. For information on dyadic societies and honor and shame, see Bruce J. Malina, *The New Testament World: Insights from Cultural Anthropology*, chaps. 2, 3. See also Halvor Moxnes, "Honor and Shame," and Bruce Malina, "Understanding New Testament Persons," in Richard L. Rohrbaugh, ed., *The Social Sciences and New Testament Interpretation* (Peabody, Mass.: Hendrickson Publishers, 1996), chaps. 1, 2.
48. Bruce J. Malina, "Jesus as Charismatic Leader?" *BTB* 14 (1984): 55–62, reprinted as "Was Jesus a Charismatic Leader?" in Bruce J. Malina, *The Social World of Jesus and the Gospels* (London: Routledge, 1996), 123–42. All references are to this version of the article.
49. Ibid., 129.

ity can get very pointed. An emerging reputational leader may convince large numbers of people that a high priest or government bureaucrat holds office not by a divine mandate but through "force, chicanery, collusion, conspiracy, or some other principle" equally unsavory.[50]

Malina identifies a number of traits of such leaders.[51] For example, they do not claim a leadership position for themselves and are often associated with traditional institutions. Jesus emerges from traditional village life and is familiar with the synagogue and its traditions of interpreting Torah. He rejects the assertive claims of Gentile rulers in favor of a service-oriented leadership in which the leader does not stand out from the group (Mark 10:42–45 pars. Matt. 20:25–28; Luke 22:24–27). A reputational leader is at home with tradition and custom. He or she does not challenge familiar ways of doing things. In spite of a traditional and customary orientation, reputational leaders do contribute to the emergence of new structures. When they arise, such leaders show their virtue by "avoidance and relinquishment and/or sharing of power."[52] Not all the characteristics listed here fit Jesus with equal comfort. While he was oriented to custom and tradition, he did not always draw on it in familiar and comfortable ways (cf. Luke 4:16–30; Matt. 5:21–48, but see Matt. 5:17–20). On what did Jesus' growing reputation depend? On his healings, his exorcisms, and his ability to best his enemies in honor-shame ripostes as well as the enthusiastic reception that greeted his proclamation of the reign of heaven. He proclaimed "a forthcoming theocracy [that] was not so much an alternative to the political ideology prevailing in Israel as a hope for its radical realization."[53] He embodied the values of Israel's past leaders, especially those figures in the Northern Kingdom like Elijah and Elisha, who advocated the values of the covenant in the midst of trying and changing times. Unlike Theudas or the Egyptian, he made no grandiose claims for himself nor did he persuade others to follow him in order to stake his claims. When he exercised power, it was on behalf of the very poor villagers from whom he came. Malina sums it up in the following way:

> But if the person in question is recognized as wielding legitimate authority because of a reputation rooted in socially verifiable influence (teaching) or beneficial power (healing), not in illusory charisma, then we shall have reputational legitimate authority in the normal and strict sense.[54]

---

50. Ibid.
51. Ibid.; for a summary of Malina's argument, see his chart comparing a Weberian charismatic leader with a reputational leader on p. 130. The traits discussed here are taken from this chart.
52. Ibid.
53. Ibid., 132.
54. Ibid., 129, 131.

All of this suggests that Jesus was a popular prophet whose roots were deeply embedded in Galilean village life. He most likely came from a peasant artisan family and shared the values of village life and its familiar customs and traditions. It may be useful to view Jesus as a peasant prophet who interpreted the Torah not as a representative of the forms of the great tradition emanating from Jerusalem but as one who read the Torah through the eyes of the various forms of the little tradition that were lodged in the villages and countryside of Galilee. At the same time, as a popular prophetic figure, he attracted crowds because he embodied the yearnings of the Galileans who were increasingly separated from their land and traditions by an alien network of Roman domination, Herodian exploitation, and temple control. Insofar as he interpreted the Torah and argued its meaning, he was a prophet in the tradition of the Deuteronomist, a prophet who continued the paradigmatic work of Moses, the prototypical prophet, and insofar as he interpreted the social, economic, and political situation in the light of the covenant promises of Yahweh, he stood in the tradition of the great oracular prophets of Israel's past. Add to this mix Jesus' own distinctive voice, rooted in his reputation as a traditional teacher and healer, and the foundation is laid for understanding Jesus as prophet. But what does such a prophet look like in action when he is engaging his adversaries over critical issues? The final section of this chapter will address this question.

THE SOURCE OF A PROPHET'S AUTHORITY

The Gospel of Mark records an incident in which the temple authorities challenge Jesus and attempt to undermine his authority (Mark 11:27–33 pars. Matt. 21:23–27; Luke 20:1–8). Mark sets the incident in the outer courtyard of the temple and identifies Jesus' opponents as "the chief priests, and the scribes and the elders" (11:27). The incident can be read as an honor/shame riposte, but it is unlikely that either the chief priests or the elders (nonpriestly aristocrats) would have challenged Jesus directly. They were too far above him in the social hierarchy to risk a confrontation. They would, most likely, have sent proxies, here called scribes, to conduct the challenge. In all probability, it would not matter whether the chief priests and elders issue their challenge directly or indirectly because the crowd would most likely have known on whose behalf and at whose behest the scribes were acting. Whether absent or present, the chief priests and elders were still involved in the incident and their honor is at stake, which may be why Mark depicts them issuing the initial challenge. It is clear that the scribes have the authority to initiate the challenge.

The proxies of the temple authorities initiate contact with Jesus by demanding that he answer two questions, both of which are aimed at undermining his political status. "By what authority are you doing these things? Who gave you this authority to do them?" (11:28). To understand the passage, we need to know what is meant by "these things." In the context of Mark, the reference seems to be to the events surrounding Jesus' entry into Jerusalem (11:15–17) or, in Matthew's version, to the healings on the temple mount that followed the entry (Matt. 21:14–17). It is equally possible that the reference could simply be to the healings and exorcisms that had marked Jesus' public activity from the beginning and had also been a source of ongoing contention (Mark 3:19b–27 and pars.). Or the scribes may be referring to Jesus' critique of the temple and his aberrant reading of the Torah.

Having been publicly challenged to debate, Jesus must decide whether to accept the challenge or ignore it. It is interesting to note in passing that scribal retainers tacitly acknowledge Jesus' public stature by engaging him in an honor challenge, a far cry from the assumption made by the scribes in Capernahum (Mark 2:1–12) that Jesus was an unworthy opponent who could be shunned and shamed but did not need to be noticed. Knowing how much is at stake, Jesus accepts the challenge, even though this means that he cannot answer their questions directly. That would put him on his opponents' ground, for their questions imply not only that they represent the only legitimate authority, the authority of the temple, but also that it is theirs to bestow. Since they have not authorized Jesus to do the works he has done, then he must be acting without proper authority. He is a rogue rabbi and a bogus prophet operating without the authorization of the temple authorities; therefore, he is a deviant. If Jesus tries to answer their questions, he will have lost the challenge and some of the social and political prominence he has gained through his public activity. So, acting as an honorable man, Jesus takes command of the exchange, setting the conditions for the riposte and demanding an answer from his adversaries (11:29). In these contests, thrust is better than parry and attack preferable to evasion. If they will answer his question, then he will answer theirs. It seems like a simple exchange, but Jesus' question springs a trap: "Was the baptism of John from heaven or of human origin? Answer me" (11:30). Notice that the insistent demand for an answer (use of the imperative implies authority and control) intensifies the conflict and puts his opponents on the defensive.

But why appeal to John the Baptist? Because John was "a real prophet" in the people's eyes, and he served in that role without either the authorization or the blessing of the temple. The prophet's authority comes from God. This is one reason why the call stories are so important in the prophetic literature (Isa. 6:1–13; Jer. 1:4–19; Ezek. 2:1–10). The authority of the true prophet derives from the Lord, which makes prophetic authority part of a system of checks and balances between temple authorities and prophetic figures who hold them to account. When Jesus appeals to John, he is identifying with the prophetic tradition, and like so many prophets, including John, Jesus serves (to use Robert Wilson's language) as a "peripheral intermediary" rather than a "central intermediary."[55] The point of appealing to John's baptism is clear. The baptism of John was approved "by heaven," an indirect way of speaking about God. It bore the stamp of divine authority even though that authority was neither sanctioned nor controlled by a priestly hierarchy. Prophetic authority, especially the authority claimed by the peripheral prophets, typically originates and flourishes outside of the borders and boundaries of commonly accepted institutional authority. So the question "Who gave you this authority?" is moot. The authority comes from Yahweh; the temple authorities are irrelevant. Therefore, the fact that they have not invested Jesus with his authority is not a liability but an asset.

Painted into a corner by Jesus' retort, the scribes try to hold the high ground by denying Jesus an answer: "We do not know" (11:33). They may be attempting to snub him by refusing to play the game that they have initiated. But Jesus' counterresponse is swift: "Neither will I tell you by what authority I do these things" (11:33). He remains a player who equally well can withhold the information they had originally sought, but his reference to John has let the cat out of the bag. Like John's baptism and most prophetic authority, Jesus' authority comes "from heaven," that is, from God. This seems to be, in part, the point of the stories of Jesus' baptism (Mark 1:9–11; Matt. 3:13–17; Luke 3:21–22), which functions like a prophetic call episode.

The challenge would appear to end in a stalemate. However, since Jesus' challengers appeared to have the upper hand at the beginning of this honor challenge and since their prominent political status as representatives of an honorable institution (the temple) and its leaders (chief priests) would predispose many to side with them, their stalemate is more of a loss than a gain. Most bystanders would have presumed that they would prevail against a peasant prophet from an insignificant village like Nazareth. Yet, by the end of the debate, Jesus stands on equal ground with the scribal proxies and forces a stalemate. In truth, at the close of the challenge, Jesus is in control, and he gets the last word. He has won by establishing himself as a figure in the prophetic tradition.

Nearly all scholars of the historical Jesus grant that he taught in parables. If so, we should expect that some of the themes of Jesus' prophetic work would be contained in them, and that is in fact the case.[56] In the parable of the rich

---

55. See Robert R. Wilson, *Prophecy and Society in Ancient Israel* (Philadelphia: Fortress Press, 1980), 32–42. *Intermediation* is Wilson's word to describe the central function of a prophet.

56. For a fuller examination of this approach to the parables, see my work, *Parables as Subversive Speech*.

man and Lazarus (Luke 16:19–31), Jesus reveals himself to be a teacher of Torah and the prophets. The parable is divided into two scenes:

16:19–22	rich and poor
16:23–31	lost and found

In the opening scene, with a few deft strokes, Jesus sketches the two-tiered society of his day, the rich who have nearly everything, and the poor who have almost nothing. Three items identify the rich man (*plousiōs*) as a member of the elite. He was "clothed in purple," the most expensive dye in the ancient world. Only the richest of the rich could afford it. He wears linen most likely imported from Egypt, and he serves great feasts, not just on special occasions but every day. He isolates and protects himself from the grim realities of the world by constructing a great ornamental gate that shuts out the world around him. By contrast, Lazarus is the poorest of the poor. He is a destitute beggar (*ptōchos*) who has been "thrown down" at the rich man's gate. How did a beggar like Lazarus come into such desperate straits? There is a familiar social script or story behind the parable. The Lazaruses of Galilee and Judea most likely began their lives as the third or fourth son of a peasant family. When they reached the age where they began to consume more than they could produce, they were turned loose on the streets to become day laborers. Day laborers lived just at or below the threshold of survival, dying slowly from the complications of malnutrition. When a day laborer, like Lazarus most likely had been, scratched or cut himself, his wounds would not heal, and he became like a leper, unclean and likely to transmit his uncleanness to others. This left begging as his last resort, but begging left one more destitute than working as a day laborer. So beggars wound up like Lazarus, too weak to move. He was too weak to fight off the unclean street curs who licked his open sores. Lazarus lay down at the gate of a rich man's house to eat the garbage thrown into the streets for the beggars and dogs to fight over; he "desired to be fed with what fell from the rich man's table," scraps of bread and bits of meat from the daily feast. Just as Jesus has sketched the rich man with a few deft strokes, so he portrays the poor beggar, full of sores, licked by street dogs, longing to eat even table scraps.

Two details leave the hearer with questions. The beggar has a name, Lazarus, which means, somewhat ironically, "Yahweh helps." The name has a jarring effect. If this is an example of God's help, who needs it! Why would the beggar have a name and the rich man have none? It is puzzling, and since this is the only instance in Jesus' parables in which anyone has a name, it is quite remarkable. The second detail is found in the verb "thrown down" (*ebeblēto*), a passive verb form implying the action of God (the divine passive).

The transition from the first scene to the second scene comes with the two death announcements (16:22). Lazarus dies, and the angels carry him to Abraham's bosom. It is implied that he was given no burial; his body was taken to a mass disposal site, either a garbage dump in the Hinnom Valley if in Jerusalem, or a similar site if elsewhere. His death is as insignificant as his life was inconsequential. By contrast, the rich man is buried in proper fashion, the honorable ending to an honorable life. But we are still left with some doubt about the fate of the poor man's body and the rich man's soul.

The second scene of the parable occurs in Hades, the abode of the dead. It is important not to identify Hades with the heaven and hell of later Christian theology. Hades is the place where all the dead go, rich and poor alike. But the geography of Hades is still important, for the rich man resides in torment in the flames while Lazarus reclines on Abraham's bosom like the honored guest at a banquet. The parable's second scene seems to be an illustration of the sayings of Jesus found in Q (Luke 13:28–30 par. Matt. 8:11–12), where the theme is also inclusion and exclusion. Yet kinship language is used throughout the scene. The rich man calls out to "father Abraham," and Abraham calls the rich man "child (*teknon*)."

The focus of the parable is on the conversation between Abraham and the rich man. The rich man makes three requests, each one of which Abraham denies. First, he demands that Abraham "have mercy on me" and send Lazarus with a drop of water to cool his tongue. Note that both "requests" are imperatives; he is still a rich man used to issuing commands and having them obeyed. Abraham refuses and asks the rich man to remember the good things he had in life while Lazarus had nothing. He seems to be saying that turnabout is fair play and serves a purpose akin to the purpose of the chasm that prevents Lazarus from taking water to the rich man. Abraham seems to think it is important to hold the rich man's feet to the fire. Turn up the heat and see if it leads to new insight for the rich man. Just as the ornamental gate shielded the rich man from seeing the consequences of his life for the poor, so looking at things from the flames on the other side of the chasm may provide him with a different perspective on his life and his wealth.

Undeterred, the rich man makes a second request, namely, to warn his father's household. The fact that he has five brothers and that they all live in his father's house indicates what a large and wealthy household it must be, very unlike the peasant or artisan household that had to turn their children like Lazarus loose on the streets to fend for themselves. To this petition, Abraham is ready with a reply: listen to Moses and the prophets. At first glance, this would seem to be a reasonable request, since the rich man believes that he is Torah obedient, but obedient to whose reading of the Torah, the reading of the Pharisees or the reading of the prophets? Does he follow the purity codes of the

Torah but forget the debt codes that speak of social justice? When Jesus, through Abraham, links Moses with the prophets, he points toward a prophetic reading of Torah. It was this reading of the Torah that inspired Amos to declare,

> For I know how many are your transgressions . . .
> you who afflict the righteous, who take a bribe,
>   and push aside the needy in the gate. . . .
> Hate evil and love good,
>   and establish justice in the gate.
>   (Amos 5:12, 15a NRSV)

In essence, Amos was appealing to a prophetic reading of the Torah as the basis for a renewal of Yahweh's covenant with his people and his call to Israel to become a contrast society. This is the impulse behind the sabbatical and jubilee provisions in the Torah (Deut. 15:1–18; Lev. 25:1–7, 8–55). The appeal to Moses is an appeal to the Torah as an expression of Yahweh's covenant with the people at Sinai, and the appeal to the prophets emphasizes the indispensable place that justice must occupy in any reading of it (Isa. 1:16–17; 5:7; Jer. 5:23–29; 21:11–14; Amos 2:6–11; Mic. 3:1–3, 9–12).

Abraham's appeal falls on deaf ears. No sooner has Abraham admonished the rich man to listen to Moses and the prophets than the rich man ignores the advice and renews his appeal by arguing that sending Lazarus as a messenger from the dead will be more effective because Lazarus will provide his father and brothers with privileged insider information. After all, Lazarus lay at the rich man's gate, a living witness to the neglect of Moses and the prophets, and neither the rich man nor his family heeded the message contained in his broken and dying body. Why would they heed his words even if he returned from the dead as an apparition? So Abraham reiterates, "If they do not hear Moses and the prophets, neither will they be convinced if someone should [return] from the dead."[57]

The kinship language becomes increasingly important as the pedagogy of the oppressor continues. Lazarus's protected location in Abraham's bosom indicates clearly that he is a child of Abraham. In fact, J. Duncan M. Derrett has argued that Lazarus is actually Abraham's steward, Eliezer (Gen. 15:2).[58] According to rabbinic tradition, Abraham would, from time to time, send his steward among his people to see how well they were fulfilling their obligation

---

57. I have repeated the verb that Luke used in the previous verse (*poreuomai*) rather than use Luke's verb (*anastē*), which seems to be a clear allusion to the resurrection of Jesus and, therefore, a Lukan addition to the parable. The brackets indicate the change.

58. J. Duncan M. Derrett, "Fresh Light on St. Luke xvi:11: Dives and Lazarus and the Preceding Sayings," *NTS* 7:364–380.

to show hospitality. Whether Lazarus can be read in this light or not, he is a part of Abraham's kinship group. So is the rich man, but all he can see is his immediate family, his father's house and his five brothers. He is concerned with their welfare but not with the well-being of Lazarus who remains for the rich man either a servant or a messenger. The rich man's view of kinship is limited to his self-interest and social class. Abraham has been attempting to elicit the recognition that, if the rich man is Abraham's "son" and if Lazarus is Abraham's son, then the rich man and Lazarus are brothers. This is what the rich man cannot see. He has neither eyes to see the destitute beggar as a brother nor ears to hear Moses and the prophets. Hence, the chasm remains.

This parable can be read as a prophetic critique of life in the two-tiered society of Herod's Galilee and the high priestly families' Jerusalem. The kinship that should link rich and poor as brothers and sisters has been broken and replaced with what we would call a class system dominated by a ruling class imitating the ways of their Roman overlords. In this context, the rich lend a deaf ear that utterly fails to hear the prophetic words of Moses and the Torah. The family who claims Abraham and Sarah as honorable ancestors has been fragmented and broken. Chasms as great as the chasm in the parable separate the rich from the poor in the family of Israel, no gap being greater than the divide between the ruling class and destitute beggars, the expendables of their society. By providing a view from the afterlife, Jesus comments on what is needed to heal the present, namely, a new reading of Moses and the prophets. This may be, in part, what Jesus means when he speaks of fulfilling the law and the prophets, not abolishing them (Matt. 5:17–20).

This chapter has attempted to establish a view of Jesus as a prophet and to examine how his teaching reflects the prophetic tradition of Israel. Since prophets in the tradition established by Moses (cf. Deut. 18:9–22) were responsible for teaching Torah and warning the people of the consequences entailed in ignoring or perverting it, it will not be surprising to learn that Jesus taught Torah. The next chapter will be devoted to understanding Jesus as a teacher of Torah.

6

"What is written in the Torah? How do you read?"

(Luke 10:26)

In the previous chapter, we suggested that Jesus quite likely did argue Torah either with Pharisees or their sympathizers and proxies in Galilee. It is time to examine more fully the issues over which they came into conflict. In the discussions that follow, it is important to note that the historical Jesus did not reject the Torah in favor of a new (Christian) theology. He says quite plainly, "Do not think that I have come to abolish the Torah or the prophets. I have not come to abolish but to fulfill" (Matt. 5:17). For Jesus, the Torah is prophetic, and he will propose prophetic readings of the Torah quite distinct from the oral Torah of the Pharisees and their political faction. In Jesus' teaching, the Torah and the prophets imply each other and amplify each other as well. In other words, the Torah is fundamentally about justice, or as Jesus puts it, "the weightier matters of the Torah [are] judgment, mercy and faithfulness" (Matt. 23:23).

THE TORAH: PURITY AND DEBT

Fernando Belo has argued that the Torah is composed of two basic codes, which he calls the purity code and the debt code.[1] It will be helpful to examine each one briefly. The purity code is rooted in an understanding of creation in which God separated incompatible pairs, for example, light from darkness or sabbath from workdays. This means that to maintain the order of creation, the Torah must continue to separate incompatible pairs. Some animals can be

---

1. Fernando Belo, *A Materialist Reading of the Gospel of Mark*, trans. Matthew J. O'Donnell (Maryknoll, N.Y.: Orbis Books, 1981).

offered as sacrifices (first-born and unblemished), but others cannot be offered. Some people are clean (Judeans) while others are not (Gentiles), and even within Israel, some people are pure (those who follow Torah) but others are not (the peasants of the land who ignore Torah). There are two kinds of food, food that has been tithed and food that has not. Deuteronomy 22:9–11 forbids planting two kinds of seeds in the same field, wearing clothes made from two kinds of cloth, or plowing with two kinds of animals. The system can be extended indefinitely so that no area of life remains untouched. The purity code will determine what food can be shared at table, what offerings can be made at the altar of the temple, and who can marry whom, for the purity codes cover all of life from the altar in the temple to the table in the household. Eventually, the world will not only be divided into incompatible pairs but will be organized into hierarchies of purity and impurity called purity maps. Jerome Neyrey summarizes one such list as it applies to people. The list moves from the most pure to the most unclean.[2]

1. Priests
2. Levites
3. Israelites
4. Converts (proselytes)
5. Freed slaves
6. Disqualified priests (illegitimate children of priests)
7. *Netins* (temple slaves)
8. *Mamzers* (bastards)
9. Eunuchs
10. Those with damaged testicles
11. Those without a penis.

(*t. Meg.* 2:7)

The same process can produce hierarchies of sacred space and time, and as the process becomes more elaborated, the combined purity maps will provide a social map of Galilean and Judean society. Just as the priest is the model for purity as applied to human beings, so the temple and its feasts will provide the most obvious model of purity for space (the holy of holies, the holy place, and the courtyards of the temple complex) and time (sabbath, day of atonement, and the major pilgrimage festivals). In other words, the purity codes define a society centered on the temple and its priests.

A community follows purity codes in order to avoid the contagion of pollution that dissolves the created order into chaos. As Belo puts it, "Pollution

2. Jerome Neyrey, "The Idea of Purity in Mark," in John H. Elliott, ed., *Social-Scientific Criticism of the New Testament and Its Social World*, Semeia 35 (Decatur, Ga.: Scholars Press, 1986), 95–96.

means confusion and dissolution of the elements involved; it is a curse; it brings death."[3] When any behavior or practice violates these prescribed boundaries, it is an "abomination" (*toebab*) or abhorrent to the Lord. An abomination describes whatever violates the boundaries set out in the purity maps. For example, women must not wear men's clothing, and men must not wear women's clothing, because their behavior violates the clear lines that separate complementary but incompatible pairs (male and female) and creates confusion (Deut. 22:5). A prophet in Israel must not resort to the practices of soothsayers, augurs, diviners, sorcerers, necromancers, and the like, because they are incompatible pairs. Prophecy is not to be identified with any of these practices. To do so invites boundary-breaking confusion and chaos (Deut. 18:9–14). This means that anyone who subverts these codes will be treated as a threat to the community that lives by them, and he or she will be labeled a deviant. The codes clearly create a prominent place for the temple and its reading of the Torah since the ultimate model of purity is the priestly caste performing sacerdotal functions in the temple. The theological goal of the purity project was to fulfill the promise of the holiness code in Leviticus: "You shall be holy, for I the LORD your God am holy" (19:2). The people of God must, therefore, reflect and embody the holiness of the God who called them into being.

The debt codes begin with the liberation from slavery in Egypt and the gift of the land. The land belongs to Yahweh and is Yahweh's to distribute as he sees fit. Leviticus picks up this theme in a very pointed manner: "The land shall not be sold in perpetuity, for the land is mine; with me you are but aliens and tenants. Throughout the land that you hold, you shall provide for the redemption of the land" (25:23–24). According to the debt codes, everyone is a debtor to Yahweh. The land was given to be a blessing to the people of the land, and that blessing was to be realized through the principle of extension, which means that the yield of the land was to be shared with all so that none would be in need. The more one gets, the more one gives. This vision of a society in which poverty had been eradicated was captured in Deuteronomy 15:

> There will, however, be no poor among you, because the Lord your God is sure to bless you in the land that the Lord God is giving you as a possession to occupy, if only you will obey the LORD your God by diligently observing this entire commandment that I command you today. (15:4–5)

All of the people were debtors to Yahweh, and all were responsible to see that the yield of the land was distributed to all. This explains why the people tithe every third year "to the Levites, the aliens, the orphans and the widows, so that

3. Belo, *A Materialist Reading*, 39.

they may eat their fill within your towns" (Deut. 26:12). The same impulse underlies the sabbatical year (Deut. 15:12–18) and the jubilee year (Lev. 25:23–55), provisions of the debt codes.

The purpose of the debt codes was to create a contrast society in which "justice would roll down like waters and righteousness like an ever flowing stream" (Amos 5:24). Belo argues that the debt codes were intended to avoid the violence that arises when a ruling class begins to exploit and oppress a peasant base. This is, he notes,

> the locus of violence that must be exorcized: the desire that is brought to bear on the other's source of subsistence, the desire that is the origin of aggressive violence. . . . This violence . . . is the source of the class system, the enrichment of some at the expense of others, and the formation of large scale ownership.[4]

Unfortunately, the debt codes harbored an inner contradiction. As the land yielded abundantly, providing the means to fulfill the principle of extension, it also triggered the desire to accumulate rather than redistribute the wealth of the land. As Belo notes, "Blessing and abundance engender the covetous desire to have more; this means that the blessing may well develop under its aegis the violence that is the curse."[5] This was certainly the case by the first century in Galilee and Judea.

These two codes of the Torah were not of equal stature. Usually, one was seen in light of the other; one of the codes was focal, and the other subsidiary. The consequences were considerable. Take the issue of poverty as an example. Seen through the lens of the purity codes, poverty is the result of impurity or uncleanness. If people lived by the purity codes of the Torah, they would be blessed and prosperous, so poverty is a sign of God's judgment on the unclean. The problem is with the poor, not the rich who are reaping the rewards of their faithfulness to Torah. Seen through the eyes of the debt codes, however, poverty is the result of covetous greed. It is the consequence of a ruling elite alienating peasants from their land and reducing them to forms of dependency such as tenants or day laborers. The problem is not with the poor but with the rich. Of course, this form of oppression can only occur if large portions of the Torah are suppressed or ignored. Although the correlation is not one to one, it is clear that the dominant forms of the great tradition treated the purity codes of Torah as focal and the debt codes as subsidiary, whereas versions of the little tradition would be more likely to read the Torah through the lens of the debt code as primary and the purity codes as secondary.

4. Ibid., 44.
5. Ibid., 54.

In the study of the passages that follow, it is assumed that Jesus was literate, that is, that he could read the Torah scroll and other scrolls that might be in a synagogue (for example, the scroll of a prophet like Isaiah or perhaps the Psalms). It is not clear that Jesus was literate and scribal, that is, that he could read and write, but he is portrayed as being able to read sacred texts. Crossan has argued against this position, assuming that a Galilean peasant would most likely not be literate. But the situation of Judeans and Galileans was different from the situation that obtained in many other ethnic communities in the ancient world. Meier puts it this way:

> For all the differences among various groups of Jews, the narratives, laws, and prophecies of their sacred texts gave them a corporate memory and common ethos. The very identity and continued existence of the people Israel were tied to a corpus of written and regularly read works in a way that was simply not true of other peoples in the Mediterranean world of the first century.[6]

Even if he could read the scrolls, it is also clear that Jesus cited texts from memory or alluded to them in his debates. This was a stock-in-trade practice for an oral teacher and storyteller, and Jesus was both.

It is time to examine how these conflicts looked in practice by examining some controversy stories.

CLEAN HANDS OR CLEAN HEART

Jesus' debate over the issue of defilement (Mark 7:1–15 par. Matt. 15:1–11; all references are to the Markan version) has long been seen as a text that attempts to combine two incompatible issues: the status of tradition (vv. 1–13) and the matter of defilement (vv. 14–23). The story also contains abrupt changes and breaks in the material. For example, the question asked in verse 5 is not answered until verse 15. This leaves the impression that the material inserted between the question and its answer reflects clumsy editing. Bultmann concluded that "the artificiality of the composition is clear as day."[7] Finally, to the degree that Jesus' reply to the charges against his disciples (v. 7) relies on the Greek version of Isaiah (the Septuagint, abbreviated as LXX) rather than the Hebrew text (abbreviated MT for Masoretic Text), it must reflect the editing hand of the early church because Jesus most likely would have used the

---

6. John Meier, *A Marginal Jew: Rethinking the Historical Jesus*, vol. 1, *The Roots of the Problem and the Person* (New York: Doubleday, 1991), 274.

7. Rudolf Bultmann, *History of the Synoptic Tradition*, trans. John Marsh (Oxford: Basil Blackwell, 1963), 47.

Hebrew text, not its Greek equivalent. Of course, it has to be determined whether this is the case. As a preliminary step, it may be useful to set the two texts side by side.

Isaiah 29:13 (Hebrew)	*Isaiah 29:13 (Greek) = Mark*
and their worship of me	in vain do they worship me
is a human commandment	teaching as doctrines
learned by rote	human precepts

We will return to this a bit later. All of these issues raise the question whether the text as it stands can be seen as a whole or is a clumsy composite of incompatible materials.

This study of the conflict will propose that it can be read as a unified whole if we understand the relationship between the form of the text and the social system within which it functioned. Bruce Malina has argued that this debate is an example of an honor challenge and riposte by noting that

> literary forms as well as literary genres derive from social systems. . . . Consequently, the place to look for both the structure of a literary form as well as the meanings mediated by that structure is in some social system. Here in Mark 7 the literary form is a challenge riposte form.[8]

The judgment that the passage is disjointed rests on the assumption that Jesus and his opponents were conducting a hostile question-and-answer session. In this setting, it is disconcerting to discover that a question asked in verse 5 is not answered until verse 15, and it is reasonable to assume that the material inserted between the question and answer is the result of awkward editing. From a contemporary point of view, the issues of tradition and defilement appear to be completely separate issues. However, if the passage presents us with an honor challenge and riposte, then we would not expect a hostile question to be answered. The proper riposte to a hostile challenge is not to answer the question but to attack the one who asked it, and this is exactly what Jesus does. Where the modern reader finds discontinuity, the ancient reader finds continuity. Let's look at the dynamics more closely.

The passage can be divided into clear blocks of material. They can be identified as follows:

vv. 1–5	initial challenge and hostile question
vv. 6–8	the Isaiah citation/the riposte and countercharge
vv. 9–13	the Corban example/illustration of the countercharge
vv. 14–15	the parable or riddle about defilement/consequence

8. Bruce Malina, "A Conflict Approach to Mark 7," *Forum* 4 (1988): 8.

After the initial challenge, we hear nothing more from Jesus' adversaries. The passage gives us a prolonged riposte, each item of which would have been debated. Even with this handicap, it may still be possible to catch a fleeting appearance of the dynamics and issues with particular attention devoted to the status and nature of Torah. In this way, we may discover that the issue of defilement is inextricably related to the status of tradition.

Jesus' adversaries are identified as "Pharisees" and "the scribes who had come down from Jerusalem" (7:1). As indicated earlier, the Pharisees were located in Jerusalem but might well be in Galilee to monitor compliance with their Torah program, and the Jerusalem scribes are most likely Pharisaic scribes. Since this passage identifies the scribes with Jerusalem but not the Pharisees, it is possible that the folks labeled Pharisees refer to local sympathizers or allies of the Jerusalem-based movement. Sanders and others dismiss the matter out of hand. Sanders calls attention to "the extraordinarily unrealistic settings of many of the conflict stories . . . nor is it credible that scribes and Pharisees made a special trip to Galilee from Jerusalem to inspect Jesus' disciples' hands."[9] He is right, of course, in saying that the scribes and Pharisees did not come down from Jerusalem for the express purpose of examining the disciples' hands, but they were in Galilee to reinforce compliance to the oral Torah, here called "the tradition of the elders" (7:5). With these authority figures moving about, eating with common hands could be seen as an act of defiance and a challenge. Since the validity of the whole edifice rests upon observing what appear to be small rituals and ceremonies, the refusal to observe any single rule can signal a challenge to the Pharisees' authority or a rejection of the whole system of oral Torah. Eating with common hands, that is, ritually unwashed hands, is a threshold issue or a presenting problem that opens up much larger questions. Since uncleanness can be communicated through touch, unclean hands pose a significant threat, especially around a table where everything and everyone the diners touch would be rendered unclean. Given the centrality of purity for table companionship in the Pharisees' program, nothing affecting the matter of eating and cleanness should be considered inconsequential or unimportant.

The Pharisees are a table companionship group and a political interest group. Their goal is to eat every meal in a state of ritual purity equal to that of the priests in the temple performing their sacerdotal tasks. Hence, they place great emphasis on the purity of those with whom they recline at table, especially their hands, the food placed on the table, and the utensils used to prepare and serve it. Only food that has been tithed to the temple can be clean, so all food must be tithed before it is consumed. In the service of this project,

9. E. P. Sanders, *Jesus and Judaism* (Minneapolis: Fortress Press, 1985), 265.

the Pharisees had generated an "oral Torah" to instruct people how to eat their meals in a state of proper purity. One foundational rule for table companionship was ritually washed hands. If unclean (literally, common) hands were not an important issue, why would scribes challenge Jesus publicly, risking their honor in a challenge-and-riposte confrontation over a trivial issue better ignored? The most obvious answer is that they understood the larger issues implied by eating with common hands. They perceived the larger implications of the practice of Jesus and his disciples, so they could not let the challenge go unanswered.

Their challenge takes the form of a hostile question that impugns Jesus' honor: "Why do your disciples not live according to the tradition of the elders, but eat with hands defiled?" (v. 5). The Pharisees align themselves with the honorable tradition of the elders. The initial assumption of some in the crowd would be that the tradition is honorable, and therefore anyone who ignores it must be shameful, deviant, or subversive. The initial attack is directed at Jesus' disciples, but in that world Jesus is responsible for the actions of his disciples, so the question still casts aspersions on him. In a highly charged political challenge, questions are not asked to gain information but are used as weapons to attack the honor of another. As already noted, Jesus cannot answer the question but must change the terms of the encounter. This explains why the terms of the discussion change so quickly.

Jesus doesn't pretend to answer the question but attacks his interlocutors. His adversaries have invoked the Torah to accuse him and his disciples of not being Torah obedient. If Jesus is to counter this accusation, he must find strong ground on which to make his case, so he turns to the prophets, in this case Isaiah: "Well did Isaiah prophesy of you actors." (Remember the discussion of "hypocrites" as stage actors.) The quotation from Isaiah sets the terms of the debate. It is a conflict between two ways of doing Torah, the lips and the heart (7:6b–7). The Pharisees are operating with a view of the human body as a symbol of the social body.[10] What occurs at one level symbolizes what is happening at the other because every member of the community is a microcosm of the larger whole. For this reason, the Pharisees rivet their attention on the purity practices of each member because the purity of the whole is at stake. Since they do attend to such matters as ritual ablutions before they eat, the Pharisees believe that they are a pure community. Contagion can only enter from the outside, brought in by unclean hands at table as they convey food to

10. For a fuller discussion of this concept, see Mary Douglas, *Natural Symbols: Explorations in Cosmology* (New York: Pantheon Books, 1982), and for an application of these views see Jerome Neyrey, "The Idea of Purity in Mark," in Elliott, ed., *Social-Scientific Criticism of the New Testament*.

the lips and mouth. Thus, they are focused on hands and lips, which are vulnerable to contagion whenever people eat.

Following a different approach, Jesus proposes that impurity comes from the heart and invokes Isaiah to set the two ways of living against each other. In this context, the Hebrew of Isaiah, "Their worship of me is a human commandment learned by rote" makes sense. Jesus compares the tradition of the elders to human directives learned by rote. This challenges its honorable status. While their adherents think they are worshiping God by scrupulously keeping the purity codes, they are doing little more than repeating what they have learned to do without comprehending the prophetic vision that emphasizes mercy and justice as the prerequisite of true worship. This is a failure with a long history as illustrated by the corpus of the prophetic literature. Jesus stands in a well-established tradition (Jer. 7:1–15; 26:1–6; Hos. 4:6; Amos 2:6–8; 4:4–5; 5:21–24; Mic. 4:1–4; Isa. 1:11–17). Not only does the citation from Isaiah fit the context of this debate, but the larger context of Isaiah fits the current debate as well. In Isaiah 29:13–14, Isaiah has challenged Judah to change. Because the people's heart is far from Yahweh and because they worship him by rote, Yahweh promises again "to do amazing things with this people, shocking and amazing" (something like a wake-up call); the wisdom of the wise shall perish, and their discernment shall be hidden. If Jesus were quoting Isaiah 29:13 for the purpose of evoking the larger section of Isaiah in which it is found, then the larger context begins to explain the "shocking and amazing" things Yahweh is doing through his broker, Jesus. He is attacking the purity codes and appealing to the hearts of Galileans and Judeans alike for a renewal of the covenant, not a multiplication of the items in the tradition of the elders.[11] Jesus' riposte then appeals to the prophetic critique of the abuses of Torah, but he is still in a vulnerable position since the Torah carries greater weight than the prophets.

With this in mind, Jesus turns to the issue of Torah obedience. The *korban* (which means dedicated) section argues that the Pharisees have abrogated the Torah in order to fulfill their tradition of the elders. Indeed, he sets "your tradition" in direct conflict with "the commandment of God" (v. 9), and this is no incidental commandment but one from the Decalogue (the Ten Commandments) itself, the very heart of the Torah. The *korban* provision has received a great deal of attention with little consensus about the details of how it worked. But its consequences were clear. Those who dedicated some portion of their wealth to the temple by declaring it *korban* deprived their parents

---

11. C. H. Dodd has argued that ancients quoted specific texts with the intention of invoking the larger section of which they were a part (*According to the Scriptures: The Sub-Structure of New Testament Theology* [London: Collins, 1965]).

of the support they could expect from their children. Yet, according to the Decalogue, sons were honor bound to support and help their parents as they grew older (Exod. 20:12; Deut. 5:16). Children were forbidden to curse their parents (Exod. 21:17; Lev. 20:9), and in this passage, Jesus seems to have enlarged the meaning of cursing parents to include the curse visited upon parents by children whose failure to fulfill their filial obligations subjected parents to poverty in their old age. In this instance, the demands of the Decalogue to care for parents were abrogated in order to support the temple by declaring some portion of one's wealth *korban*, that is, dedicated to God. How ironic that the God who gave the Decalogue is portrayed as annulling his own commandment! But the deeper issue is related to the covenant. When collected together, the passages from the Decalogue (Exod. 20:12; Deut. 5:16) and other Torah texts (Exod. 21:17; Lev. 20:9) articulate a familiar covenantal theology of blessing for fulfilling the commandments and curse for failing to observe them. It is as though Jesus were invoking a memory of the Shechem covenant renewal ceremony (Deut. 27:1–26). If Jesus began his riposte with an appeal to the prophets, he concludes the riposte with a solemn appeal to the heart of the Torah itself. His reading of the tradition of the elders reduces it to a shameful human contraption that actually subverts the Torah given at Sinai.

But how would this matter of *korban* resonate with peasants who do not have enough wealth to dedicate to the temple? They cannot even pay their tithes. It would seem to be an issue for the wealthy but not for peasants, but this appearance may prove to be wrong. At the heart of *korban* is a decision to serve the needs of the temple at the expense of one's family, a conflict that runs deep in peasant life. When the temple demanded its tithes and offerings from peasants living at a subsistence level, it was forcing them to choose between temple and family. Peasants could support their parents and other elders in the village or pay their tithes and offerings. When they chose to support their families, they were vilified as unclean and Torah disobedient. With his attack on *korban*, Jesus escalated the conflict with the Pharisees and their scribes by declaring that their decision to place temple before family and kinship obligations was a distortion of Torah and an abrogation of one of its most important commandments. By the time he completed his riposte, Jesus had depicted his opponents not as teachers of the Torah but as enemies of Torah who threaten to bring a curse upon the land by encouraging people to abandon their familial and kinship obligations in order to serve the needs of the temple. What began as an honorable tradition of the elders is now "your tradition" which "you hand on." Jesus declares that the responsibility for what has happened is in their hands and on their heads.

The covenantal implications of Jesus' riposte suggest that he is building a fictive kinship movement that will gather around his reading of Torah. If so, the beginnings of a political faction are emerging. Having dispensed his enemies, Jesus then appeals to the crowd, finally answering the question that began the political debate, but he is no longer speaking to the Pharisees or their scribes. His answer is in the form of a riddle or parable (vv. 14–15). Once again, Jesus contrasts two ways of doing Torah, from the inside out (the heart/lips) or from the outside in (hands/lips). Although the vice list in verses 20–23 probably contains the ethical reflection of the early church, the vices listed pretty much cover the sixth through the tenth commandments. Jesus' debate with the Pharisees provided rich source material for the theological and ethical reflection of the early church.

"ONE THING YOU LACK"

One of the most interesting passages in the Gospels is the meeting between Jesus and a rich ruler (Mark 10:17–22 pars. Matt. 19:16–22; Luke 18:18–23; all references are to the Markan version unless noted). In the nature of things, it would have been unusual for Jesus, a peasant villager, to encounter a member of the ruling class. Luke identifies him as a ruler (*archōn*), a term implying that he had political power and held office, although neither Mark nor Matthew makes this identification. Mark simply says that "he had great estates," implying that he belonged to the ruling elites. Why would such a figure speak with Jesus? It is possible that if Jesus had gained a reputation as a teacher of Torah (rabbi?), then an observant ruler might have sought his insight, but this remains a matter of speculation. Much depends on whether one reads the ruler's challenge as a positive honor challenge or a negative honor challenge. It is also possible that he was attempting to bait Jesus or undermine his public standing. Once again, the encounter is framed in terms of an honor challenge and riposte, except in this case, we get a sense of the give-and-take characteristic of such an encounter. It is also important to remember that individuals represent groups so that what one says to an individual is actually being addressed to his or her group. In this case, it means that Jesus is addressing the invisible ruling class of Galilee or Judea through its visible representative, and his prescription for the rich ruler applies to his class as well.

At heart, this dialogue is about the Torah, the Decalogue in particular, and since the discussion alludes to the Decalogue and cites it selectively, it may be helpful to note the parallels between the two.

The Decalogue (Exodus 20:1–17)	The Dialogue (Mark 10:17–22)
1. No other gods before me	1.
2. No idols	2.
3. No wrongful use of God's name	3.
4. Keep the sabbath holy	4.
5. Honor father and mother	5. Honor father and mother
6. You shall not murder	6. Do not kill
7. You shall not commit adultery	7. Do not commit adultery
8. You shall not steal	8. Do not steal
9. You shall not bear false witness	9. Do not bear false witness [do not defraud?]
10. You shall not covet	10. [do not defraud?]

A comparison of the lists indicates that Jesus cited either five or six commandments, depending on the interpretation of the phrase "Do not defraud," and he omitted either four or five of the commandments. A quick glance at Matthew's version (19:18–19) indicates that he omitted the phrase "Do not defraud," perhaps because he considered it an elaboration of the commandment against bearing false witness, but it can convey a meaning closer to the prohibition of covetousness, as we shall see below. So, for the moment it is safe to say that, in this story of the exchange with the ruler, Jesus cited either five or six commandments and omitted the others.

The flow of the honor challenge and riposte can be outlined as follows:

10:17	The Rich Man Statement (address; hostile compliment) Question/positive (?) honor challenge
10:18–19	Jesus Counterquestion (rejects hostile compliment) Counterstatement (a reading of the Decalogue)
10:20	The Rich Man Second challenge: got it covered from my youth!
10:21	Jesus Second counterstatement (riposte: one thing you lack) A second reading of the (omitted portions of the) Decalogue
10:22	The outcome: rich man leaves, stunned

Most interpreters of this passage think the rich man's initial address, "Good teacher, what must I do to inherit the life of the age to come?" (10:17), is a form of flattery, as though he were trying to get on Jesus' good side. Indeed, Kenneth Bailey believes that the ruler expects Jesus to receive his compliment and respond with an equivalent display of respect like "noble ruler." [12] But Malina and Rohrbaugh detect a hostile challenge in the address: "In a limited good society, compliments indicate aggression; they implicitly accuse a person of rising above the rest of one's fellows at their expense. Compliments conceal envy, not unlike the evil eye."[13] If this is the case, Jesus fends off the challenge with a sharp retort, "Why do you call me good? No one is good but God alone." With this remark, Jesus denies that he has overstepped any boundaries by claiming honor for himself at the expense of God or others. It may be that Jesus is separating himself from the ruler's acquisitive tendencies by refusing to accept the rich man's view of him as accumulating goodness the way he has accumulated goods.

Having defused the initial remark, Jesus can address the basic honor challenge by citing the commandments. The phrase "Do not defraud" carries a variety of meanings. The verb (*apostereō*) has three meanings: (1) appropriating "property held on deposit," presumably as collateral on a loan or other debt instrument; (2) refusing to pay laborers their wages; or (3) acquiring assets through embezzlement. Leviticus captures these concerns:

> When any of you sin and commit a trespass by deceiving a neighbor in the matter of a deposit, or a pledge, or by robbery, or if you have defrauded a neighbor, or have found something lost and lied about it— if you swear falsely regarding any of the various things [then make restitution by paying the original amount plus one-fifth]. (Lev. 6:2–5)

A similar cluster of concerns is found in Malachi 3:5 and James 5:4–6. The most natural reading of these texts would suggest that "do not defraud" is an example of bearing false witness but we will hold the matter open until we finish discussing the dialogue.

The ruler has put the matter in terms of inheritance: "What must I do to inherit the life of the age to come?" Inheritance is a way of transferring wealth from one generation to the next, but most forms of inheritance carry stipulations. Perhaps he is thinking of those stipulations in terms of the covenant with Abraham, or in terms of the covenant with Moses at Sinai. His questions indicate that he is assessing his situation. Since his question carries covenantal implications, Jesus turns to the covenant at Sinai, reciting four or five of the commandments. The ruler must have felt relieved because he responds immediately by saying, "All these I have observed from my youth." This is no idle boast. He has never murdered another person; he has remained a devoted

---

12. Kenneth E. Bailey, *Through Peasant Eyes: More Lucan Parables, Their Culture and Style* (Grand Rapids: Wm. B. Eerdmans Publishing Co., 1980), 162.

13. Bruce J. Malina and Richard L. Rohrbaugh, *Social-Science Commentary on the Synoptic Gospels* (Minneapolis: Fortress Press, 1992), 244.

husband; he is too wealthy to need to steal; he speaks truthfully at public forums; and he honors his parents as a faithful son. He is a model of Torah obedience, selective Torah obedience. He is moral, but selectively moral. The character of that selective morality will be tested in Jesus' second reading of the Torah.

In his first recitation of the Torah, Jesus mentioned five or six commandments, but he omitted the first four commandments, all of which reflect on the honor of God. The first commandment declares that the people of Israel shall have no other gods before Yahweh. Why? The answer was given in the exodus: "I am the LORD your God, who brought you out of the land of Egypt, out of the house of slavery" (Exod. 20:2). God's character is different from the other gods and baals, for God is a God of liberation, not a god who enslaves. To have no other gods before Yahweh is to keep the project of liberation alive and well. To honor the peculiar nature of Yahweh means creating a society that reflects God's liberating character. It is not possible to worship Yahweh and enslave Yahweh's people by foreclosing on peasants and seizing the land that Yahweh has given them. The first commandment carries both a theological and an ethical imperative. Reserve loyalty to Yahweh alone, and continue the project of liberation begun in the exodus and confirmed at Sinai.

The second commandment prohibits the making of idols. It is a corollary of the first commandment. As soon as the people abandon their exclusive loyalty to Yahweh the God of liberation and freedom, they will begin making counterfeit gods to justify their oppression and exploitation of the land and its people. The consequences cannot be contained, so the second commandment comes with a threat and a promise. The threat is that God's judgment will continue to the third and fourth generations, but the promise is that God's covenant love (steadfast love or *ḥesed*) will endure to the thousandth generation for all who are covenant keepers. The second commandment recognizes quite frankly that there will be continual conflict between the makers of idols and the keepers of the covenant. This means that the work of judgment and covenant renewal will exist together. The third commandment prohibits the wrongful use of Yahweh's name because, in the ancient world, maintaining one's honorable name is most important. Therefore, any abuse of God's name will bring God's reprisal. As we shall see, the commandment includes far more than profane use of God's name. The fourth commandment relates to the sabbath, keeping it holy. Perhaps the most important aspect of sabbath observance for the peasants and villagers of Galilee is that it afforded a day of rest, a respite from the endless toil and labor that marked their daily lives. But keeping the sabbath meant that God had provided rest for rich and poor alike. If the first commandment was rooted in the exodus, the fourth commandment was rooted in creation. Both commandments reinforce the notion that the land is a gift, an expression of the bounty of God's creation.

How might these four or five commandments apply to a member of the ruling class of Judea or a Herodian aristocrat in Galilee? The Q tradition contains a saying of Jesus that fits the discussion of the first commandment: "You cannot serve God and Mammon" (Q: Luke 16:13). Mammon came to mean not just wealth but the unjust and dishonest means by which it could be acquired: "It denotes the dishonest profit which a man makes in a matter or transaction by selfishly exploiting the situation of another."[14] In short, it is a good description of the rich ruler whose class was accumulating wealth at the expense of the peasant villages of Galilee. His wealth was less a sign of blessing than it was the mark of a social predator. When confronted with a choice between his wealth and the poverty of the reign of God, he retains his wealth and chooses to serve Mammon (10:22). So the first commandment may still have a prophetic word to speak to his class and to him. Not only has he set another god before Yahweh, but he has created an idol of Mammon whom he serves. In light of this situation, Jesus' omission of the first two commandments may be a silent commentary on the ruler's political and economic attachments, which are masked beneath his veneer of piety and Torah obedience. He will follow Torah only insofar as it enables him to maintain his wealth, power, and prestige.

In his case, to have no other gods before Yahweh would mean, at the very least, respecting the land as Yahweh's gift and extending the blessings of its yield as far and wide as possible. He could become a model of the principle of extension. But he has chosen to accumulate wealth and power while losing covenantal perspectives in the process. Deuteronomy warned the people against exalting themselves and confusing God's gift with their own success.

> Take care that you do not forget the Lord your God, by failing to keep his commandments. . . . Do not say to yourself, "My power and the might of my own hand have gotten me this wealth." (Deut. 8:11–14, 17)

Yet this is what the rich ruler and his class have done. Through their exercise of power and economic maneuvering, they have been alienating peasants from their patrimonial plots of land, the visible embodiment of their covenant with Yahweh, and transforming the land into a commodity to be exploited rather than a gift to be nurtured.

The third commandment forbids the wrongful use of the Lord's name. How could this apply to the ruler? In order to legitimate their increasing wealth and power, the ruling classes in Galilee and Judea have invoked God's name to justify their actions and policies, insisting that their wealth is the result of Yahweh's blessing rather than the spoils of their exploitive and extractive practices. To use God's name in this way is to abuse God's name by calling on

14. F. Hauck, *"mamonas"* in *TDNT* 4:389.

God to bless their oppressive schemes. In this process, they have ignored the fact that they have invoked the very God who led the people out of slavery and gave the land as a gift to bless the return to economic servitude and political bondage! Even if he has never used profanity, the ruler has lifted God's name up to emptiness when he solemnly conjures God's name to bless oppression.

The provision of the sabbath day was part of a larger picture in the Torah. The sabbath provided for one day of rest in seven; the sabbatical year provided for cancellation of debts; and the year after the seventh sabbatical year, the jubilee, provided for the redemption of land, freeing of debt slaves, and forgiving debt (Deut. 15:1–11; Lev. 23:18–55). It is not possible to know how the rich ruler treated his peasants. Did he provide for a sabbath rest? Or did he work them so hard on his land that they had to use the sabbath to care for their own small plots? While he took his sabbath rest, did he allow or make it possible for his peasants and servants to do the same? We do know that his class undermined the provision for canceling debts during sabbatical years through the introduction of the *prozbul*. When the rabbis discovered that the rich refused to make loans to peasants in the year leading up to the sabbatical year, they introduced the *prozbul*, an oath taken by a debtor vowing that he would repay the loan whenever the lender stipulated (sabbatical or no sabbatical). The effect of the provision was to annul the Torah provision for cancellation of debt, so that debt became perpetual. Just as sabbath provided a physical respite from the endless toil of life, so the sabbatical provided debt relief from the endless cycle of poverty and misery. But it appears that both were undermined and eventually abrogated by the ruling class.

Finally, Jesus omitted the tenth commandment, against covetousness. The reasons are so obvious that they hardly need to be stated. Suffice it to say that the rich man has devoted his life to coveting what belonged to others, using any means at his disposal to get it. But whether he has used high interest on loans to peasants followed by foreclosure on their debts to possess their land or high rents and heavy extractions of labor, his covetousness discloses a deeper problem—the violation of the covenant expressed in the Decalogue. He is not Torah obedient, as he would like to believe; he is Torah disobedient.

But how can Jesus unveil the hidden contradiction in the rich ruler's question and response? Even as he says, "All these, I have observed from my youth," he is abrogating the larger meaning of the Torah by condemning others to grinding poverty so he can live in luxury. The polite exchange turns pointed very quickly. Jesus begins innocuously enough: "One thing you lack," but then turns prophetic by issuing four strong imperatives (in italics below), very much like Isaiah (1:16–17) clustered imperatives in his address to Judah or like Amos combined an imperative and promise pattern (5:14–15) to place a challenge before Israel. So Jesus commands,

go
sell what you have (dispossess)
give (redistribute) to the destitute (*ptōchoi*), and you will have treasure in
   heaven
follow me, coming along (join the faction or movement)

At one level, this is an invitation to follow the principle of extension, "the more
you get, the more you give," and fulfill the promise of the debt codes of the
Torah; but at another level Jesus' challenge is much more radical because he
is calling on the rich ruler to dispossess himself. Little wonder he goes away
stunned by what he has heard.

In another place, I argued that these four imperatives interpret the meaning of the debt code for the rich ruler and his class. If so, then Jesus' drastic
words are neither an abrogation of the Torah nor a "Christian" reading of its
message. We do not see here an example of Jesus' "higher righteousness," as
Matthew might have assumed, but a prophet of the justice of the reign of God
spelling out the meaning of God's Torah for his troubled time. This reading
entailed the need to restore the debt codes of the Torah, with special emphasis on the principle of extension contained within them. Only a radical redistribution of the wealth of the land would make it possible to create the contrast
society that God's people were supposed to be. No doubt, Jesus earned powerful enemies as his reading of Torah became more widely known.

JUSTICE AT THE GATE?

It is widely accepted that Jesus taught by means of parables, so it should not
be surprising to discover a concern for the Torah in the parables of Jesus. The
parable of the widow and the judge (Luke 18:2b–5) is set in a Torah court. (For
an outline of Luke 18:1–8, see chapter 2.) Given what we have been describing, the story is probably set on a market day or at a synagogue gathering at
the village gate or town square (see chapter 4). It is important to remember
that this is a parable, not a description of a historical event, but even stories
will reflect familiar social scenes and social scripts. If Jesus told parables like
this in synagogue gatherings, they would have captured the ears of the gathered crowd, for it was a story about what they were doing regularly at their village gatherings.[15] This parable conveyed a prophetic critique of Torah judges
who undermined the justice of the Torah by means of their actions.

15. I have dealt with this parable in more detail in Herzog, *Parables as Subversive
Speech*, 215–232 (see note 39, chap. 1).

It is difficult if not impossible to know how the parable would have been heard in the villages of Galilee. Why was the widow and not her male relatives petitioning a Torah judge? It would have been most unusual for a woman to appeal directly to the court. The most likely answer is that the widow is alone in the world without any male relatives to plead her case. What is the case she is bringing to the court? Since she is identified as a widow, it is probable to infer that a dispute has arisen over her rights as a widow. Perhaps she is claiming her right to retrieve her dowry (her *kethubah*) from her deceased husband's family. While her husband would have access to the usufruct of the property and inheritance she brought into their marriage, her wealth would revert to her in the event of his death. It is also possible that she is claiming her right to be sustained by her husband's property and goods as long as she remains in his household. Usually such matters were part of written prenuptial agreements so that their wealth would revert to each household in previously agreed-on ways. But if the agreements were oral, then disputes could arise and need to be adjudicated. The widow's desperation suggests that she needs to reclaim her *kethubah* in order to sustain herself in the absence of any male kin who can plead her case. She is alone and vulnerable. She would not be anxious to remain in her deceased husband's household where she would be reduced to humiliating roles, and she could even threaten the equilibrium of the family if she were to insist on her rights to a levirate marriage to one of her dead husband's brothers. She probably wants out but needs her bridewealth if she is to survive.[16]

Bailey is convinced that the parable assumes three things: 1) "the widow is in the right (and is being denied justice)"; 2) "for some reason the judge does not want to serve her (she has paid no bribes?)"; 3) "the judge prefers to favor her adversary (either the adversary is influential or he has paid bribes)."[17] If we follow these clues, we can propose a reading of the parable that may reflect the concerns of the historical Jesus. In an agrarian society like we have described, the poor are vulnerable, and the more desperate the poor are, the more vulnerable they become. Nowhere is this illustrated better than in the Torah and the prophets where widows and orphans receive special attention. It is as though they become test cases for the justice of the Torah. One of the more important texts in this regard is found in Exod. 22:21–24, in which God promises to hear the cry of widows and orphans as surely as he heard the people's cry when they were enslaved in Egypt. The linking of the fate of widows and orphans to the fate of the people liberated from slavery in Egypt would

16. For a discussion of dowries and bridewealth, see K. C. Hanson and Douglas Oakman, *Palestine in the Time of Jesus* (Minneapolis: Fortress Press, 1998), chap. 2.

17. Bailey, *Through Peasant Eyes*, 133–34.

seem to provide a powerful incentive to treat these vulnerable ones well, yet the persistent concern for widows and orphans in Torah and the prophets suggests that this was not always the case (cf. Deut. 10:16–18; 14:28–29; 24:17–18; 26:12–13; 27:19; Isa. 1:16–17, 23; 10:1–2; Jer. 7:5–7; 22:3; Ezek. 22:6–7; Zech. 7:8–12; Ps. 68:5; 94:6; 146:9). What is clear in this parable is that the widow's cry has fallen on deaf ears.

Those deaf ears belong to a Torah judge, probably a local official with authority to interpret the Torah to settle disputes. The judge may be part of a larger council of elders, or he may be acting on his own. One thing seems reasonably clear. He intends to ignore the widow and refuse her claim, probably because he is waiting to receive a bribe from the unidentified "adversary," possibly because the amount in dispute is considerable, at least substantial enough to warrant the payment of what Lenski calls "honest graft." But the adversary hesitates because he is in a powerful position, being set against a widow alone in the world without any male kin to advocate for her rights. Since it is an open-and-closed case, why should the adversary pay the judge to do what he must do anyway?

This gridlock between judge and adversary provides the desperate widow a window of opportunity to make her case. If the widow remains silent, she will be on the streets and in desperate straits. She belongs to what Freire called "the culture of silence" in which she is immersed. If the judge has his way, she will soon lose everything. All that is required of her for the system of injustice to work is her silence, yet that is precisely what she fails to offer. Instead, she cries out to the unjust judge. She is bold and persistent because she, in part, also has an open-and-shut case; the Torah honors the plight of widows and orphans. She is protected by Torah when Torah is interpreted by just judges, but even Torah can be subverted in the interests of corrupt judges and their powerful patrons. This may be why texts like Sir. 35:14–26 and 2 Chr. 19:4–7 focus on the character of those who adjudicate Torah. So Jehoshaphat charged the judges he appointed to

> Consider what you are doing, for you judge not on behalf of human beings but on the LORD's behalf; he is with you in giving judgment. Now, let the fear of the LORD be upon you; take care what you do, for there is no perversion of justice with the LORD our God, or partiality, or taking of bribes. (2 Chron. 19:6–7)

By contrast, the judge in the parable "neither fears God nor respects human beings" (author's trans.). This means that the woman's status as vulnerable widow evokes neither compassion nor caring. The absence of any fear of God is especially troubling, and Bailey speculates that this describes a man who has no shame and, therefore, no honor, since honor requires a finely tuned sense of shame. Add to this the belief that "the fear of the LORD is the beginning of wisdom" (Prov. 1:7), and the figure of the judge would be seen as even more alarming. Little wonder that Bernard Brandon Scott calls him "an outlaw judge."[18] How can one adjudicate Torah without wisdom or compassionate honor? The widow's case looks hopeless. It would appear that the silent alliance between a locally powerful family and their client judge is about to trump the Torah's concern for a vulnerable and desperate widow.

Yet just the opposite occurs! The widow assails the judge until he decides in her favor. The language of the parable is humorous. The judge declares that he will decide in her favor "so that she may not wear me out with her continual bruising" (*hypōpiazō* is a boxing term that refers to repeated blows that give a black eye). The language is metaphorical in more ways than one. The widow is not attacking the judge but assaulting his reputation; she is giving him a black eye. Since he needs to maintain the facade of righteousness in order to retain his role as judge, this is a cause for alarm. If the unseen adversary chooses to delay too long, then the judge will have to act in order to preserve his public persona. The widow is blowing open the lies and cover stories that maintain the oppressive use of Torah courts to deny justice at the gate. In speaking of what he calls the domination system, Walter Wink notes that

> when anyone steps out of the system and tells the truth, lives the truth, that enables everyone else to peer behind the curtain, too. Anyone who steps out of line therefore *denies it in principle and threatens it in its entirety*. . . . If the main pillar of the system is living a lie, then it is not surprising that the fundamental threat to it is living the truth.[19]

The judge's delay affords everyone listening to the widow's plea an opportunity to peer behind the curtain, offstage, where in clear violation of the Torah the judge is quietly negotiating with a wealthy family to throw another widow onto the streets. How can the Torah be highjacked and put to such mean use? The problem is not the Torah but those who judge in its name while denying its meaning and purpose. Jesus' parable codifies how the justice of the Torah might be undermined by an unjust judge. Torah is more than a covenant; it is a covenant that requires just and faithful interpreters. Perhaps this is one reason why Deuteronomy includes this curse in the covenant renewal ceremony: "'Cursed be anyone who deprives the alien, the orphan and the widow of justice.' All the people shall say, 'Amen!'" (27:19).

18. Bernard Brandon Scott, *Hear Then the Parable: A Commentary on the Parables of Jesus* (Minneapolis: Fortress Press, 1989), 180.

19. Walter Wink, *Engaging the Powers: Discernment and Resistance in a World of Domination* (Minneapolis: Fortress Press, 1992), 98.

It would not be stretching matters too far to say that the parable of the widow and the judge provides a glimpse of a prophetic critique of how the Torah is applied to favor the wealthy and influential at the expense of the poor and destitute. Yet even in these circumstances Jesus proposes a course of action that can wring justice out of a corrupt system. If Jesus used the parables as tools of social analysis that propose courses of action, then this parable would have served as a lively discussion starter, for it provides a glimpse of how a widow gained justice when all the odds were stacked against her. To use Freire's language, the parable codifies a limit situation that seems to afford no exit from a profound dilemma. Yet the widow's actions illustrate the kind of "limit act" that can transform the dead-end dilemma into an opportunity to do justice. But this outcome would not have been possible if it were not for the framework of justice provided by the Torah. In effect, the parable problematizes the relationship between Torah and Torah judges to make it clear that corrupt judges cannot corrupt Torah but have to be reckoned with. The villagers hearing the parable would be encouraged to decode what is said about judges, especially when it places them beyond criticism. They would also be encouraged to study and analyze how the widow subverted the very system that was fixed against her. This reading of the parable provides an insight into the way Jesus used parables as tools of social analysis and as codifications of how systems of oppression were at work with the intent of undermining the prophetic and protective care of the Torah's provisions. In this case, the parable presented a widow whose desperation motivated her to break the culture of silence and shame the judge into doing what he was required to do.

"FOR THE LAND IS MINE . . ." (LEV. 25:23)

Throughout the first century, two views of the land clashed with each other. The Torah viewed the land as a gift of Yahweh. This is the attitude expressed by Naboth when he refused to sell his land to Ahab or trade it for a better vineyard: "The LORD forbid that I should give you my ancestral inheritance" (1 Kgs. 21:3). Every peasant's plot of land was a reminder of Yahweh's covenant with the people. The land was invested with theological import. By contrast, the Romans and their Herodian clients viewed the land as an asset to be managed and a commodity to be exploited. For this reason, they were willing to foreclose on peasants who could not repay their loans and seize the land as a way of increasing their holdings.

To justify their predatory behavior, the ruling class established an ideology that would mystify what was happening and blame the victims of their practices.[20]

---

20. See William Ryan, *Blaming the Victim* (New York: Vintage Books, 1976), chap. 1.

Their ideology blamed the poor for their poverty, as though it were their sole responsibility, and mystified the system that rigged the economic game against them, although it must be said that peasants do not seem to be confused by the mystification. They usually have a clear understanding of what is happening and who is responsible. The banking education of the elites only added to the economic burdens of peasants by casting them as the cause of their own demise when they failed to repay a loan and lost their land. Each time this scenario played out in the villages of Galilee, it must have seemed as though it was the implacable outcome of an irresistable fate. There was nothing that peasant villagers could do about it. After all, if one borrowed, one must pay it back, even though the terms were dictated by the elites. Their interest rates might be usurious (from 30 to 60 percent), but loans still had to be repaid. There were no alternatives. This ideology portrayed every failure as a peasant failure that reflected on their inability to cope with their condition. No one asked whether interest rates were fair, nor why the elites used debt instruments in violation of the Torah's prohibition against taking interest, especially from the poor. The basic principle was stated in Exod. 22:25: "If you lend money to my people, to the poor among you, you shall not deal with them as a creditor; you shall not exact interest from them."[21]

A similar provision in Lev. 25:36–37 prohibited taking interest from any kin who had fallen on hard times, and Deut. 23:19–20 forbids taking interest from an Israelite but permits charging interest to a foreigner. After his return to Jerusalem, Nehemiah had to act to stop Israelites from taking interest from one another (Neh. 5:1–13). Clearly the Torah tradition was biased against taking interest because it disrupted community and violated the principles that Yahweh had enunciated at Sinai. Of course, an ideology that focused on blaming the victim would mask these portions of the Torah and mystify the source of current practices that traced to the covetous greed of the ruling elites, not to the peasant villagers losing their land as they sank into debt servitude. (For other texts addressing the question of interest, see Ps. 15:5; Ezek. 18:8, 13, 17; 22:12.)

The peasants of the land needed a teacher who would demystify what the elites had done and expose their policies for what they were. The parable of the workers in the vineyard (Matt. 20:1–16) can be read in this light as a codification intended to unveil their mystifications and examine them more closely. When this is done, Freire says, "that which had existed objectively but had not been perceived in its deeper implications . . . begins to 'stand out,' assuming the character of a problem and therefore a challenge."[22] The process

21. For a fuller discussion see Jacob Neusner, *The Economics of the Mishnah* (Chicago: University of Chicago Press, 1990).

22. Paulo Freire, *Pedagogy of the Oppressed*, 9th ed., trans. Myra Bergman Ramos (New York: Seabury, 1973, orig. pub. 1968), 70.

of creating a parable/codification as a focus for discussion functions something like revelation, disclosing God's will in a way that brings both judgment and covenant love.

The parable can be analyzed as follows:[23]

Introduction	1a
Act 1, the hiring	1b–7
Act 2, payday	8–15
Scene 1, payment	9–10
Scene 2, debate	11–15
Conclusion	16

For the moment, we will take the introduction (v. 1a) and conclusion (v. 16) to be the result of Matthew's framing of the parable. So the parable that Jesus told begins in v. 1b, "A householder went out early in the morning to hire day laborers for his vineyard," and it ends with the householder's final retort, "Do you begrudge my generosity?" This comment reads literally in Greek, "Or is your eye evil because I am good" (Matt. 20:15b, author's trans.).

The parable brings together the extremes of Galilean society. The house-holder (*oikodespotēs*, cf. the Latin *paterfamilias*) is a wealthy landowner, as indicated by the number of day laborers he must hire to bring in his grape harvest, a number that implies he has large vineyards. Since vineyards yield wine, he is most likely involved in the business of exporting his wine for profit. If peasants had vineyards at all, they would have been small, producing wine for local consumption only. If the householder is near the apex of the social pyramid, a member of the local aristocracy, then the day laborers are at the bottom of the social scale. To use Lenski's diagram (see chapter 3), they belong, for the most part, to the "expendables." Day laborers have lost their land and with it, their safety net, or they are the excess sons of peasant families who had to turn them out on the streets when they began to consume more than they could produce. They do not even have the security of a contract with an elite landowner as tenants do (see Mark 12:1–12 for a picture of tenancy). Day laborers congregate at known locations and wait to be hired. As the parable shows, they do not always get their wish.

The householder is pictured going to the marketplace to hire day laborers for the harvest. It is unlikely that a member of the ruling class would do this work himself; it is more likely that he would have sent his steward to do the hiring. Why then does Jesus depict the householder as taking such an active role? One reason may be that Jesus wants to make the invisible elites visible in

23. For an extended description of the parable, see Herzog, *Parables as Subversive Speech*, chap. 5.

this parabolic codification. Normally elites and day laborers would never meet. They were from different worlds, but in this parable, they will encounter each other. When the householder reaches the square where the workers are gathered, he agrees to pay each laborer he has hired a denarius a day. In subsequent trips to the *agora* (marketplace) at the third, sixth, and ninth hours, he selects them, saying, "Whatever is right (*dikaios*), I will give you." But he will determine what is "just" (*dikaios*), and now he is no longer paying the laborers but giving them what he determines to give. When he goes out at the eleventh hour, he doesn't even promise to give them what is right. He simply orders them, "You, too, go into the vineyard." These changing descriptions progressively emphasize the unilateral power of the householder. His word determines what is "right" and defines what is "just." The day laborers, growing more anxious as the day passes, are willing to go into the vineyard on the householder's promise of payment or even without such a promise. They are desperate. Note also how the householder views the day laborers left in the marketplace: "Why do you stand here idle all day?" The assumption that the workers are idle and lazy, rather than waiting to be hired, fits the way elites view the poor. It is all part of blaming the victim. With the hiring of the eleventh-hour workers, the first part of the parable comes to a close.

The second scene begins as the first scene did, with the action of the householder. Just as he sets the rules in hiring, so he now sets the rules for payment, but this time he alters the customary order for paying workers. Usually, the first hired are the first paid, but the householder instructs his steward to reverse the order and pay the eleventh-hour workers first. He has also ordered his steward to pay these last hired a full denarius. No steward would determine payment on his own when the master is present. What could the eleventh-hour workers reasonably expect to be paid since they worked only an hour? In spite of a number of clever efforts to determine a first-century version of a minimum wage, no proposal has answered the question in a satisfactory way. It is possible that a laborer hired after midday could expect to receive something like half of a denarius, but no more. The fact of payment at the end of the day was crucial. Deuteronomy 24:14–15 prohibited the practice of withholding the wages of a day laborer because he needed it for survival.

Although the specifics can no longer be reconstructed, it is likely that a laborer hired late in the day could expect a minimum payment but certainly not as much as the laborers who had worked all day. All of this means that the householder has set up the laborers he hired first. He has put them at the back of the line and forced them to watch as the last hired workers get a full day's pay. Of course, when they witness this unexpected boon, they assume that they will receive a benefit proportionate to the one received by the laborers he hired last. Their hopes are dashed when they receive a denarius, as they had agreed.

It is important to note that a denarius is not a generous wage. Scott observes that "of itself the wage is not generous. . . . A denarius a day would be sufficient to support a worker and his family at a subsistence level, that is, at the level of a peasant."[24] The problem with Scott's assessment of the situation is that day laborers belonging to the class of expendables were finally unable to support themselves. Once they left the village, they lost all hope of sustaining their life. They were able to earn malnutrition wages, probably because their work was so sporadic. If a denarius could support a day laborer for four days, and a day laborer worked sixty days a year, he would have enough food to cover two hundred and forty days or about two-thirds of a year. The rest of the time he would have to beg. It is not surprising that Jeremias called the denarius "a bare subsistence wage."[25] Most day laborers live for about five to seven years after they lose their kinship and village networks. Their situation is truly desperate.

It is important to understand who these day laborers are in order to understand their reaction to receiving a denarius. The reversed order of payment and the pay given to the last hired were deliberate provocations. They functioned like the beginning of an honor shame challenge, except this owner is so far above the workers that it doesn't make sense. Still, the workers respond like men who have been shamed. Note their mumbling: "These last worked only one hour, and you have made them equal to us who have borne the burden of the day and the scorching heat" (v. 12). In short, they accuse the householder of shaming their labor. As day laborers who have nothing left of their honor but their animal energy and capacity to work, they know that the householder has insulted them and shamed them. Their day-long labor was worth no more than the last hired workers' single hour. For men who have worked a twelve-hour day, this is an unforgettable insult. They must respond, or they will be shamed forever because if they do not, they would be colluding in their own degradation. More to the point, if they consent to the owner's valuing of their labor, they will never work for a denarius a day again but will be forced to work a full day for less than a denarius. So they do the unthinkable; they respond to the householder's provocation. In doing so, these laborers react like any peasant would react whose source of subsistence has been threatened. It would take a truly desperate situation to induce a peasant to challenge an elite.

In turn, their response to the challenge is met by the householder's final speech (20:13–15). Notice that he replied to one of them; he did not address the whole group. He singles out one of the workers to make an example out of him, an effective way to control the group. His form of address, friend (*hetaire*) is not friendly but is used of a superior speaking to inferiors. So Jesus and Socrates call their disciples "friend." It is also used in a situation where the speaker does not know the name of the person he is addressing, again a sign of social distance.[26] The final response contains three arguments. First, the owner reminds the worker that he agreed for a denarius. As our earlier analysis revealed, the so-called bargaining really masked the unilateral power of the landowner. So the negotiation probably followed this line: "All willing to work for a denarius, follow me." This is what "agreeing with me for a denarius" most likely means. The willingness of the day laborers to settle for a denarius is held against them, but the argument overlooks the changed circumstances, especially the extra pay for the shortest shift. In verse 14a, the owner turns on the laborer and shuns him: "Take what belongs to you and get." He is blacklisted and blackballed. He will not work for this landowner again and, as word spreads, he may not work in that area again.

Second, the owner claims that he is not paying wages but giving a gift. The wages are no longer seen as something earned but as a handout from the owner: "I choose to give to this last one as I give to you. Am I not allowed to do what I choose with what belongs to me?" (v. 15). On the surface, it seems like a reasonable claim, and no doubt the peasants who heard this parable would have assented to the owner's claim. But a moment's reflection would reveal that neither the land nor its usufruct belongs to the vineyard owner. If we hearken back to the by-now-familiar text, Lev. 25:23, we will remember Yahweh's word, "The land shall not be sold in perpetuity, for the land is mine; with me you are but aliens and tenants." This presents quite a different claim from the one advanced by the householder. Indeed, the debt codes of the Torah mean that the yield of the land belongs to all, especially the poor, the widow, and the orphan. Now the claim to "give to this last as I give to you" can be seen for what it is, a distortion and abuse of the debt codes of the Torah. The householder's malnutrition wages represent a grotesque imitation of Yahweh's bounty and a distortion of the principle of extension found in the debt codes of the Torah.

Finally, the householder tries to mystify the whole transaction by confusing good and evil. The Greek reads literally, "or is your eye evil because I am good," translated as "or do you begrudge my generosity" (v. 15b). The point of the saying is to stigmatize everything the laborer has said as evil and to dress the owner's words in the cloak of "what is just." In this fashion, the owner declares the day laborers to be evil so that he can dismiss what they have seen, while declaring his own vision of things to be good. He tries to reassert the political and economic order of the world.

---

26. BAGD, 314.

If this reading is arguable, then Jesus has told a powerful parable that exposes the ideological claims of the ruling class for what they are: blasphemous denials of the debt codes of the Torah, misuse of the land, and an arrogation to themselves of the prerogatives of Yahweh. More to the point, the fate of the workers in the parable represents the victimization of the poor at the hands of the rich. The workers' failure is not their doing but an arranged insult intended to paralyze them and keep them immersed in self-hatred. The owner's attack against the "friend" who spoke out is a blatant attempt to reimpose and reinforce the culture of silence in which the workers are buried. The parable also codifies what happens when the elites can pick out one of the workers and turn him into an example. Their solidarity was broken; they can die one at a time or risk acting together. This parable presents a limit situation that fails to produce the kind of limit acts that can transform the world. But people can learn from their failures as well as their successes.

At its heart, this parable is an argument for a Torah reading of the situation in Galilee where Herod and the Herodians have turned the land into a source of wealth while driving the peasants into increasingly serious forms of dependence. Their policies created a rural underclass of expendables drawn from those alienated from their land or those turned out of their families because they became too great a drain on their family's resources. Yet not even day laborers are without hope and power, so Jesus tells a story when those at the top are most dependent on those at the bottom. The grape harvest has to be completed within very narrow time parameters or the value of the grapes is compromised. The shaming of the workers concludes the harvest as the ruling class's effort to perpetuate the appearance of their power and the powerlessness of the day laborers. In this way, they seek to restore the normal order and hide their vulnerability.

If Jesus used the parables as subversive speech, his story might stimulate his peasant audience to reflect on the generative themes found in the parable and to catch a glimpse of another thematic universe.

CONCLUSION

This chapter has attempted to show that Jesus was familiar with the Torah and argued its meaning in a variety of settings. In the debate about clean or common hands, Jesus promoted a reading of Torah that sublimated a purity reading of the Torah to a reading emphasizing its debt codes. In his encounter with a ruling elite, Jesus championed a reading of Torah focusing on its meaning for the economy of his day. The parable of the widow and the judge indicts the misuse of power by Torah judges who forsake the widow for the promise of a bribe. The Jesus traditions show us a picture of Jesus who appeals to Torah and argues its meaning more than a Jesus who abandons Torah for a [Christian] theology. The parable of the laborers in the vineyard exposes the ideology of the ruling class and their blasphemous claims to own the land when in truth it belongs to Yahweh.

The Torah was intricately tied to the temple. This means that any assault on the great traditions' readings of the Torah was also, quite possibly, an attack on the temple. To this topic, we will turn in the next chapter.

7

"Something greater than the temple is here."

(Matthew 12:6)

TEMPLES IN AGRARIAN SOCIETIES

Temples play a crucial role in agrarian societies. Rulers of agrarian societies often come to power through the use of violence, and they value the traditional forms of legitimization that temples can provide because they reinforce tradition, stability, and certainty, values that rulers favor after they come to power. Temples also provide divine sanction and blessing, leaving the impression that a ruler has come to power by the will of the gods or a mandate from heaven. Temples can also provide rituals of social cohesion that bring together the center and the periphery by means of pilgrimage festivals and other regularly recurring events. In this way, temples contribute to the "image of an ordered state" that reinforces the symbolic world of its subjects and communicates the values of the ruling elites to all other members of the state (see chapter 3).

Temples can also contribute to the economy of an empire through the collection of various forms of tribute, offerings, and gifts, or in the case of the temple in Jerusalem, the collection of tithes. In agrarian societies, temples play a critical role in separating peasants from the wealth they produce. Lenski and Lenski put is this way:

> Technological advance creates the possibility of a surplus, but to translate that possibility into reality requires an ideology that motivates farmers to produce more than they need . . . and persuades them to turn that surplus over to someone else. . . . a system of beliefs that defined people's obligations with reference to the supernatural was best suited to play this critical role.[1]

---

1. Gerhard Lenski and Jean Lenski, *Human Societies: An Introduction to Macrosociology*, 4th ed. (New York: McGraw-Hill, 1982), 173.

They are considered so valuable that rulers often exempt temples and their priests from paying tribute.

John Lundquist has argued that building a temple is an essential element in the formation of a centralized state.[2] Not until a nascent state demonstrates its ability to organize massive public building projects can it be considered fully developed. The first building project that most societies undertake is the building of a temple, for the reasons previously noted. This may explain, in part, why David was so anxious to build a temple in Jerusalem, his seat of power. Only the prophetic intervention of Nathan prevented David from beginning this project (2 Sam. 7:1–17). Although he heeded Nathan's prophetic word, David knew that his monarchy was not complete as long as the temple remained a dream. Solomon, of course, fulfilled his father's dream. The report of the dedication of the temple, found in 1 Kgs. 8–9, illustrates its dynastic significance. In 1 Kgs. 8:25–26 and again in 1 Kgs. 9:4–5, Solomon repeats the promise that Yahweh had made to David. But there is a catch. The dynastic promise is not unqualified but comes with an important string attached.

> If you then turn aside from following me . . . and do not keep my commandments and my statutes that I have set before you . . . then I will cut Israel off from the land that I am giving them; and the house that I have consecrated for my name I will cast out of my sight; and Israel will become a proverb and a taunt among all peoples. (9:6–7)

The covenant is conditional, and the rulers are held accountable to keep the covenant, unlike other agrarian rulers who were a law unto themselves.

The temple was not Solomon's first building project. He had first built his own palace and then constructed the temple beside it. This fits a pattern common in the Near East and expresses a commonly held belief. By means of the proximity of palace and temple

> the legitimizing decisions of the cosmic deities are transferred to earth and to the earthly monarch, the whole process symbolized by and centered in the building of the temple. . . . There is thus a tie between the temple as the abode of the king of the gods and the temple as a dynastic shrine of the earthly king.[3]

To oppose the king was to oppose god. This important role of the temple helps us understand why Herod the Great devoted so many resources and so much attention to renovating the Second Temple (*Ant.* 15.380–425). Through his efforts, Herod was trying to establish his credentials as "king of the Jews" and

---

2. John Lundquist, "The Legitimating Role of the Temple in the Origin of the State," *SBLSP* 21 (1982): 271–97.
3. Ibid., 291.

mute his role as Rome's client ruler. Although he gave us a resplendent temple mount, he never succeeded in overcoming the suspicion that attached to his Idumean roots.

THE SYMBOLIC WORLD OF THE TEMPLE

Most temples embodied a symbolic architecture; they were considered to be microcosms of the cosmos itself. For this reason, everything was important when building a temple. It started with location. Most temples were built on mountains or high places. The temple in Jerusalem is built on what is called the Temple Mount, understood to be the place where heaven and earth intersect. Temples usually were built as a series of increasingly secluded courtyards or chambers, so it is not surprising to learn that the temple precincts in Jerusalem contained an increasingly inaccessible set of courtyards that separated Jew from Gentile, women from men, laity from priests, and eventually the high priest from all ordinary priests. The temple was usually constructed on a series of raised platforms that reinforced the idea of hierarchy while symbolizing the temple as a successive ascent toward heaven. The temple in Jerusalem followed this common pattern. Its outer courtyard (perhaps called the courtyard of the Gentiles) was the lowest courtyard and was separated from the temple precincts by a low wall whose gates were adorned with solemn warnings against trespassing. The courtyard of the Israelite women was the lowest courtyard in the actual temple precincts. From there, a male Israelite would climb steps leading to the Nicanor Gate and the court of the Israelite laymen. This court was separated from the court of the priests by a low balustrade. While the courtyard of the priests was on the same level as the court of the laymen, the barrier prevented laity from entering the work space of the priests. Furthermore, priests could enter the temple building itself by climbing another set of steps leading to a yet higher platform. Only priests could enter the temple building to burn the daily incense in the Holy Place. On the same level but beyond that was the Holy of Holies, which the high priest alone could enter and only on the Day of Atonement. If we put all the pieces together, it is clear that the temple embodied a social ideology and a political theology. Commenting on a specific aspect of the temple furnishings, Josephus mused, "Nor was the mixture of materials without its mystic meaning; it typified the universe" (*War* 5.210–14). The architecture and symbolic world of the temple in Jerusalem declared that Judeans were more important than Gentiles, that men were more important than women, and that priests were superior to laity. At the pinnacle of the symbolic order was the high priest and the high priestly families who controlled the temple. One can understand why the

Pharisees modeled their table companionship project on the temple. The priest was the model for humanity, especially the priest in the temple performing his sacred duties.

The temple embodied the purity codes of the Torah, whose way of ordering the world was transferable to every area of life. To order the world in line with purity concerns and holiness was to continue the work of creation. Two examples may reinforce this point. (For a third example, see the previous chapter.) Although these materials are taken from the Mishnah (second century CE), they reflect the values and concerns of earlier periods of time. The first purity map orders space from lesser to greater purity.

> There are ten degrees of holiness.
> The land of Israel is holier than any other land.
> The walled cities [of Israel] are holier still. . . .
> Within the walls of Jerusalem is still more holy. . . .
> The Temple mount is still more holy. . . .
> The Rampart [surrounding the temple precincts] still more holy. . . .
> The Court of the Women is still more holy. . . .
> The Court of the Israelites still more holy. . . .
> The Court of the Priests is still more holy. . . .
> Between the Porch and the Altar is still more holy. . . .
> The Sanctuary [the holy place] is still more holy. . . .
> And the Holy of Holies is still more holy.[4]

The second purity map organizes time and moves from the lesser festivals to the more important pilgrimage festivals. The material is found throughout the Second Division of the Mishnah, *Moed* (Set Feasts), and implies an ordering of sacred time. Not surprisingly, the major festivals of Tabernacles (4), the Day of Atonement (3), and Passover (2) are high on the list, but it may surprise some to learn that Sabbath (1) is considered the most sacred time of all, holier even than the major festivals. This should give an edge to Jesus' controversies surrounding the sabbath. The point to be made here is that the very structure of the temple and the theology it promulgated encouraged the endlessly unfinished task of mapping the world and organizing the results in the form of purity maps in order to maintain the structure of creation. Peter Berger would identify this work as "world construction," the making of a "sacred canopy," and "world maintenance," reinforcing the status quo.[5] Jesus would take a very different approach.

4. Jerome Neyrey, "The Idea of Purity in Mark," in John H. Elliott, ed., *Social-Scientific Criticism of the New Testament and Its Social World*, Semeia 35 (Decatur, Ga.: Scholars Press, 1986), 95–96.
5. For a fuller discussion of these important roles, see Peter L. Berger, *The Sacred Canopy: Elements of a Sociological Theory of Religion* (Garden City, N.Y.: Doubleday/Anchor Books, 1969), 3–51.

THE TEMPLE IN JERUSALEM

Few would dispute that the temple in Jerusalem was at the center of the political religion of Judea and Galilee, cutting across the political landscape created by Herodian client rule in Galilee and high priestly rule in Judea.[6] In the world of Jesus, temple religion served the interests of the dominant elites by supplying a religious justification for their oppressive and exploitive order while reinforcing that order through its demands for tithes and offerings, represented as divine obligations demanded by Yahweh. When Jesus visited the temple for the Passover celebration, somewhere around 30 CE, he was visiting an institution in crisis. As noted earlier in this study, the province of Judea (which included Samaria) had been under the control of a Roman prefect since Archelaus was deposed in 6 CE. The prefect serving in 30 CE was Pontius Pilate, who served in that capacity from 26 to 36 CE. His counterpart in the temple was the high priest, in this case, Caiaphas, who also enjoyed a long tenure, serving as high priest from 18 to 36 CE. The Roman prefect appointed the high priest and kept the high priest's robes in his possession, releasing them only for the ceremonial occasions on which the high priest would officiate, primarily the Day of Atonement.

Essentially, four high priestly families controlled the high priesthood from the time that Herod the Great converted the high priesthood into an appointive office (about 37 BCE) to the destruction of the temple in 70 CE (*Ant.* 15.39–41). They were, however, caught between two worlds, being minions of Rome on the one hand yet chosen to represent the people of Israel before Yahweh, on the other hand. By the time Jesus entered Jerusalem, the high priests had compromised their standing with the people of the land in order to maintain their position of power and privilege in the temple state that was Judea. The more they fulfilled their priestly role in the temple, the more they alienated themselves from the Romans, who regarded the temple as a symbol of the Judeans' obstinate refusal to acculturate to the world of the Roman gods. The more they accommodated to the Roman political order, the more they alienated themselves from their own people. Perhaps no event brought their conflicted role to the surface more clearly than the Passover festival, a celebration of Yahweh's power to liberate the people from oppression and slavery, presided over by a high priest who held his office at the pleasure of Rome, the occupying colonial power. This may explain, in part, why the pilgrimage festivals also became focal points for protest against Roman rule (see *War* 2.10 par. *Ant.* 17.213; Mark 11:15–18 and pars.).

---

6. For a fuller description of the role of the temple, see K. C. Hanson and Douglas Oakman, *Palestine in the Time of Jesus* (Minneapolis: Fortress Press, 1998), chap. 5.

Still, for all of the limitations placed on the temple by Roman rule, it was the center of political and economic power for Galilee and Judea. The Sanhedrin, which met in the temple precincts in the chamber of hewn stone, controlled the interpretation of the Torah and, through its officially sanctioned readings of Torah, aspired to control the system of Torah courts in villages and market towns, although the judges (elders?) who served in those courts may have been motivated by other more pressing concerns, as the parable of the widow and the judge illustrates (Luke 18:1–8).[7] The temple was the source of the great tradition, possibly several versions of the great tradition, which interpreted and legitimized the central focus on the temple.

The temple's demand for tithes and offerings, as well as the temple tax collected from every observant Jewish male between the ages of fifteen and sixty-five (estimates of the age range vary) ensured that great amounts of money would flow into the temple treasury each year. When the demand for tithes was connected with the quest for purity, as a result of the Pharisees' insistence that all food be tithed in order to be clean, the temple gained a powerful motivation for emphasizing tithes and a powerful tool for enforcing that emphasis. Needless to say, the peasants of Galilee and Judea would take a very different view of the matter. The economic strain placed on the peasantry may explain why they kept their distance from the temple even while attempting to support it to the degree that they were able. Peasants valued the temple because they believed that the sacrifices offered there ensured timely rains and bountiful harvests. In the end, however, the temple authorities read peasant reluctance to pay their tithes as defiance of Torah rather than desperation born of exploitation. As Jesus' debate with the Pharisees over purity suggests (Mark 7:1–16), many were faced with the choice between supporting family and giving support to the temple.

JESUS' ATTITUDE TOWARD THE TEMPLE

Jesus seems to have held an ambivalent, though predominantly critical, view of the temple. After cleansing a leper (Mark 1:40–45 pars. Matt. 8:1–4; Luke 5:12–16), he charges the cleansed leper to "go [and] show yourself to the priest, and offer for your cleansing what Moses commanded" (1:44). Jesus may be referring to Lev. 14:1–9, part of a much longer passage, Lev. 14:1–32, which prescribes a lengthy ritual for confirming a leper's cleansing, including the provision of a sacrifice that even the poor could afford. If Jesus is sending the leper to the temple, his examination would be conducted by a priest in the Chamber

---

7. For a fuller description, ibid., 146–57.

of the Lepers in the temple precincts. Of course, there were ordinary priests in many of the towns and villages of the area, so it is possible that Jesus may simply be sending the leper to a local priest. The final phrase, do that "as a witness or testimony to them" (*eis marturion autois*), carries the hint of a challenge. In sending the leper to the temple, Jesus is also sending a message to the temple as a broker of God's healing power, which through his public work is restoring the lost, a power that the temple can acknowledge and confirm but cannot exercise. It is something like the message Yahweh speaks through Mic. 4:4–8: "In that day, says the LORD, I will assemble the lame and gather those who have been driven away, and those whom I have afflicted. The lame I will make the remnant, and those who were cast off, a strong nation" (4:6–7). The motif of restoration and renewal remains at the heart of Jesus' proclamation of the reign of heaven.

Since the healing of the leper can be read in this light, Jesus' final instructions to the leper conform to the attitude toward the temple expressed in the healing of the paralytic (Mark 2:1–12 pars. Matt. 9:1–8; Luke 5:17–26). We have already argued earlier (see chapter 4) that, in this healing, Jesus claims to be a reliable broker of God's healing power and, in that role, proffers God's forgiveness to the paralytic. If this reading is plausible, it is clear that Jesus believes that neither the priests nor the high priests, through their control of the sacrificial system, are fulfilling their role as brokers of God's patronal power and covenant love. By healing the man on the mat, Jesus does an end run around the sacrificial system altogether and offers Yahweh's forgiveness without recourse to it. This would be reason enough for the scribes to accuse him of blasphemy and assume that he is acting as God alone can act. When Jesus steps into his role as a broker of God's healing power, he steps on the toes of the priests who have arrogated that power to themselves. If they believe that they hold a monopoly on God's power, Jesus demonstrates through his healing and exorcisms that he has broken that monopoly, thereby opening other channels through which that power can flow to the benefit of the poor, the lame, and the blind, in short, "the least, the last, and the lost."

In Matthew's version of the incident of plucking grain on the sabbath, Jesus justifies the actions of his disciples by arguing Torah with a twist:

> Have you not read in the [Torah] how on the sabbath the priests in the temple profane the sabbath and are guiltless? I tell you, something greater than the temple is here. And if you had known what this means, "I desire mercy, not sacrifice," you would not have condemned the guiltless. (12:5–7)

The sayings contain two different arguments, verses 5–6 and verse 7, although they are related. The first is an argument from the Torah. On the sabbath, the

priests perform their normal duties in the temple, preparing and offering sacrifices. By working on the sabbath, they profane the sabbath, yet they are held
guiltless, because, by virtue of their priestly privilege, they are excepted, or
loosed, from a strict reading of the Torah in order to be freed for their priestly
service in the temple. In this situation, the temple's sacrifices take precedence
over the sabbath. What is good for the priest does not, however, apply to the
laity who are bound by the strictures of the Torah's sabbath regulations. Having established the principle by observing priestly behavior, Jesus argues from
the lesser to the greater. If the priests can set aside the prohibitions against
working on the sabbath, then how much more should his disciples be able to
do so in light of the "something greater" that is here and justifies the disciples
plucking grain on the sabbath. "Something greater than the temple is here,"
and this "something greater" changes the rules surrounding the sabbath and
to whom they apply. The Q tradition contains two sayings that use this formula, "something greater than . . . is here" (see Q: Luke 11:31–32 par. Matt.
12:41–42). In these two instances, that something is greater than the wisdom
of Solomon and the proclamation of Jonah; the something greater is presumably the wisdom and proclamation of Jesus. If we read this instance from
Matthew 12 in the context of the historical Jesus, however, the something
greater may be the prophetic reading of the Torah that traces to Jesus, perhaps
summarized by his proclamation that the reign of heaven is at hand (Mark
1:14–15). It is a reading of the Torah that frees ordinary people to address their
own survival needs even on the sabbath rather than serving a system that prohibits their efforts to find subsistence in a grainfield.

The second commentary on the incident turns to Hos. 6:6, which reads in
Hebrew, "I desire steadfast love [ḥesed], not sacrifice." This is translated into
Greek as, "I desire mercy [eleos], not sacrifice" (the Septuagint [LXX] rendering of the Hebrew). Clearly, if the use of Hosea traces to Jesus, the emphasis
needs to fall on the Hebrew, "I desire steadfast love, not sacrifice." The reference to "steadfast love," which could also be translated as "covenant love," fits
the context rather well. God's steadfast love, which ensures and honors the
covenant with his people, is the "something greater" than the sacrificial system, even though the sacrificial system was originally intended to express that
steadfast love and to provide people an opportunity to express their gratitude
for God's patronage and generous beneficence. In Mark 2:23–28, covenant
love looses the disciples from restrictive readings of Torah that serve the interests of a priestly caste and their retainers while, at the same time, Torah
encourages them to help themselves to the bounty of the land as an expression
of the principle of extension behind the debt codes of the Torah. Marcus Borg
has argued that the central contrast between mercy and sacrifice in this pas-

sage provides an important clue to what Jesus was all about, namely, substituting the mercy code for the holiness code. Although in his later work Borg has changed his language from mercy code to "compassion code,"[8] his point is essentially the same.

This much seems clear. Jesus appeals to a prophetic critique of the temple and its sacrificial system found in a portion of Hosea where Yahweh determines to turn his face away from his people because they have attempted to return to him without acknowledging their guilt. They are seeking repentance without remorse (5:15–6:3). Yahweh then reviews what he has done to the people to get their attention: "I have hewn them by the prophets; I have killed them by the words of my mouth" (6:4–5). Hosea 6:6 concludes the section by contrasting what God wants, steadfast love and the knowledge of God, with what the people seem willing to give, sacrifices and burnt offerings but little else. The first two terms (steadfast love and knowledge of God) pick up the theme of covenant whereas the latter two items (burnt offerings and sacrifices) identify what happens when the sacrificial system becomes an end in itself and is detached from the obligations of covenant love and knowledge of the justice provisions of the Torah. By appropriating Hosea in this fashion, Jesus may be implying that he is continuing the prophetic hewing to which Hosea refers.

Since his own honor is at stake in the behavior of his followers, Jesus' purpose is to exonerate his disciples from the charges leveled against them: "You would not have condemned the guiltless." As the priests break the Torah every sabbath yet are guiltless, so his disciples are guiltless even though they are breaking the Torah. Why? Because their actions are covered by God's steadfast love. In this case, "mercy" would not be a bad translation of "steadfast love," for mercy takes into consideration the condition of the disciples, whose hunger drives them to glean on the sabbath. The rejoinder Jesus makes, "You would not have condemned the guiltless," applies to more than his disciples. It is an indictment of a temple system and its priestly caste that spends too much time and effort condemning those in need, abandoning in the process Yahweh's steadfast love and covenant loyalty. The demands of a sacrificial system have obliterated God's covenant love, condemning guiltless peasants for trying to survive even when their efforts mean that they cannot pay their tithes to the temple. The conflict between sacrifice and steadfast love is sharp. When does sacrifice become merciless, as the contrast implies? It does so when it loses sight of God's love and turns God's peasant people into slaves of the sacrificial system. The temple condemns what steadfast love condones.

---

8. See Marcus Borg, *Conflict, Holiness and Politics in the Teaching of Jesus* (Harrisburg, Pa.: Trinity Press International, 1998, orig. pub. 1984), 135–46.

A HOUSE OF PRAYER FOR ALL PEOPLE

Jesus used the temple as a setting for one of his parables, the parable of the Pharisee and the publican (Luke 18:9–14). Allowing for the Lukan framing (v. 9) and the generalizing conclusion (v. 14b) enables us to identify the parable of Jesus with verses 10–14a. It is also possible that verse 14a is a Lukan addition to clarify what is implied in the parable but not stated directly.

v. 9	Lukan framing
vv. 10–13	core parable of Jesus
v. 10	the setting
vv. 11–12	the Pharisee
v. 13	the toll collector
v. 14a	possible ending or Lukan addition
v. 14b	Lukan generalizing conclusion

The setting for the story appears to be the courtyard of the women in the temple precincts, the place where people would gather ("go up into the temple to pray") for the morning and afternoon sacrifices. Many believed that the afternoon sacrifice was an especially propitious time to offer prayers to God, so they gathered in the courtyard to watch for the smoke rising from the altar. When they saw the smoke, they would utter their prayers with the conviction that they were being carried up to God with the aroma of the acceptable sacrifice. For this purpose, even sinners were allowed to gather in the courtyard. By simply specifying that "two men went up to the temple to pray," Jesus has sketched the physical setting and time for his hearers.[9]

The scene of the parable sets up a dramatic confrontation in the form of an honor-and-shame conflict. Verse 11 can be read in two ways: 1) "the Pharisee stood and prayed thus with himself"; or 2) "the Pharisee stood by himself and prayed thus." In the first instance, the phrase *pros heauton* modifies how he prayed, and in the second instance, it explains where he stood. The second reading fits the details of the parable better than the first. As the Pharisee stood by himself, apart from the crowd gathered in the courtyard, so the toll collector stands "far off," isolating himself from the congregation but for reasons very different from those of the Pharisee. The parallel descriptions of the two figures set them both apart. But the parable gives a brief description of the Pharisee, who utters a long prayer, and a long description of the toll collector, who utters a short prayer.

---

9. For a full discussion of the parable, see Kenneth E. Bailey, *Through Peasant Eyes: More Lucan Parables, Their Culture and Style* (Grand Rapids: Wm. B. Eerdmans Publishing Co., 1980), 142–56. My reading is indebted to Bailey's reconstruction of the scene in the parable.

The Pharisee's prayer explains why he stands apart from others. His prayer divides into two sections, a condemnation of sinners and a commendation of the Pharisees' way of life. The condemnation appears to be aimed at the toll collector. It depends on how we read the phrase "or even like this" (*ē kai hōs*) toll collector, which can also be read, "or just like" this toll collector. In the first instance, the phrase adds the toll collector to the list of incorrigible sinners, and in the second it identifies him as all three: extortioner, unjust, adulterer. In either case, the Pharisee is engaged in some serious negative labeling for the purpose of stigmatizing the toll collector. If the attack on the toll collector focuses on shaming, the second part of the prayer recites two key reasons why Pharisees are honorable. They surpass the requirements of the Torah. They fast twice a week, not just once a year, and they tithe whatever they purchase in case the growers were lax in the matter of tithing. The contrast would appear to be complete. The goodness of the Pharisees shames the evil of the toll collectors. What is left to say?

This is where the parable takes an unexpected twist. The toll collector hears the condemnation and consents to it. He bows his head to the ground and beats his breast, in a gesture of extreme grief. As Bailey and others have noted, his prayer is more than a general appeal for mercy. He cries out, "God be merciful [*hilasthēti*] to me a sinner." The verb refers to the sacrifice taking place in the temple. He is saying, "Let this sacrifice be an expiation/propitiation for me." There is no better example of what it would mean for the temple to become "a house of prayer for all the peoples" (Mark 11:17). At this point, the hearers of the parable might well be confused. They expected the parable to set the righteous against the wicked, concluding with a ringing condemnation of the toll collector and a rousing celebration of the righteous Pharisee. But the toll collector's depth of grief has altered the picture, and his prayer reveals a heartfelt repentance unanticipated from a figure like a toll collector. As if this were not enough confusion to process, Jesus steps out of the narrator's role and says, with solemn intensity (if this verse is a part of the parable that Jesus told and is not a later or Lukan addition), "I tell you, this one went down to his house justified rather than the other."[10] Much depends on how one interprets the phrase "I tell you." If it functions as an attachment formula, then it would indicate that verse 14 is a later addition. If it functions as an intensifier, then it belongs to the parable as a closing punch line to increase the hearer's vertigo. Indeed, it may well function as part of the three-fold process of orientation,

10. It is also possible that this verse is a later addition to the parable to make its implicit meaning so clear that nobody could miss the point. If this verse is from the early church, then justification may be read as a theological term reflecting the theology of the early church.

disorientation, reorientation. The verb (*dikaioō*) does not need to carry the full weight of the theology of the early church but can mean here "acquitted." The divine passive indicates that the work of declaring the toll collector acquitted is the work of God. If this is a saying of Jesus, it reveals once again his role as broker of God's acquittal and forgiveness. The parable presents in imaginative form the very forgiveness that Jesus has already extended through his healings and exorcisms, a forgiveness offered and operating independently of the temple.

The reversal of expectations at the close of the parable may cause its hearers to reassess and problematize the two figures who appeared in it, and when they do, they may discover that the Pharisee and the toll collector are more complicated than they seem. Toll collectors (*telōnai*)[11] were the folks who worked in the tollbooths along the roads, at borders, and at the gates of towns and cities, collecting the indirect tolls and posts imposed on travelers, merchants, or peasants hoping to come to town to sell their goods. They defrauded and cheated those with whom they dealt but did not profit from their work. They were paid daily wages that placed them at subsistence level, and the job turnover was high, because the chief toll collectors (Luke 19:1–10, the story of Zaccheaus) who hired them did not trust them. Toll collectors took the brunt of the hostility from folks who came into contact with them, working in what was essentially a dead-end job until they were fired and put out on the streets. Meanwhile, the chief toll collectors got rich at their expense. They were considered unclean and beyond redemption because they could never repay all the people they had defrauded. Extremely vulnerable and without security, they were low-level functionaries in the system of tribute taking that marked the Galilee of Herod Antipas and the province of Judea overseen by the high priestly houses.

As the Pharisee's prayer reveals, he too is part of a system of tribute taking. He specifically mentions tithes in his prayer, not just tithing crops, animals, and the fruit of orchards and vineyards, but tithing everything that one purchases for meals. Tithing to the temple is, from one point of view, just another form of tribute taking, although one justified in the Torah (Lev. 27:30–33; Num. 18:21–32; Deut. 14:22–29; 26:1–15). When the priestly redactors of the Torah studied the two traditions regarding tithing, they combined them into one, thereby ensuring that peasants and others would be liable to a double tithe, a tithe to be given to the temple and a second tithe to be spent in Jerusalem. The dual system of tribute worked hardship on the peasants of the land, so both figures, the Pharisee and the toll collector, play roles in parallel systems of tribute, but one system of extraction is considered prominent while

---

11. For a discussion of toll collectors, see John Donahue, "Tax Collectors and Sinners: An Attempt at Identification," *CBQ* 33 (1971): 39–61.

the other is considered deviant. Read in this context, the toll collector repents of his role in an oppressive system, but the Pharisee does not. Not only does the Pharisee refuse to repent on the issue of tithing, but he holds up the more rigorous Pharisaic standard as a position to be emulated by all. In truth, this makes him an unjust extortioner condemning the peasants of the land to perpetual indebtedness to the temple. This may be why the toll collector experiences God's acquittal while the Pharisee stands guilty of the very activities he has accused the toll collector of pursuing.

If Jesus used this parable in a manner parallel to the way Freire used codifications, then the parable presented an opportunity to discuss tribute: who collected it, who provided the ideological justification for it, and how the figures involved in tribute taking were being perceived and evaluated. In other words, the peasants would have had the opportunity to decode the figures in the parable and their public facades in order to discern who was behind the mask (remember the discussion of *hypokritēs*). Then they would problematize their assumptions against the social types and scripts contained in the parable and problem pose what they thought was the case against what now appears in the parable. Contrary to popular belief, this parable reveals that Pharisees and toll collectors play similar roles in parallel systems of tribute taking, yet one is admired as a model of piety and the other despised as an example of collaboration. Yet the toll collector appeals for mercy and receives it, presumably because his prayer is heard. In the world of the parable, Jesus reverses the roles of the two figures, so that the Pharisee reinforces oppressive tribute (tithing everything that he gets) while the toll collector repents and seeks mercy. As the story was discussed, peasants might begin to decode tribute taking by realizing that tribute is tribute, however it is packaged and even when it is packaged as pious duty. The parable problematizes the matter of tribute. Seen in this light, Jesus subverts the temple's claim to tithes as divine obligation and re-presents it as another example of tribute taking.

"A CAVE OF SOCIAL BANDITS"

The most important key to unlocking Jesus' attitude toward the temple will most likely be found in the episode usually called "the cleansing of the temple" (Mark 11:15–17; Matt. 21:12–13; Luke 19:45–46; John 2:13–17). As noted in chapter 1 of this study, Sanders believes that the incident in the temple is one of the indisputable facts on which historians can construct a view of Jesus' public work. He is convinced that Jesus prophesied the destruction of the temple as a prelude to the appearing of a new temple that would be part of a new heaven and new earth. The temple was, in short, a major theme in what Sanders calls

"Jewish restoration eschatology." The difficulty with this position is that it seems to be little more than another, more drastic, version of the cleansing of the temple, this time with an eschatological spin. In both the traditional view of the cleansing of the temple and Sanders's vision of the coming of a new temple, the temple remains the essential centerpiece of the discussion. The issue in both of the approaches noted previously is the reformation and renewing of the temple as an institution. It is at least possible that Jesus did not share this view but believed that the temple was beyond reformation and needed to be destroyed altogether. This is certainly how Mark reads the event as indicated by the way he intercalates the temple incident between the cursing of the fig tree episodes (Mark 11:12–14, 15–19, 20–24). Given what we have gleaned so far about Jesus' view of the temple, this would not be out of character with his prophetic critique.

At first glance, the incident seems to be a protest against the commercialization of the temple's outer courtyard, but further exploration will reveal that Jesus' actions are directed against the temple itself, not commerce in the courtyard of the Gentiles. Mark depicts Jesus engaged in four activities:

1. Drive out those who sold and those who bought.
2. Overturn the tables of the money changers.
3. Overturn the seats of those who sold doves.
4. Prohibit vessels from being carried through the temple.

Most of the commercial activity occurring on the Temple Mount was essential for the sacrificial system to work. Money changers changed coins into temple-approved currency (the Tyrian didrachma), which allowed pilgrims to purchase what they needed to offer sacrifices. Nor is there any evidence that the money changers charged exploitive or onerous fees for their labors. The phrase "those who sold and those who bought" most likely refers to the sale and purchase of sacrificial animals and related necessities, such as oil, wine, or grain. The sellers of pigeons sold the birds to the poor who could not afford to offer a larger sacrifice. As Sanders has noted, "the business arrangements around the temple were necessary if the commandments were to be obeyed."[12]

Then why did Jesus focus his symbolic prophetic actions on people who were just doing their jobs, business as usual, keeping the sacrificial system in operation? Why focus on the retainers who are taking care of business and making it possible for pilgrims to participate in the sacrificial system? Because they represent interests much greater than themselves. Myers proposes that the money changers, for example, who engaged in their activities in the outer

---

12. E. P. Sanders, *Jesus and Judaism* (Minneapolis: Fortress Press, 1985), 65.

courtyard were controlled by the high priestly families who, along with their allies, benefitted from the business conducted there. So Myers urges that "we must see the moneychangers as street level representatives of banking interests of considerable power."[13] In this light, Jesus' attack on the sellers of doves makes sense because they represent one important way that the temple exploits the poor.[14] Jesus' actions are symbolic of his critique of the entire temple system. Therefore, they are more than a critique of commercialism. As Myers puts it so well, "It is the *ruling-class interests* in control of commercial enterprises in the temple market that Jesus is attacking."[15] If so, Jesus' prophetic action would have sent ripples throughout the temple hierarchy.

To understand Jesus' protest and actions, it is important to understand what it meant to look at the world as a place of limited good and limited goods. In the eyes of peasants, all things were in short supply; all goods were limited. This applied to everything from a concrete good like land, which was always being divided and subdivided but never increased, to a symbolic good like honor. Since everything had already been distributed, the only way to acquire more was to deprive somebody else. In this view of the world, the rich are those who can impose their will on others and appropriate their land and goods, while the poor are those who cannot prevent the loss of their honor and inherited land. This is why the rich are seen as the greedy who take what belongs to others by means of fraud and deceit. So the rich (for example, the high priestly families) are powerful enough to accumulate wealth, and the poor are vulnerable and unable to prevent their own oppression and exploitation. What does all of this mean for the temple and for Jesus' actions in the temple? Malina and Rohrbaugh put the matter in the following way:

> Given the limited-good view of the world, if the Jerusalem Temple personnel and their supporters were amassing wealth stored in the "den of thieves," then large numbers of persons were simultaneously becoming poor and unable to maintain their honor as "sons of Israel."[16]

In Judea and to a lesser degree in Galilee, the wealth of the temple was an inevitable corollary of the poverty of the peasantry, and the means by which the temple extracted tribute from peasants was through the temple tax, tithes, and sacrifices. The money changers were needed for collecting the temple tax and the purchase of sacrifices every bit as much as those who actually bought

13. Ched Myers, *Binding the Strong Man: A Political Reading of Mark's Story of Jesus* (Maryknoll, N.Y.: Orbis Books, 1988), 301.

14. Ibid., 299.

15. Ibid., 300.

16. Bruce J. Malina and Richard L. Rohrbaugh, *Social-Science Commentary on the Synoptic Gospels* (Minneapolis: Fortress Press, 1992), 251–52.

and sold the sacrificial animals. Of those who sold victims, Jesus targeted those who sold doves because they kept the poor indebted to the temple and entwined in its larger system. What appeared to be a concession was actually a condition for keeping the poor involved in the system that exploited them.

Jesus interprets his actions by two appeals to the prophets (Isa. 56:7 and Jer. 7:11). Both passages are significant, especially if the citation of a part is intended to evoke a memory of the whole prophetic passage in which it is found. By reciting Jer. 7:11, Jesus may well be invoking Jeremiah's whole temple sermon (7:1–15). Yahweh instructs Jeremiah to go to the gate to the temple and declare, "Do not trust in these deceptive words: 'This is the temple of the LORD, the temple of the LORD, the temple of the LORD'" (7:4). Saying doesn't make it so, yet the people of Judah seem to think that they can invoke the temple as a talisman against misfortune. What are they missing? Why can the temple not save them? In response to these questions, Jeremiah speaks a judgment oracle that carries a counterappeal and set of conditions: "If you do not oppress the alien, the orphan and the widow, or shed innocent blood in this place, and if you do not go after strange gods . . . I will dwell in this place" (7:6–7). The necessary condition for Yahweh's elusive presence is a commitment to justice and compassion. Jeremiah explains that the phrase "the temple of the LORD" is just a deceitful phrase because the people "steal, murder, commit adultery, swear falsely and make offerings to Baal" and then have the gall to appear before Yahweh to seek safety. The vice list found in verses 9–10 reads almost like an anti-Decalogue, an indication that Jeremiah is holding the rulers of Judah to account for ignoring the Decalogue and thereby forsaking the covenant. Insofar as their actions are motivated by greed resulting in the exploitation of the poor, they have turned the temple into little more than "a den of robbers" (7:11).

How does all of this connect with Jesus' prophetic action in the temple? In both cases, a ruling elite was using the temple for its own purposes so that the temple became a source of exploitation of the poor. Worship became a travesty because the rulers who came to the temple had savaged the Decalogue and destroyed the covenant. In both instances, those in charge of the temple had turned it into an instrument of oppression. But Jesus recites more than Jeremiah. If Jeremiah provided the basis for a prophetic critique, Isaiah provides a vision of what the temple could be.

Isaiah 56 belongs to the portion of Isaiah called Third Isaiah (chapters 56–66), a collection of largely postexilic prophecies addressed to the conflicts and problems that the exiles faced upon their return to Zion. When the exiles returned, they had to define what kind of community they would be. Would they cleanse themselves of foreigners through mass divorce (Ezra) and seal themselves off from strangers and aliens by rebuilding the walls around Jerusalem (Nehemiah), or would they become inclusive and welcoming to foreigners and strangers (Third Isaiah)? Isaiah 56:1–8 is one of the most dramatically inclusive statements in the prophetic literature. In this vision, even eunuchs will have a place in God's house, "a monument and a name better than sons and daughters" (v. 5). The promise to eunuchs is astonishing in light of Deut. 23:1, which prohibits eunuchs from being admitted to the assembly of Israel. (A similar statement in Lev. 21:18–20 appears to apply only to the offspring of Aaron, that is, to priests.) For Isaiah, the return from exile is not an end but a beginning of a much greater ingathering.

> Thus says the Lord GOD,
> who gathers the outcasts of Israel,
> I will gather others to them
> besides those already gathered.
> (56:8)

Following in Isaiah's footsteps, Jesus has been conducting his own "postexilic" prophetic work aimed at gathering the outcasts of Israel and restoring the blind, lame, mutilated, and broken. But Isaiah imagines the Lord bringing in the exiles and outcasts to his holy mountain (the temple), where they will offer burnt offerings and sacrifices acceptable to Yahweh. It is this inclusive temple that shall be called "a house of prayer for all peoples" (56:7). The contrast between the temple envisioned by Isaiah and the temple Jesus entered in Jerusalem could hardly have been greater. Whereas Isaiah's temple was dedicated to inclusiveness, the Jerusalem temple was constructed to separate Judeans from Gentiles. The balustrade separating the temple precincts from the outer courtyard of the Gentiles symbolized the separation of Judean and Gentile. Even more pointedly, the demands of the temple created two categories of Judeans, clean and unclean, and effectively excluded peasants and other poor folks from participation in the temple system. It followed an agenda of exclusion no less rigorous than the program proposed by Ezra and Nehemiah.

Clearly, Jesus' prophetic citations were germane to the temple of his day. By invoking the prophets, he identifies himself with the tradition of Israel's great prophets and develops his critique of the temple from that tradition, but Jesus may be even more drastic than Isaiah, for Jesus does not envisage a reformed or even a transformed temple. For him, the die is cast. The temple is beyond redemption. With this view, Neusner agrees. In his study of the temple incident, he concludes that only a person who "rejected the Torah's explicit teaching concerning the daily whole offering could have overturned the tables."[17]

17. Jacob Neusner, "Moneychangers in the Temple: The Mishnah's Explanation," *NTS* 35 (1989): 287–90.

This means that the money changers may have been more than incidental retainers, as we have assumed. Neusner's remarks suggest that they were indispensable to the effective working of the sacrificial system. Since they were essential figures for collecting the temple tax, and since the moneys collected in this manner purchased the daily whole offering for the whole people of Israel, Jesus' actions represented not only a "rejection of the most important rite of the Israelite cult"[18] but a rejection of the cult itself. If this is the case, then Jesus' actions in the outer courtyard would have reverberated all the way to the altar in the court of the priests.

CONCLUSION

From the evidence and inferences gathered to this point, we can propose that the incident in the temple was closer to a prophetic act symbolizing the destruction of the temple than an attempt to cleanse or reform the temple. From Jesus' point of view, the high priests and their priestly counterparts had inverted the meaning and role of the temple: "Is it not written, 'My house shall be called a house of prayer for all nations?' But you have made it a cave of social bandits [*spēlaion lēstōn*]." The last line can also be translated "a den of thieves." In the latter translation, the elites who go to the temple are compared to thieves who escape to their hideouts "just as bandits lie low until pursuit dies down, and then go out to commit fresh depradations."[19] Depicting the ruling elites as bandits serves to remind us that they take, often forcibly, what belongs to others. If we translate *lēstai* as "social bandits," we evoke a different picture of the high priestly establishment. Social bandits often attack elites and rob them to support their movement, usually a violent reaction to the loss of some security previously enjoyed by peasants. They represent a prepolitical form of protest and are considered deviant by the political establishment. If Jesus is referring to social bandits, he is most likely playing with the deviant/prominent theme. Most folks would think of the priests and high priests as prominent and the social bandits hiding in the caves in the Judean wilderness as deviant. So Jesus reverses the judgment. The real social bandits are not the brigands hiding in caves but the priestly establishment who steal what little the poor have left to keep the temple running. Once again, as we saw with the Pharisee and the toll collector, the prominent becomes deviant, and the deviant, prominent.

In the reading of the incident in the temple proposed here, Jesus enacts a symbolic destruction of the temple while providing a prophetic critique of its

18. Ibid., 289–90.
19. John Bright, *Jeremiah* (Garden City, N.Y.: Doubleday, 1965), 56.

failures. This action would have set Jesus in sharp opposition to the rulers in Jerusalem, especially those high priestly families who controlled the temple and profited from their control. The Gospels will speak of that political cadre as "the chief priests, the scribes and the elders" (see, for example, Mark 8:31–33; 10:32–34). They perceived Jesus as a great enough threat to arrest him and choreograph an elaborate status degradation ritual that we will call a "show trial." If this chapter has accurately portrayed Jesus' attitude toward the temple, their hostility towards him may have been justified.

8

The View from the Village

The Great Tradition and the Little Tradition
in Conflict over Tribute

GALILEE IN CONFLICT

Palestine in the first century was a world in conflict. From the point of view
of the rulers and their historians, it might have appeared, as Tacitus noted, that
"under Tiberius all was quiet" (*Hist.* 5.9–10), but to the peasant villagers who
labored to survive under the harsh conditions of oppression and exploitation,
the situation looked quite different. History from below rarely looks like history from above. Although the causes of conflict were varied, this study has
mentioned three. First, the world of Jesus was dominated by advanced agrarian societies built on systemic tensions and conflicts between the rulers and
the ruled. Second, the presence of the temple in Jerusalem further complicated
an already-difficult political relationship between Judea and Galilee because
of its demand for tithes. Third, Palestine was under the colonial domination
of the Roman Empire through the client kingship of the Herods in Galilee and
its environs and through the high priestly houses in Jerusalem. These conflicts
were fueled by an ideological conflict that took the form of a clash between
the great tradition of the ruling class, based in their urban centers, and the little tradition of the peasant villagers. This level of conflict expresses the fact
that empire does not stop at physical occupation but seeks to establish ideological domination as well.[1]

---

1. It would be more accurate to speak of great traditions and little traditions in the
plural. In Jerusalem, the high priestly houses promulgated one form of the great tradition, focused on the priests and the temple, while the Pharisees pursued their own
version of the great tradition (expressed through the oral Torah), which focused on the
laity and their households. It could be properly said that the Essenes developed their

CONFLICT IN AGRARIAN SOCIETIES:
THE ISSUE OF TRIBUTE

Jesus conducted his public work in a world of advanced agrarian societies, which are characteristically divided into two groups, the ruling class who live in luxury and the majority of the population who live at a subsistence level or worse, at the edge of destitution and ruin. The peasant class produces the wealth on which agrarian societies are based, primarily through the cultivation of crops, orchards, and vineyards. Yet by means of a redistributive or tributary economy, the rulers are able to appropriate the lion's share of the harvest, the so-called surplus, while leaving the peasant producers barely enough to maintain a subsistence existence. This redistribution of wealth occurs primarily through taking tribute. Taking tribute was an economic expression of domination because it established the ability of the ruling class to take the yield of the land from the hands of those who had produced it and to appropriate it for their own political purposes and social ends.

In Palestine, these dynamics apply whether we are discussing the client kingship of the Herods or the internal rule of the high priestly houses of Judea under the control of the Roman prefect of Judea. The references to client kingship and ruling priestly houses under Roman control indicate that peasants were subjected to more than one level of tribute. The peasants of Galilee were most likely subjected to three levels of tribute: the tribute extracted by imperial Rome; the tribute collected by the Herods; and the tithes demanded by the high priestly houses in order to maintain the temple as well as their own power and prominence. This confluence of tribute takers meant that the peasants of Galilee would be under extreme stress. If we remember that tribute is taken from what is left after the rulers claim their portion of the harvest, we may be able to imagine the burden this placed on small holders and to appreciate the threat each collection of tribute posed to their livelihood and their future.

---

own version of the great tradition. Although we do not have any literary remains of peasant versions of the little tradition, we can infer what they might have looked like. Why then not speak of great traditions and little traditions in the plural instead of in the singular? Because the many versions of the great and little traditions worked off of commonly held traditions and texts, such as the Torah and the prophets. So even disparate versions of the little tradition would also demonstrate some unified perspectives (e.g., resistance to tribute and colonial rule). In addition, speaking of great tradition and little tradition in the singular reinforces the simple fact that agrarian societies and aristocratic empires were divided between the rulers and the ruled, the powerful and the vulnerable. So this study will use both the singular and the plural to describe these ideological formations called the great tradition and the little tradition.

Roman tribute took two forms, tribute based on land and the head tax.[2] The philosophy behind both forms of tribute reflects clearly what Lenski has called "the proprietary theory of the state," the notion that land controlled by Caesar or Herod was their personal estate to be exploited and distributed as they saw fit.[3] Nor was it unusual for rulers to impose layer upon layer of tribute on peasants, forcing them to pay more than their subsistence existence could absorb. In his study of what he calls "aristocratic empires," John Kautsky noted that such empires (like the Roman Empire) neither replace the governments they conquer nor "disturb local hereditary interests"; rather, "they simply added themselves to the top" while leaving the other levels of extraction untouched.[4] This was certainly the case in Galilee and Judea.

Since the continuing rule of aristocratic elites in agrarian societies depended directly on their ability to extract tribute and keep the peasant villagers in subjection to them, and since peasants did not accept their oppression and exploitation without resistance, conflict was built into the very structure of agrarian societies. One of the forms this conflict took was the clash between the great tradition and the little tradition.

THE GREAT TRADITION AND THE LITTLE TRADITION

The great tradition contained the interpretation of the world as seen by the rulers, history seen from above. It was usually centered in urban areas and propagated from there to the villages of the countryside. More often than not, it was written. Of course, the great tradition had its guardians, who controlled its parameters and determined its interpretation. These guardians might be hereditary sacral elites, such as high priests, or their retainers (such as scribes or a political faction like the Pharisees). The great tradition, while propagating a "social ideology of patronage," would usually legitimize "inequalities in material and cultural resources as foreordained" and celebrate "the positive value of stratification."[5]

In Jesus' day, interpretations of the Torah functioned as the basis of various forms of the great tradition, whose influence extended throughout Judea and

2. David Fiensy, *The Social History of Palestine in the Herodian Period: The Land is Mine* (Lewiston, N.Y.: Edwin Mellen Press, 1991), 99–101.

3. Gerhard Lenski, *Power and Privilege: A Theory of Social Stratification* (New York: McGraw-Hill, 1966), 215–19.

4. John Kautsky, *The Politics of Aristocratic Empires* (Chapel Hill: University of North Carolina Press, 1982), 124.

5. James C. Scott, "Protest and Profanation," *Theory and Society* 4 (1977): 14.

Galilee, even though Galilee was ruled by Herod Antipas and not under the jurisdiction of the high priestly houses in Jerusalem. This chapter proposes that a particular reading of the Torah functioned as a great tradition that sustained the rule of the high priestly families in Jerusalem, along with a lay aristocracy in Judea, and perhaps the rule of the Herods in Galilee (though this seems less likely because the legitimacy of the Herods depended primarily on their ties to Rome). This "oral Torah" or "tradition of the elders" specified what in the great bulk of Torah was "binding" and what could be "loosed." It seems likely that the great tradition focused primarily on matters of purity and how they should be applied to the people of Judea and Galilee, since this issue could be used to maximize the social distance between elites and peasants while reinforcing the control of the few over the many. In fact, forcing peasants to accept the great tradition would actually serve to intensify their marginalization, for

> whether it is a matter of knowing the sacred texts, of speaking and dressing properly, of performing the elaborate ceremonies of initiation, marriage or burial, peasants are asked, in effect, to revere a standard which is impossible for them to achieve.[6]

The same holds true for the ceremonies of purity surrounding the consumption of meals and the temple's demand for tithes. Saldarini understands the Pharisees' oral Torah as a covertly political program.[7] The very act of carving out an area of ritual purity created a space that the colonizer could not easily penetrate, and offering tithes replicated the imperial demands for tribute but in a context of support for the temple. Of course, this same agenda marginalized the peasants of Galilee, who could neither keep the purity codes nor pay the tribute demanded by the temple in the form of tithes.

For all of these reasons the great tradition, even when it appeared as a reading of Torah, could neither support the lives of peasant villagers nor serve their interests. As Scott has noted, the farther down the scale of social stratification one moves, the less binding the great tradition becomes, and the farther one moves away from the center toward the periphery, the weaker the great tradition becomes. This cultural and geographical distance provides space for the little tradition to take root and grow.[8] Scott defines the little tradition as "the distinctive patterns of belief and behavior which are valued by the peasantry of an agrarian society."[9] The little tradition expresses the values of peasants

---

6. Ibid., 17.

7. See Anthony J. Saldarini, *Pharisees, Scribes and Sadducees in Palestinian Society* (Grand Rapids: Wm. B. Eerdmans Publishing Co., 2001).

8. For an early discussion of the great tradition and the little tradition, see Robert Redfield, *Society and Culture* (Chicago: University of Chicago Press, 1956), 70 ff.

9. Scott, "Protest and Profanation," 8.

and incorporates their grasp and selective appropriation of the great tradition in a way that sustains their life, culture, and values; it is history seen from below.[10] It also becomes a source and resource for resisting the imposition of the great tradition by the ruling elites. In spite of their determined efforts, elites are usually unable to impose their construction of reality and social world on peasant villagers. Peasants find ways to manage what Scott calls a "negotiated subordination,"[11] that is, they can neither deny nor disregard the imposition of the great tradition by ruling elites, but they can and do resist. More often than not, the little tradition will embody forms of this resistance. By combining elements of the great tradition with its own indigenous characteristics and perspectives, the little tradition may be more local and syncretistic than the great tradition, which strives to define the common norms sponsored and encouraged by the ruling powers. Redfield rather scornfully contrasts the two traditions in this way:

> In a civilization, there is a great tradition of the reflective few, and there is a little tradition of the unreflective many. The great tradition is cultivated in schools and temples; the little tradition works itself out and keeps itself going in the lives of the unlettered in their village communities.[12]

His remarks reveal an evident blindness to the strength, wisdom, and resistance found in the little tradition. Just as Sanders and Gray (see chapter 5) assumed that peasants were apolitical because they did not participate in politics in the same ways that elites did, so Redfield assumes that peasants are ignorant and unreflective because they do not express their forms of reflection in a public and literate manner shaped by a formal education.

FORMS OF RESISTANCE

But what forms might this resistance take? In his study of what he calls "the weapons of the weak," James C. Scott has focused his attention on the "everyday forms of peasant resistance, the prosaic but constant struggle between the peasantry and those who seek to extract labor, food, taxes, rents and interest from them."[13] But this

10. See the following collection of essays: Frederick Krantz, ed., *History from Below: Studies in Popular Protest and Popular Ideology* (Montreal: Concordia University, 1985).
11. Scott, "Protest and Profanation," 12–16.
12. Redfield, *Society and Culture*, 70.
13. James C. Scott, *Weapons of the Weak: Everyday Forms of Peasant Resistance* (New Haven, Conn.: Yale University Press, 1985), xvi.

struggle between rich and poor is not merely a struggle over work, property rights, grain and cash. It is also a struggle over the appropriation of symbols, a struggle over how the past and the present shall be understood and labeled, a struggle to identify causes and assess blame, a contentious effort to give partisan meaning to local history.[14]

If Scott is right, then we might reasonably expect that the little tradition would reflect some of these basic issues as they are experienced by the peasants in Galilee, since the focus of conflict is "the material nexus of class struggle—the appropriation of land, labor, taxes, rents and so forth."[15]

Up to this point, it may seem as though the great tradition and the little tradition are equally accessible and can, for all intents and purposes, be placed side by side for analysis and comparison, but in light of the power relations between rulers and ruled, this could not be the case. In a political environment where an oppressive ruling class dominates a suppressed population, there will be at least two versions of what is happening, a "public transcript" of events controlled by the rulers and a "hidden transcript" of the same events and conditions as seen through the eyes of the peasants. Although the hidden transcript is not identical with the little tradition, they will overlap. The public transcript is a "shorthand way of describing the open interaction between subordinates and those who dominate," whereas the hidden transcript covers the "discourse that takes place 'offstage,' beyond the direct observation of the power holders."[16] Put differently, the hidden transcript captures what the oppressed say to each other and distills what they really think about their rulers but are too intimidated to express openly. The public transcript is the "*self-portrait of dominant elites as they would have themselves seen.*"[17] Quite clearly, there will be a significant discrepancy between the public transcript of the dominant rulers and the hidden transcript of the oppressed.

This discrepancy would appear to create a chasm as great as the one separating the rich man from Lazarus. How can we ever get from one to the other? What makes the difficulty even greater is that the public transcript of the elites may appear in a variety of written forms while peasants generally live in an illiterate oral culture, so that their perspectives are even harder to discern and describe and often must be inferred from the hostile descriptions of the rulers or their historians. The task would be impossible were it not for a third form of political discourse found among the oppressed classes that Scott describes

14. Ibid., xvii.
15. Ibid., 33.
16. James C. Scott, *Domination and the Arts of Resistance: Hidden Transcripts* (New Haven, Conn.: Yale University Press, 1990), 2, 4.
17. Ibid., 18.

as "a politics of disguise and anonymity that takes place in public view but is designed to have a double meaning or to shield the identity of the actors."[18] This means, in effect, that "a partly sanitized, ambiguous and coded version of the hidden transcript is always present in the public discourse of subordinate groups."[19] One place that version might surface is in the little tradition. In Mark 12:13–17, the conflict over what belongs to Caesar and what belongs to God may capture an attempt to expose and disclose the hidden transcript of resistance to paying tribute to Rome,[20] a position that will be spelled out later in this chapter.

With the assistance of Scott's work on the little tradition, the weapons of the weak, and the role of public and hidden transcripts, we have some tools and a framework for discerning what might have been part of the little tradition of the peasants of Galilee. At least, we might be able to identify some examples in the texts of the Synoptic Gospels.

THE LITTLE TRADITION AS RESISTANCE TO TEMPLE TRIBUTE (MATTHEW 17:24–27)

If Jesus' remarks about paying back to Caesar what is Caesar's and rendering to God what is God's is an incitement to resist the payment of tribute, then the charge brought against Jesus, remembered in Luke, makes some sense. "They began to accuse him, saying, 'We found this man perverting our nation and forbidding us to give tribute to Caesar'" (23:2). Jesus may have been vilified as "a friend to toll collectors and sinners" (Q: Luke 7:34), but that does not mean that he was a friend of tribute and tolls. This is what makes the puzzling "miracle story" in Matt. 17:24–27 so intriguing. The material is found only in Matthew; hence it either belongs to Matthew's special traditional materials (M) or is a composition of the evangelist himself, a position argued by Gundry.[21] At the outset we concede that the text as it stands reflects the compositional hand of Matthew.

18. Ibid., 18–19.

19. Ibid., 19.

20. See Herzog, *Jesus, Justice, and the Reign of God* (Louisville, Ky.: Westminster John Knox Press, 2000), 224–32, and Herzog, "Onstage and Offstage With Jesus of Nazareth: Public Transcripts, Hidden Transcripts, and Gospel Texts" in Richard Horsley, ed., *Hidden Transcripts and the Arts of Resistance: Applying the Work of James C. Scott to Jesus and Paul,* Semeia Studies 48 (Atlanta: Society of Biblical Literature, 2004), 41–60.

21. Robert Gundry, *Matthew: A Commentary on His Literary and Theological Art* (Grand Rapids: William B. Eerdmans Publishing Co., 1982), 355–57.

From a form-critical point of view, the story hardly qualifies as a miracle story, since the text narrates no miracle. The core story (*chreia*) seems to have two parts and concludes with Jesus' pronouncement "Then the sons are free."

vv. 24–25a   the collectors question Peter in public (onstage)
vv. 25b–26   Jesus questions Peter in private (offstage)

Meier finds the story structured into two parallel parts.

> At the end of this parallel structure Jesus makes the pronouncement that is the climax and point of the whole dispute story. . . . The theological point is clear: Jesus and his disciples are exempt from paying the temple tax.[22]

The dispute story, as Meier calls it, moves from onstage, the public confrontation between the tribute collectors and Peter, to offstage when Peter enters the house (v. 25b). Peter's quick-witted response to his interrogators produced an example of a public transcript, while Jesus' instruction provides a glimpse of a hidden transcript. If the tribute in dispute is the tribute owed to the temple, then the tribute collectors, unlike their Herodian and Roman counterparts, must persuade and cajole but cannot compel its payment. Jesus' argument seems to be an argument from the lesser to the greater. If the kings of the earth exempt their sons (family) from the payment of tribute, then how much more will Yahweh free his sons (and daughters) from the onerous burden. To a peasant population excluded from the temple because they could not afford to pay their tithes and offerings, this was a welcome word and a response in keeping with Jesus' emphasis on the forgiveness of sin or cancellation of debt (see the discussion of Mark 2:1–12 in chapter 4).

While it is true that the origin of the temple tax was rooted in the liberating event of the exodus (Exod. 30:11–16) and reaffirmed as part of the renewal of the covenant in the postexilic period (Neh. 10:32–33), it is equally clear that by the time of Jesus, the temple tax had become part of an onerous system of multiple tribute taking that left the peasants of Galilee struggling to survive. Therefore, Jesus' announcement that "the sons are free" would have resonated with the peasants among whom he conducted much of his public, prophetic work. Jesus' declaration was a liberating affirmation.

Even if the core dispute story originally included verses 24–26, this still leaves the status of verse 27 in doubt. Meier argues that verse 27 has its own clear structure. After announcing a "new theological principle" ("lest we scandalize them"), Jesus "issues an order made up of four clauses, each beginning

---

22. John P. Meier, *A Marginal Jew: Rethinking the Historical Jesus*, vol. 2, 880.

with an aorist participle, which is then followed by an aorist imperative (or . . . an equivalent future tense)."

Participle	+	Command
going to the sea		throw in a hook
the fish coming up first		take
and opening its mouth		you will find a *statēr* [= two didrachma]
taking it		give it to them for me and for you[23]

But what does the saying mean, and why has Matthew added it to the core dispute story? Gundry believes that Matthew "wanted to portray Peter as a paradigm of obedient discipleship in paying the temple tax—and this in order that Jewish Christians might not cause unbelieving Jews to reject the gospel."[24] This would necessitate placing Matthew before 70 CE, which Gundry is willing to do. By contrast, Warren Carter thinks the setting is post-70 CE and refers to the *fiscus judaicus*, the tribute that Vespasian imposed on all Jews after the revolt of 66–73 CE[25] (*War*, 7.218). Carter thinks the provision of the tribute from the fish's mouth emphasizes God's sovereignty. Paying the tribute gathered in this way makes no concessions to Rome. Juvenal might boast that "every rare and beautiful thing in the wide ocean . . . belongs to the imperial treasury" (*Sat.* 4.51–55), but this story reveals God as sovereign over all the fish of the sea. Jesus has no option but to pay the tribute, but he does so in a manner that avoids the fight-or-flight options forced on a colonized population. Meier is convinced that, Mattheanisms aside, the pericope contains some sort of dispute about whether Jewish Christians should pay the temple tax. He notes that even Bultmann thought the dispute referred originally to something other than the temple tax but would not hazard a guess what it might be.[26] For the purposes of this reading, we will assume that the issue is the temple tax.

If verse 27 belongs with the original unit, can it be read in a manner consistent with what has already been proposed? It does address the fundamental struggle in agrarian societies, namely, "the material nexus of the class struggle—the appropriation of land, labor, taxes, rents and so forth."[27] Taking a cue from Scott, it is possible to read verse 27 as a humorous profaning of the great tradition. In this light, the dispute contrasts two responses to paying tribute. The collectors represent the great tradition's demands for tribute. They do not

23. Ibid., 880–81.
24. Gundry, *Matthew*, 356–57.
25. Warren Carter, *Matthew and the Margins: A Sociopolitical and Religious Reading* (Maryknoll, N.Y.: Orbis Books, 2000), 356–60.
26. Meier, *A Marginal Jew*, 2:883–84.
27. Scott, *Weapons of the Weak*, 33.

hesitate to shame Peter or Jesus in order to gain compliance. In a different key, the dialogue between Peter and Jesus represents the little tradition's response. This means that the ludicrous comments about catching a fish and taking a coin out of its mouth reflect what Meier called "a humorous and folkloric touch but also something more."[28] It is a profanation of the great tradition's obsession with tribute. Notice that Jesus' discourse is offstage, out of the earshot of the tribute collectors. In the secure environment of the house, Jesus can speak freely with Peter, giving his imagination full play. We do not need to pay tribute, Peter, and this is how we will do it!

The story was remembered and passed down among a population of peasants for whom Jesus' words were good news indeed. The lampooning of the need to pay tribute only added to the enjoyment of the story while reinforcing its basic message, "Then the sons are free." Scott has already noted that profanation can take the form of folk tales and jokes.[29] If this reading is not satisfactory in every detail, then it stands on the same ground as every other attempt to explain this puzzling text.

THE LITTLE TRADITION AS RESISTANCE TO ROMAN TRIBUTE (MARK 12:13–17)

The clash between the public transcript and hidden transcript is also evident in the incident where Jesus debates the Pharisees and Herodians on the question of Roman tribute. Mark has placed the incident on the Temple Mount, but there is nothing in the passage to suggest that it must be placed there, and the presence of Herodians may argue for a Galilean context. It is probable that villagers discussed the question of tribute since it affected their lives so directly. Since the setting does not appreciably affect the reading of the incident proposed here, we will leave the question of location (temple courtyard or peasant village square) unresolved.

Whatever the original context, the incident depicts a conflict disguised as an inquiry, but this is no civics class discussion about the duties of citizens in a democratic society; it is an attempt at political entrapment with lethal consequences. All of the basic elements of the encounter point in this direction: 1) the political character of the inquiry; 2) the use of flattery to force Jesus to take a stand on a hot issue; 3) the explosive question about tribute; 4) the use of the denarius; and 5) the exchange culminating in Jesus' elusive aphorism.

---

28. Meier, *A Marginal Jew*, 2:882.
29. Scott, "Protest and Profanation," 20.

Not everyone reads the debate in this way. J. Duncan M. Derrett, for example, has argued that the scene depicts the Pharisees and the Herodians addressing a technical question to Jesus. He bases this reading on the use of the term *apokrisis* in the Lukan version of the story, a verb that became "a technical term for a *rescript*; it is what we lawyers call a *responsum*, a technical answer to a technical question, particularly in the field of behavior."[30] He discovers support for his reading by noting the reference to Jesus as teaching "the way of God" (Luke 20:21). Jesus is not being asked for his personal opinion about paying tribute but is being asked to speak as a teacher and an interpreter of the Torah. More pointedly, the question could read, What does the Torah say about paying tribute to Caesar? If this is the setting, then Jesus' response cannot be "merely a piece of evasion," since this would defeat the purpose for which the question was asked. Jesus is being asked to update the Torah for the age of Tiberius.

The difficulty with this reading is that it tends to overlook the elements of entrapment that surround the account and assumes that the scene is more akin to a courtroom or a covenant renewal ceremony than it is a scene of political intrigue. By contrast, Malina and Rohrbaugh propose reading the incident as an example of a "challenge-riposte encounter,"[31] a hostile honor challenge directed at Jesus with the intent of discrediting him and shaming him publicly. This is why Jesus does not respond to his adversaries' flattery but "answers with an insulting counterquestion."[32] An honorable man cannot cede the terms of the debate to his opponents but must establish his own terms. If this is the case, then Jesus will neither quote nor debate the Torah (*pace* Derrett) because he knows that the initial question is not a disinterested inquiry but a trap.

One shortcoming of Malina and Rohrbaugh's reading of the incident is that it minimizes the political and economic dimensions of this public encounter. In their reading, the challenge and riposte is part of a larger battle to preserve or gain honor and to avoid being shamed, but this reading loses track of what is at stake politically in this clash between a public transcript that justifies paying tribute and a hidden transcript that resists paying tribute. The ruling class retainers who initiate the conflict with Jesus are ultimately beholden to Rome for their power and prestige, and they know that the system of colonial domination is dependent upon the orderly and timely payment of tribute. The ability to rule

---

30. J. Duncan M. Derrett, "Luke's Perspective on Tribute to Caesar," in Richard J. Cassidy and Phillip Scharper, eds., *Political Issues in Luke-Acts* (Maryknoll, N.Y.: Orbis Books, 1983), 39–40.

31. Bruce J. Malina and Richard L. Rohrbaugh, *Social-Science Commentary on the Synoptic Gospels* (Minneapolis: Fortress Press, 1992), 256.

32. Ibid.

depends on the collection of tribute, so the question about the payment of tribute is politically loaded. An incident from the reign of Nero illustrates the centrality of tribute to Roman rule. Upon learning how difficult it was to collect
taxes and tribute, Nero pondered whether he should abolish all indirect taxation
and "present the reform as the noblest gift of all to the human race." He was
eventually prevented from executing his plan by his senior advisors who argued
"that the dissolution of the empire was certain if the revenues on which the state
subsisted were to be curtailed" (Tacitus, *Ann.* 13.50; also cited in Carter).[33]

One could add to this dynamic the class conflict between the rulers who
demand tribute and the ruled who must pay it, another aspect of the debate
that Malina and Rohrbaugh minimize. Since they believe that the encounter
is between those who are roughly social equals, they can miss the class conflict
implicit in the debate between the proxies of the ruling class and the prophet
who speaks for the people of the land. Scott's work brings these dimensions of
the encounter to the surface. Having sketched the nature of the incident, it is
time to look at its elements more closely.

The initial flattery may appear to be ineffective since it fails to deceive Jesus,
but it was not intended for Jesus' ears but the ears of the crowd. The flatter-
ers are preparing the crowd for Jesus to disavow the tribute. By describing
Jesus as a teacher who does not judge people by their social standing or curry
favor with the rich and powerful, they are, in effect, "daring Jesus to commit
himself in this loaded political situation."[34] Every seemingly complimentary
reference raises the stakes by forcing Jesus to "save face" before the crowd by
opposing the payment of tribute. The flattery throws down the gauntlet by
attempting to force Jesus to deny the payment of tribute.

The question posed by the Pharisees and the Herodians was not a general
question about the inevitability of death and taxes; it was a specific question
about paying tribute. The payment of tribute to Rome had been a volatile issue
since Pompey had imposed tribute on Jerusalem and Judea in 63 BCE as a
symbol of their subjection to Rome. The Romans collected tribute on land
and people as a way of asserting their domination over the bodies of their subjects and the lands they had conquered. In 6 CE when Augustus converted
Archelaus's failed kingdom into a Roman province, he conducted a census in
order to develop an inventory of assets on which tribute could be calculated.
As Finney notes, "the census constituted the numerical basis (computed in
hectares and human heads) from which the Romans levied their so-called poll

---

33. Warren Carter, *Matthew and Empire: Initial Explorations* (Harrisburg, Pa.: Trinity Press International, 2001), 14.

34. Ched Myers, *Binding the Strong Man: A Political Reading of Mark's Story of Jesus*
(Maryknoll, N.Y.: Orbis Books, 1988), 311.

(or head) tax," which all nonelites were expected to pay in "imperial specie."[35] It was this census that triggered the revolt of Judas of Gamala, who evidently argued that "the payment of tribute to the Romans was incompatible with Israel's theocratic ideals."[36] Myers highlights the conflict in the sharpest of terms when he declares that the encounter was "a test of loyalty that divided collaborators from subversives against the backdrop of revolt."[37] At its deepest level, the conflict reflected Israel's covenantal insistence that God alone should rule Israel, a claim that excluded all other rulers, whether Roman, Herodian, or priestly.

When tribute was collected in Roman coinage, it was part and parcel of Roman political propaganda. The denarius was the most stable and extensively circulated coin of Tiberius's reign, a coin that doubled as currency and propaganda. The obverse of the coin contained a profile of Tiberius's head "adorned with the laurel wreath, the sign of divinity,"[38] and was inscribed with an epigram that claimed divinity for both Augustus and Tiberius. Written in full with abbreviations omitted, the epigram read, *Tiberius Caesar Divi Augusti Filius Augustus*. The reverse side depicted the emperor's mother, Livia, "sitting on the throne of the gods, in her right hand the Olympian scepter, in her left hand the olive branch to symbolize her incarnation as the heavenly *Pax*, the divine counterpart to the *Pax Romana*."[39] The coin was inscribed on this side with the phrase *pontifex maximus*, or high priest. The enduring presence of the denarius and its ubiquity made it a familiar symbol of Caesar's presence and power. It was no ordinary Roman coin! The Roman denarius was a piece of political propaganda that asserted Rome's claim to rule the cosmos, thereby reinforcing the ideological basis of Roman domination. It summarized the public transcript of imperial rule.

Against this background, Jesus' demand for a denarius makes sense. To deflect his opponents' momentum and to defuse their question, Jesus combines a counterquestion with a demand to find a denarius. In doing so, he seizes the initiative from his interlocutors and determines the course of the encounter.

35. Paul Finney, "The Rabbi and the Coin Portrait (Mark 12:15b, 16): Rigorism Manque," *JBL* 112 (1993): 632.

36. F. F. Bruce, "Render to Caesar," in E. Bammel and C. F. D. Moule, eds., *Jesus and the Politics of His Day* (Cambridge: Cambridge University Press, 1984), 254–55. See also Josephus, *War* 2.118; *Ant.* 18.23.

37. Myers, *Binding the Strong Man*, 310.

38. H. St. J. Hart, "The Coin of 'Render unto Caesar . . .' (A Note on Some Aspects of Mark 12:13–17; Matt 22:15–22; Luke 20:20–26)," in Bammel and Moule, eds., *Jesus and the Politics of His Day*, 248; Ethelbert Stauffer, *Christ and the Caesars*, trans. K. and R. Gregor Smith (Philadelphia: Westminster Press, 1955), 124 (122–128).

39. Stauffer, *Christ and the Caesars*, 125.

This is why the coin is so central. Finney is quite right when he observes that the request for the coin "interrupts the dialogue and redirects its flow."[40] By focusing attention on the coin, Jesus seems to refocus the controversy away from the Torah. He does not intend to debate Torah because he knows his adversaries' apparent interest in "the way of God" is a ruse. Better to establish other ground for the conflict. If he argues Torah, as they would like to argue it, Jesus would be on their turf as representatives of the great tradition. So Jesus seeks to position himself in a manner more congruent with the little tradition.

The denarius also distinguishes Jesus from his adversaries. By the way they have formulated their question, they have implied that they are actually on the same side. "Should *we* pay tribute or should *we* not?" Jesus' strategy separates him from them. By asking for a denarius, Jesus reveals that he does not have one but his opponents are able to procure one, whether they have to scurry about and find a money changer or have one among themselves. The point is clear: they have access to a denarius; Jesus does not. As Belo noted, the coin embodies "the uncleanness inflicted on the country by the occupying power" and, as such, it symbolizes the economic exploitation and political suppression of the so-called *Pax Romana*.[41]

The encounter escalates as soon as the Pharisees and Herodians produce the denarius. Jesus asks a nasty question: "Whose image [*eikōn*] and inscription [*epigraphē*] is this?" If the act of producing the coin did not shame his opponents, the question did. Everyone knew what was on the despised coin. It was a blasphemous statement and an idolatrous claim, so the Pharisees and Herodians seek the most innocuous answer possible. They cannot refuse to answer lest they seem to be ashamed of their Roman masters, in which case their role as collaborators could be compromised. So they have to answer the question, however embarrassing it might be to do so and however much it casts them in a negative light. So they mutter, "Caesar's."

Based on the Gospel accounts of these events, it is not possible to know exactly what happened and how. If Jesus was holding the coin, his very act of holding up the coin and playing dumb borders on the sarcastic. Imagine him holding up the denarius and asking pseudo-innocently of the most powerful man in the Mediterranean world with the most familiar profile, "Who is this guy and what does he say about himself?" Playing dumb can be an effective weapon of the weak. It is also possible that this is an example of the humor used by the weak. Humor can provide a most engaging way to undermine the strong while denying any such purpose. Just kidding! Both the images and the epigram

40. Finney, "The Rabbi and the Coin Portrait," 631.
41. Fernando Belo, *A Materialist Reading of the Gospel of Mark*, trans. Matthew J. O'Donnell (Maryknoll, N.Y.: Orbis Books, 1981), 187.

condemn the coin. It violates Deut. 8:5, which forbids making any graven images of things on the earth, below the earth, or in heaven. More importantly, the coin violates the first and second commandments of the Decalogue (Exod. 20:1–6). The coin is a living denial and disavowal of the covenant received at Sinai. Above all, the exchange over the coin identifies Jesus' enemies with the idolatrous coin. Even if he is holding the coin that his opponents have produced, Jesus distances himself from it by forcing them to procure it and acknowledge what it proclaims. They have been skewered, but Jesus is still on the spot. He has, in this sense, already prevailed in the political challenge. But the public challenge by the Pharisees and Herodians has set up an expectation that Jesus would address the question of tribute. Some of the crowd no doubt expects Jesus to use the little tradition to defuse the claims of the great tradition.

Jesus responds to the challenge with an aphoristic riddle: "The things of Caesar pay back to Caesar, and the things of God to God" (author's trans.). Until more recent times, the majority opinion has been that Jesus counseled paying tribute. Bruce, for example, compares Jesus' "counsel on non-resistance to Rome" with Jeremiah's counsel of submission to Babylon.[42] As Jeremiah advised Judah not to resist the Babylonian empire, Jesus counsels cooperation with Rome by paying tribute. The reason lies with the coin itself: "A coin which by its very form and appearance contravenes [God's] law cannot be regarded as [God's]." Throughout his discussion, Bruce assumes that Jesus would be more aligned with the longstanding tradition of the prophets rather than the newly emerging "fourth philosophy" that considered any tribute payment a compromise of Israel's theocratic ideal. He does not seem to think there is any other position. Stauffer, who shares this basic conclusion, parallels the two halves of the saying, the first of which advocates paying tribute and the second of which counsels paying the temple tax and tithes. The latter is what belongs to God.[43] In a variation of this theme, Kennard believes that Jesus' advice is limited to those who originally asked the question, namely, "the upper class quislings" and aristocrats who collaborated with Rome and benefitted from their collusion.[44] Since they possessed the denarii, Jesus advised them to repay Caesar, whose policies and patronage had brought them so much wealth.

When Jesus' aphorism is understood as counseling the payment of tribute, his interpreters assume that the aphorism is spelling out parallel obligations. The aphorism is conjunctive rather than disjunctive. Tannehill, however, entertained the notion that the aphorism might be an antithetical aphorism, a position that he argued persuasively before changing his mind in the light of his conviction

---

42. Bruce, "Render to Caesar," 260.
43. Stauffer, *Christ and the Caesars*, 129–34.
44. J. S. Kennard, *Render to God* (New York: Oxford University Press, 1950), 113–19.

that Jesus was something like a centrist politician, staking out a compromise "middle position" according to which it is permissible to pay tribute but also, even more important, to contemplate the things that are God's and render them to God.[45] The difficulty with this position is that it seems to be governed by his prior conviction that Jesus was seeking middle ground as an effort to avoid conflict over a hot-button issue like tribute. In light of this conviction, he seems to abandon, or at least minimize, his careful and persuasive analysis of the antithetical nature of Jesus' aphorism.

There are good reasons for questioning the readings that attribute to Jesus support for paying tribute. Taking a cue from Tannehill, Myers contends that Jesus did utter an antithetical aphorism to set competing loyalties in sharp contrast to each other. The tribute laid a heavy burden on the peasantry, who were exploited to raise it and whose land could be expropriated when it appeared that the demands could not be met through the usual practices of tribute collecting. Since Jesus devoted so much of his public activity to the very people who would be most adversely affected by tributary demands, it seems unlikely that he would readily have accepted their validity. With this conclusion, Horsley agrees,[46] and James Scott has also argued that the ideological fractures in agrarian societies more or less follow class lines.

The shift of verbs from the initial challenge to Jesus' response is significant. His opponents ask him, "Should we give [*dounai*] tribute to Caesar?" Jesus' retort speaks of paying back (*apodote*) to Caesar what is his. The verb *apodidōmi* refers to paying back a debt that is owed. As Horsley notes, the verb evokes "the imperial situation of domination and subjugation."[47] This is in keeping with what Lenski has called "the proprietary theory of the state" so common in agrarian societies.[48] The demand for tribute and the forceful collection of tribute are expressions of this right assumed by agrarian rulers. So the question about paying tribute is not raising an incidental issue but an essential matter that goes straight to the heart of the Roman occupation of Galilee and Judea. In brief, the question of tribute struck at the very heart of the legitimacy of the Roman Empire by addressing its most essential function. The question was an effort to reinforce the public transcript on the right of Rome to occupy Palestine.

45. Robert Tannehill, *The Sword of His Mouth* (Philadelphia: Fortress Press, 1975), 173–76.

46. Richard Horsley, *Jesus and the Spiral of Violence: Popular Jewish Resistance in Roman Palestine* (San Francisco: Harper & Row, 1987), 308–14.

47. Ibid., 309.

48. Gerhard Lenski, *Power and Privilege: A Theory of Social Stratification* (New York: McGraw-Hill, 1966), 214–19.

This imperial situation convinces Horsley that Jesus escalated the issue from the question of tribute to the question of lordship, where the conflict can be even more sharply drawn. What "things" belong to God? In the middle of the last century, Kennard rightly saw that all things belong to God: the land, the earth and the fullness thereof, the heavens and the riches of the earth (Ps. 19).[49] What then can belong to Caesar? One thing only. The coin which he minted in his image and likeness. That can be returned (paid back) to Caesar because it came from Caesar. Indeed, it must be paid back because it is blasphemous and idolatrous.

But this is exactly what cannot be said openly "onstage" in the form of a public transcript. The Pharisees and Herodians have attempted to force Jesus to disclose and declare the hidden transcript of resistance to tribute as a form of resisting Roman rule. Jesus responds with an antithetical aphorism that acts like a riddle. It is his version of that third kind of speech identified by Scott, a disguised, ambiguous, and coded form of speech dedicated to maintaining the hidden transcript of resistance while leaving a public transcript that is in no way actionable. Jesus has created for himself enough "plausible deniability" to prevent his adversaries from moving against him. He seems to be saying, "Return the coins to Caesar. Caesar has imposed the coins on the land; pay him back in the same coinage he foisted on us in violation of the first and second commandments." But this is not a call to pay tribute as a recognition of Rome's right to rule. Tannehill's instinct was correct. It is an antithetical aphorism but uttered in a way that raises as many questions as it answers.

Jesus has been forced to play a role onstage in a political drama whose purpose was to reinforce Rome's right to take tribute. In the process of accomplishing this goal, the Pharisees and Herodians perceived an opportunity to trap Jesus and shame him before a crowd of people sympathetic to him. Impressed into the role of an actor in this form of political street theater, Jesus is seemingly forced to choose between deference to Rome, a choice that alienates him from his popular base of peasant support, or defiance of Rome and denial of Rome's right to take tribute, a choice that threatens serious consequences from the powers that be. Caught between a rock and a hard place, Jesus dissembles and communicates a coded message of resistance while appearing to remain deferential to Roman power. He dissembles to avoid entrapment but his peasant supporters who use ruses like this in order to survive understand what he is doing and what he intends to communicate.

His enemies can only marvel at his quick-witted response. It is likely that they had an inkling of what Jesus was doing, but his dissembling was effective

49. J. S. Kennard, *Render to God*, 123–25.

enough that it left them powerless to arrest him. Yet it provided Jesus an opportunity to speak a coded message for those "who had ears to hear." Make no mistake about it. The peasants and common people of the land who heard this
exchange knew what Jesus was doing and saying. His coded word for those with
ears to hear and eyes to see was an encouragement to resist, even though the
public transcript of his reply was in no way provocative or inflammatory. To
those listening, Jesus was offering both an inducement and the encouragement
to resist by using the full arsenal of what Scott calls "the weapons of the weak."

It could easily be argued that nothing changed as the result of Jesus' decep-
tion. The triumph was a pyrrhic victory. True, peasants still had to pay tribute, but now they could pay their poll tax or *tributum capitis* not as an act of
acquiescence but as an act of resistance, even defiance. They were returning
the denarius to the blasphemer who had minted it yet without acknowledging
Rome's claim to rule either their bodies, which belong to the Creator, not Caesar, or their land, which belongs to the Liberator, not the oppressor. Jesus' hidden transcript of resistance reinterpreted their actions while maintaining the
facade of conformity to the colonizer's demands. In societies where peasants
exercise so little control over so much of what happens in their lives, this little tradition reading of the payment of tribute offered a source of encouragement and resolve. Now the payment of the denarius was not a test of Rome's
right to rule but an act of removing the blasphemous coins from the land.
Their actions would bear witness to the fact that the ideological domination
of the people of the land by their colonial masters and local elites was not complete. They were still able to carve out zones of resistance.

CONCLUSION

This chapter has argued that Jesus counseled resistance to the taking of tribute.
In both the story of the coin in the fish's mouth (Matt. 17:24–27) and the conflict over paying tribute to Caesar (Mark 12:13–17), he follows a consistent line
of action, maintaining the hidden transcript of resistance even when he or Peter
were subjected to attempted entrapment. Jesus appears to have maintained the
distinction between the political arena "onstage" where the rulers and their
retainers write the script and control the scenes of their political street theater
and the peasant arena offstage where the hidden transcripts can be revealed and
discussed more readily. Scott's work has helped us to discern Jesus' support for
the hidden transcript of resistance through his ambiguous and coded response
to his adversaries and through his use of humor with Peter.

But why would Jesus take such a stand toward tribute? If Jesus proclaimed
the coming reign of God (Mark 1:15), then it would be inappropriate to rec-

ognize Roman hegemony or participate in its rituals of domination. In terms of local politics, both the temple's demands for tithes and Herod's collection of tribute were ruining the lives of peasant families, increasing their load of debt while threatening to alienate them from their land when they were unable to service their indebtedness. The more tribute collected, the greater the hardships on peasant families. The loss of land and breakup of families was more than a social problem; it was a theological issue related to the covenant and the Torah. While the rulers in Galilee and Judea alike were busy redistributing wealth through their tribute taking, they were also ignoring the Torah's systems of redistribution of wealth as found in the sabbatical and jubilee traditions. The covenant at Sinai was clear: if the people of Yahweh obeyed his commandments, they would banish poverty from the land, and if they took their covenant responsibilities seriously, they would redistribute the wealth of the land (which was, after all, Yahweh's gift) to those in need (Deut. 15:1–18; Lev. 25:1–55, especially 23). But rather than following the covenant's provisions for redistributing the wealth of the land so that none would be poor, the rulers in Jerusalem and Tiberius were greedily hoarding the wealth of the land to create and maintain their power in collaboration with Rome.

In his public activity and teaching, Jesus had been echoing sabbatical and jubilee themes, such as the forgiveness of debt/sin and the release from bondage ("be loosed" or freed from your disease or possession). As a prophet in the Deuteronomic tradition, Jesus opened up these covenant themes. It would be highly unlikely that a popular prophet in this tradition would sanction the paying of tribute, although he would need to be indirect and discreet in the ways he addressed these topics. In Jesus' day, the public transcript being written by the rulers and their proxies counseled payment of tribute, and the Torah's covenant themes had become hidden transcripts disclosed cautiously and covertly in events like healings and exorcisms or spoken in parables and riddles.

This may be why Jesus does not speak a clear, straightforward word but still develops covenant themes in the midst of a world in which it is dangerous to develop those themes in too direct a way. To transpose these matters into a Freirean key, Jesus acted like a true pedagogue of the oppressed in his debate over the denarius. When Jesus employed the coin as an audiovisual aid, he was using it as a codification for all to see of the contradiction between payment of tribute and preserving the covenant, and his subsequent riddle was an invitation to those who had "ears to hear" to gather offstage to discuss the matter in a friendlier environment.

The way in which Jesus silences his opponents strikes other chords. Luke notes that "they were not able in the presence of the people to catch him by what he said; but, marveling at his answer, they were silent" (20:26). In his work with rural peasants and urban laborers, Freire discovered that they lived in a culture of enforced silence, created by the oppressors' unending efforts to intimidate and brutalize those who dared to break the silence or question the social construction of reality imposed on them by their rulers. So it is ironic that Jesus gives voice to the hidden transcript of the silenced even in indirect ways and silences those whose voices usually dominate the discussion. In this setting, every clash between Jesus and the rulers or their proxies became an example of what Freire called a "codification." Jesus was using his own public activity in general and encounters like this one in particular to disclose generative themes that could be used to construct an alternative world from which peasants could decode, problematize, and recodify the propaganda of the ruling elites. In the case of Jesus and the question of tribute, Jesus used the denarius to problematize the issue of tribute and the identity of God. Once the claims on the coin were made public, the contradiction of paying was clear. But how to recodify the necessity of paying the denarius demanded by the Romans who had the military power to discourage either rebellion or refusal to pay? Jesus' antithetical aphorism provided just the paradox needed to encourage his readers to seek the limit acts (in this case, paying tribute as an act of resistance) that could transform the limit situation in which they found themselves from an admission of defeat and despondency to an affirmation of bending but not breaking under colonial rule. In the universe of the Romans and Herodians, peasants were being intimidated into paying tribute and silenced if they objected. In the alternate universe created by the subversive pedagogue, peasants were resisting Roman rule by ridding the land of blasphemous coins and returning them to the false divinity who had issued them. As they followed with interest Jesus' controversy with the scribal proxies of the powers that be, they were learning how to turn the intractable givens of their world into problems to be analyzed and courses of actions to be contemplated. Even severely limited options are better than no options at all.

What was liberating about Freire's pedagogy and Jesus' as well was the way they restored the humanity of those who had been dehumanized. Jesus' public activity revealed that it was possible even for peasants to recreate themselves as subjects of their own history rather than to settle for being the objects in the world of their oppressors. The ultimate sanction for this step was the character of the covenant God who created all his people, not just the rulers. Created in the image of the covenant God, peasants were subjects in the history of the people of God no less than their rulers. But in the colonial history of Roman rule and the derivative history of the house of Herod, this was not the case. Jesus' role as subversive pedagogue was to turn this situation into a problem to be posed and solved. In this environment, Jesus' roles as prophet and pedagogue came together in ways that strengthened both roles.

9

The Village as Shadow Society and Alternate Moral Universe

In advanced agrarian societies, the power brokers and rulers generally live in urban areas while the peasantry lives in the countryside in villages, market towns, and hamlets. From their location at the heart of things, rulers seek to impose their will on the peasants not only by taking tribute, taxes, tolls, rents, and other less visible goods and services but also by asserting their ideological domination over the countryside. Given this situation, it should not be surprising to learn that the villages and hamlets of the countryside become pockets for nurturing resistance to the great tradition of the ruling elites and places for nourishing the growth of a little tradition, a constant reminder that the ideological domination of the great tradition is never complete.

This chapter proposes that some of Jesus' teachings and activities can be seen as an expression of the little tradition at work in Galilee. His words and actions reveal what Scott calls "a struggle over the appropriation of symbols, a struggle over how the past and present shall be understood and labeled, a struggle to identify causes and assess blame, a contentious effort to give partisan meaning to local history."[1] These episodes and lessons may be little more than "small arms fire in the class war," to use Scott's apt phrase, but they are important nevertheless.

PROFANING THE GREAT TRADITION

One path that resistance might take is the formation of what Scott calls "a shadow society, a pattern of structural, stylistic and normative opposition to

---

1. James C. Scott, *Weapons of the Weak: Everyday Forms of Peasant Resistance* (New Haven, Conn.: Yale University Press, 1985), xvii.

the politico-religious tradition of the ruling elites."[2] In a strange way, the emergence of this shadow society reflects the way hegemony engenders its opposite:

> what matters for our purposes, however, is that the material and symbolic hegemony normally exercised by ruling institutions does not preclude, but rather engenders, a set of contrary values which represent in their entirety a kind of shadow society.[3]

This society comes to expression in a variety of social and cultural forms, both onstage and offstage, that is, in the public places controlled by the rulers and in the security of peasant villages beyond the reach of the rulers, in the form of "millennial dreams . . . popular theatre, folk tales, folk sayings, myths, poetry, jokes and songs."[4]

The shadow society affords peasants an opportunity to profane the great tradition and subvert its power over their lives. Scott readily acknowledges that

> the radical strain of the little tradition may take the form of rituals of reversal in which, for a time, the poor become aristocrats; the prevailing hierarchy of power and piety are openly mocked; and deference is suspended. Popular sacrilege is at the core of these "moments of madness."[5]

However much the rulers try to control these unsanctioned forms of the little tradition, their profanations serve as a constant reminder that "the symbolic hegemony of ruling groups is not complete" while, at the same time, revealing "an alternate moral universe" and "a latent normative subculture" that cannot be eradicated or controlled. Jesus' table companionship with toll collectors and sinners represents one such ritual of reversal or "moment of madness," a profanation of the Pharisees' goal to eat every meal in a condition of ritual purity equal to the priests in the temple. To this text we will turn next.

IN RIDDLES: TABLE COMPANIONSHIP WITH TOLL COLLECTORS AND SINNERS

Using Scott's work as a guide, it is possible to reconstruct the nature of the conflict involved in the dispute over table companionship. Mark 2:15–17 depicts a conflict between Jesus and "the scribes of the Pharisees" over eating

---

2. James C. Scott, "Protest and Profanation: Agrarian Revolt and the Little Tradition," *Theory and Society* 4 (1977): 1–38, 211–46.
3. Ibid., 19.
4. Ibid., 20.
5. Ibid., 29.

with "toll collectors and sinners." It has already been noted that the Pharisees were, to some extent, a table companionship group with a purity agenda. Jacob Neusner has observed that

> Pharisaic table-fellowship required keeping everywhere the laws of ritual purity that normally applied only in the Jerusalem temple, so Pharisees ate their private meals in the same condition of ritual purity as did the priests of the holy cult.[6]

This meant that the Pharisees were oriented to the temple in Jerusalem as the center of their symbolic world. They took their models of purity from the Torah's concerns about the ritual purity of priests in the temple and attempted to impose them on every table in Israel. The way to become the people of God was to become a nation of priests. The crucial link that joined household to temple was the meals consumed at table. This is why the Pharisees insisted that the laws of ritual purity were to be followed whether in the temple or in one's own house.

> Therefore, one must eat secular food . . . in a state of ritual purity *as if one were a Temple priest*. The Pharisees thus arrogated to themselves— and to all Jews equally—the status of temple priests. . . . The table of every Jew in his home was seen as being like the table of the Lord in the Jerusalem Temple.[7]

Such a regimen imposed a "perpetual ritualization" on daily life, including the preparation of food, the vessels in which it was prepared and consumed, and the hands and bodies of those who prepared it, served it, and consumed it at table. To be considered clean, all food had to be tithed to the temple. This included all food purchased in the marketplace because the purchaser could not be certain whether the original growers of the food had been scrupulous in their tithing habits. For this reason, tithing came to occupy a central place in Pharisaic belief and practice.

According to Anthony Saldarini, the Pharisees were also a political interest group aligned with powerful elites for the purpose of promoting their politics of holiness and imposing it on all Israel. Their program does seem to be shaped by the imperial situation to some extent, for the Pharisees were trying to isolate and create an area of life that the colonizers could not easily control or undermine because they did not have easy access to it. What better place to begin than with shared meals from which most were excluded on purity concerns alone.

---

6. Jacob Neusner, *From Politics to Piety: The Emergence of Pharisaic Judaism* (New York: KTAV, 1979), 67.

7. Ibid., 83.

It is in this context that Jesus' reclining at table with toll collectors and sinners makes a serious symbolic statement about the Pharisees' project to replicate in their houses the meals that occur in the temple. But the very conditions that led to pure table companionship excluded the peasants of Galilee and created an odd assortment of outcasts and outlaws identified in the Gospels by phrases like "toll collectors and sinners." If emulation of the Pharisees' program is not within the realm of possibility, then undermining it certainly is. So Jesus joins the toll collectors and sinners onstage in an act of popular political theater that "engenders a set of contrary values which represent . . . a kind of shadow society."[8]

The clash between traditions is echoed in the conflict between Jesus and "the scribes of the Pharisees." Jesus provokes the hostile exchange by reclining at table with the unclean and the undesirables. Toll collectors (*telōnai*) were at the bottom of the economic scale.[9] They worked the tollbooths and cheated as many as they could in order to earn money for the chief toll collector who employed them. Because they were conveniently visible figures, they absorbed a lot of the hostility and anger intended for the more invisible elites and high retainers whose dirty work they did (see chapter 7). The word "sinners" refers to those who fail to keep Torah in the Pharisaic way, especially those who are chronically negligent of its purity concerns. From the Pharisees' point of view, uncleanness could be contracted through touch, so when Jesus reclines at table and eats out of common dishes, he is rendering himself unclean. Every time he broke off a piece of bread and dipped it in a common dish, he would contract the impurity of anyone else eating from the same dishes, although Jesus did not view the matter in the same way.

At table with outcasts and outlaws, Jesus was acting out an alternative political vision for the renewal of Israel that includes the ingathering of those who were made outcasts by the propagation of the great tradition of the elders. What is at stake is who will be welcomed to the table and who will be included in the meal. For example, Jesus proclaims that "many will come from the east and west, and from the north and south, and sit at table in the reign of God" (Q: Luke 13:29 par. Matt. 8:11). If Jesus gathers with toll collectors and sinners, he would seem to be announcing by means of this enacted parable that the purity codes of Torah, so important for the great tradition, are irrelevant at best and an obstruction at worst to the work of God's covenant renewal. The meal not only lampoons the Pharisees' efforts to replicate the holiness of the temple but probably reflects the theme of social reversal when the outcasts will

8. Scott, "Protest and Profanation," 19.
9. See John Donahue, "Tax Collectors and Sinners: An Attempt at Identification," *CBQ* 33 (1971): 39–61.

feast while the pure and the powerful are excluded. The following parable of exclusion in Q embodies a stark reversal. After those excluded appeal to the householder who has closed his door to them, he replies,

> I tell you, I do not know where you come from; depart from me, all you workers of iniquity! There you will weep and gnash your teeth when you see Abraham and Isaac and Jacob and all the prophets in the reign of God and you yourselves thrust out. (Q: Luke 13:27–28)

In the actions and sayings of Jesus, it is possible to see the "struggle over the appropriation of symbols." Who can claim the ancestors (Abraham, Isaac, and Jacob) and who belongs to the company of the prophets? For whom is the great banquet intended? Will it be a gathering of the Pharisees and their like, or is it a gathering of prophets open to all directions, inviting the exiles and the dispersed to come home from the four corners of the earth?

A great deal is at stake in the issue of who eats with whom. Using the work of anthropologists Peter Farb and George Armelagos, Crossan summarizes the broader social significance of commensality:

> It means the rules of tabling and eating as miniature models for the rules of association and socialization. It means table fellowship as a map of economic discrimination, social hierarchy and political differentiation.[10]

This would indicate that Jesus chose well when he chose to use table companionship as a forum for making a symbolic statement. Farb and Armelagos do not exaggerate when they conclude, "To know what, where, how, when and with whom people eat is to know the character of their society."[11] The Pharisees' meal and Jesus' meal embody two different visions of what it means to be the people of God. With so much at stake, it is not surprising that the Pharisees respond to the challenge posed by Jesus' behavior. Their question addressed to Jesus' disciples, "Why does he recline at table with toll collectors and sinners?" is, by their standards, an entirely reasonable one. Nothing good can come of it. He will only wind up as unclean as they already are. Why risk so much?

Jesus responds to the attack with a proverb and an aphorism. The proverb appeals to common sense. Where should a physician be if not with the sick? It also reflects Jesus' own interpretation of the work of God. Both N. T. Wright and John Meier think that the "symbolic praxis" of eating with all sorts of

---

10. John Dominic Crossan, *Jesus: A Revolutionary Biography* (San Francisco: Harper-Collins, 1994), 68, citing the work of Peter Farb and George Armelagos, *Consuming Passions: The Anthropology of Eating* (Boston: Houghton Mifflin, 1980).

11. Farb and Armelagos, *Consuming Passions*, 222.

people was a regular part of Jesus' activity, but they relate it to Jesus' own theological convictions. Meier elaborates the theological point of such meals more fully when he suggests that

> his meals with sinners and the disreputable were celebrations of the lost being found, of God's eschatological mercy reaching out and embracing [sinners]. His banquets with sinful Israelites were a preparation and foretaste of the coming banquet in the kingdom of God.[12]

What is clear is that Jesus used the meals as opportunities for the inclusion of the very folk who were excluded from the Pharisees' table gatherings. This strongly suggests, as Wright notes, that table companionship was intimately related to Jesus' announcement of the coming reign of God and represented an acting out of the messianic banquet.

Though extremely valuable, both Wright's and Meier's comments tend to sublimate the political and economic dimensions of this conflict in order to develop their theological readings. Emphasizing the future or eschatological nature of the meal leads them to overlook or minimize its more immediate social significance. For them, the meal is more like an anticipation of the Christian eschatological banquet than a class conflict in which the great and little traditions confront each other and, in truth, it may be a bit of both.

Seen through Scott's eyes, the meal with toll collectors and sinners can be interpreted as a profanation of one version of the great tradition represented by the oral Torah of the Pharisees. Jesus' table companionship represents just such a ritual of reversal, in which those invited to the table are those who are normally rejected as table guests. The hospitality of the reign of God mocks the concern for purity when it dominates and dictates the Pharisaic table gatherings and determines who is included and who excluded. Normally, elites try to control such profanations by limiting them to particular occasions and places in the hope that they may act to "drain off the tensions which any political order engenders,"[13] especially a ruthlessly exploitive and oppressive political order with its accompanying moral sanctions.

It is possible that every time Jesus gathered at table with sinners, he was acting out of an alternate moral universe that refused to be controlled by the normative order of the great tradition circulating in Judea and Galilee. This sense of just such an alternative symbolic universe underlies Jesus' final aphorism, "I came not to call the righteous but sinners." The aphorism has a playful, perhaps ironic tone, for Jesus does not deny the label "righteous" to the scribal Pharisees but declares their status irrelevant to what God is about. The reign

---

12. John Meier, *A Marginal Jew: Rethinking the Historical Jesus*, vol. 2, 303.
13. Ibid.

of God and the renewal of Israel are about sinners, not the righteous. Since the righteous are beside the point, their purity concerns cannot be determinative for Jesus' table companionship. This aphorism reverses the significance of sinners and righteous while denying the existence of neither.

Two of Jesus' parables speak to some of the themes disclosed by this examination of his table companionship with toll collectors and sinners. In the parable of the rich man and Lazarus (Luke 16:19–31), the rich man's exclusion of Lazarus in this life is reversed, after death, when Abraham makes Lazarus the guest of honor who reclines on his bosom. Throughout the parable (discussed in more detail in chapter 5), Abraham seeks to elicit from the rich man the insight that he and Lazarus are brothers who belong to the same family and, therefore, belong at the same table. But the rich man cannot see Lazarus as his brother and so excludes himself from Abraham's banquet. In similar fashion, the parable of the great banquet (Luke 14:15–24, see below) is built around the theme of reversal. The invited guests are excluded while those normally excluded are invited. This parable also reads as an attempt to claim the symbol of the great banquet for the poor of Galilee and Judea. In the parable, the one who gives the banquet initially invites the folks one would expect to be present, but their insulting refusals lead him to fill his banquet hall with the unexpected, "the poor, the maimed, the blind and the lame" (v. 21). This ritual of reversal depicts a scene in which the ones invited unwittingly open the door to those who would normally have no hope of being invited to such a banquet.

HISTORY FROM BELOW:
ANOTHER LOOK AT THE VINEYARD

The parable of the wicked tenants (Mark 12:1–12) has long been understood as an allegorical reading of Israel's history echoing the vineyard parable in Isa. 5:1–7. The Markan parable and its parallels (Matt. 21:33–46; Luke 20:9–19) give evidence of being infused with theological themes, culminating in the murder of the son and the judgment that follows. In this section, I will propose that the parable does contain a view of history as seen from below, a peasant critique of the ruling high priestly houses in Jerusalem and the Herodians in Galilee.

A brief examination of the Isaiah passage may provide some clues for reading the vineyard parable. The Isaianic text breaks into three parts:

5:1–2	a love song
5:3–4	a judicial plea
5:5–7	a judgment oracle

The love song appears to describe unrequited love; after all the loving prepa-rations, the vineyard produces wild grapes. In the second section, the beloved, seeking exoneration, speaks directly to the hearer like a prosecutor soliciting a verdict. Finally, in the third section, the beloved announces an impending judgment on the vineyard. The time for regrets is past; the time for judgment has arrived. The Lord "expected justice, but saw bloodshed; righteousness, but heard a cry" (v. 7). The differences between the two parables are also impor-tant. The issue in Isaiah is the appearance of an unexpected and unfruitful har-vest. In spite of his efforts in his vineyard, Yahweh gathers nothing but wild grapes. The issue in Jesus' parable is the behavior of the tenants. Although the imagery differs, the two parables may not be as far apart as they appear.[14]

The similarities between Isaiah 5 and Mark 12 are strong enough to sug-gest that the Markan parable is drawing upon intertextual echoes from Isaiah. But in the Markan parable, the issue shifts to the tenants. If the vineyard maker is Yahweh and the vineyard is "the house of Israel and the people of Judah" (Isa. 5:7), who then are the tenants? And how do we understand their behav-ior? To answer these questions, a bit of background is in order. The popula-tion of rural cultivators in an agrarian society typically falls into one of three categories: small holders, tenants, and day laborers. The small holder is essen-tially a peasant villager who enjoys the safety net of the village and kinship group. But when a small holder loses his land, he is forced into a contractual tenancy with a landowner on terms pretty much dictated by the landowner. The tenant is a lowly figure without much status or prestige because he has lost his land and now works the land that belongs to someone else on terms determined by them. At the very bottom of the ladder in an agrarian society is the day laborer, who has lost even the protection of a contractual relation-ship with an elite and works for a day at a time only when hired.

Seen from the point of view of the Torah, the tenant is not an inappropri-ate figure to describe the leadership of "the house of Israel and the people of Judah." Myers says it well: "Jesus here tells a story in which the Jerusalem lead-ership, who were *in fact* the absentee landowning class, appear as *tenants* of an absentee landlord—that is, Yahweh."[15]

Throughout the Pentateuch, it is clear that the land is a gift from Yahweh; it does not belong to the people, to a ruling class, or to a king but belongs to

14. For the inordinately curious, I have developed another view of the parable of the wicked tenants in my *Parables as Subversive Speech: Jesus as Pedagogue of the Oppressed* (Louisville, Ky.: Westminster John Knox Press, 1994), chap. 6, "Peasant Revolt and the Spiral of Violence," where I argue that the parable codifies what Dom Helder Camara called "the spiral of violence" and the peasants' response to it.

15. Ched Myers, *Binding the Strong Man: A Political Reading of Mark's Story of Jesus* (Maryknoll, N.Y.: Orbis Books, 1988), 308.

God alone (see chapter 6 for details on the debt codes of the Torah). In this parable, the land clearly belongs to the landowner, who contracts with the tenants. They are selected and called to serve in the vineyard, and they are responsible for fulfilling their part of the contract and returning a designated portion of the yield of the vineyard to the owner. This view of the land, however, conflicts with the view of the land shared by agrarian rulers, who believe that the land is theirs to distribute and redistribute as they please. The land is an asset to be managed for the well-being of the ruling house and the houses of the aristocrats supportive of its rule. The yield of the land is theirs to seize in the form of tribute.

When the tenants in the parable refuse to return the portion of the yield of the vineyard to the owner, they are both denying and shaming the "lord of the vineyard" (*ho kurios tou ampelōnos*) in order to claim the land for themselves, all the while forgetting that they are merely tenants who serve the owner. In short, they are claiming their right to the yield of the vineyard as though they were the "lords" of the vineyard. The parable represents the rulers as tenants, emphasizing their lowly position before Yahweh, a decidedly "little tradition" view of the ruling class that clashes with the rulers' self-understanding. The behavior of the tenants in the parable, then, reflects the actions of agrarian rulers like Herod Antipas and the members of the high priestly houses in Jerusalem. They refuse to distribute the yield of the vineyard as the owner has commanded, and they reject the prophetic servants sent by Yahweh to correct their behavior and restore them to their rightful role as tenants in the vineyard. The violence meted out to the prophetic servants may reflect widespread remembrance of the career and death of John the Baptist, or interest in some of the popular prophets of the types mentioned in Josephus or in the Elijah and Elisha cycle of stories, or the popularity that the great oracular prophets like Isaiah and Jeremiah continued to enjoy in the synagogue gatherings of the peasant villages. Matthew 23:29–35, which speaks of a long line of persecuted prophets, may reflect a "little tradition" view of the rejection of the prophets as a major theme in the unfolding of Israel's history. It needs to be said that, when the tenants reject the lord of the vineyard, they also reject the debt codes of the Torah, which include the sabbatical and jubilee provisions for breaking the cycle of debt and indentured service.

If the servants in the parable represent the prophets, perhaps based on a characterization like the one in Amos 3:7, "Surely the Lord GOD does nothing, without revealing his secret to his servants, the prophets," then the parable stands in a long tradition of prophetic critiques of ruling classes and rulers. Jeremiah brings both shepherd and vineyard imagery together in a lament: "Many shepherds have destroyed my vineyard; they have trampled down my portion; they have made my pleasant portion a desolate wilderness"(12:10).

This tradition of political criticism could be traced through Ezekiel (34:1–24), Jeremiah (10:21; 23:1–4), and Zechariah (13:7–9), to name just a few instances where this prophetic voice is heard, although in these cases, the prophets use primarily shepherd imagery. But Isaiah launches similar judgments, once again using vineyard imagery as he did in 5:1–7:

> The LORD enters into judgment with the elders and princes of his people;
> It is you who have devoured the vineyard;
>   the spoil of the poor is in your houses.
> What do you mean by crushing my people,
>   by grinding the face of the poor?
> says the Lord GOD of hosts.
>
>   (3:14–15 NRSV)

The difference between these prophetic passages and Jesus' parable is, in part, the social location of the prophet. The great oracular prophets came to their prophetic task as insiders to the corridors of power, but Jesus speaks as a popular or peasant prophet. Therefore, his parable provides a glimpse of what a prophetic perspective from below might look like.

The parable of the tenants can be read as providing historical perspective shaped by the little tradition. In this view, the rulers are seen as tenants in the service of the owner of the vineyard, tenants who attempt to throw off their humble role and seize control of the vineyard by breaking their contract (covenant) with the owner and rejecting the prophetic servants sent to set them right. As Isaiah put it, "[God] expected justice but saw bloodshed" (5:7). As a critique of the political rulers, the parable represents an attempt to limit their power in a manner similar to the attempt to circumscribe the power of the king in Deut. 17:14–20. In both parable and Torah text, the authors remind the mighty that they are nothing more than servants of Yahweh, hoping that their appeal will curtail the exploitive and acquisitive tendencies of the rulers.

The parable seems to fit this scenario until the appearance of the son, which appears to introduce a christological dimension to the story. What then are we to make of the appearance of the son? Myers argues that, in Ps. 118:22, David was seen as the rejected one,[16] and as God restored David to the throne, so Jesus becomes the one who restores the promise to David.[17] Based on the enthronement psalms, which portray kings as God's sons (Ps. 2:7; 89:26–27), it is also possible to suggest that the son is a reference to a righteous king in the mold of Deut. 17:14–20, a hope that would find expression in the tradition of popular kingship. The appearance of the son could also reflect the presence of some little tradi-

16. Ibid., 309.
17. Ibid.

tion theologizing on the fate of Jesus in Jerusalem, paving the way for the beginnings of more developed christological thought. Within the narrative of the parable, the arrival of the son intensifies the escalating violence directed toward the prophets while raising the question of inheritance. If the heir to the vineyard can be killed, then the tenants can become the rulers after all. Their hostile takeover of the vineyard would be complete. The emergence of the house of Herod from the ashes of the Hasmonaean dynasty and the emergence of the high priestly houses in Jerusalem, the very place known as the city of David, must have seemed like the victory of the tenants over the vineyard owner's son.

The parable ends on an altogether different note. The quick reversal at the end of the parable speaks of swift judgment upon the tenants and their sure destruction: "He will come and destroy the tenants and give the vineyard to others." The parable ends on a note of strong and sudden retribution and the redistribution of the vineyard to those for whom it was intended. So the ending of the parable reaffirms the debt codes of the Torah. The owner will deal justly with the true inheritors of the vineyard, "the house of Israel and the people of Judah" (Isa. 5:7). They will receive the land as an inheritance just as Yahweh intended (Deut. 15). Have they become "the stone which the builders rejected"? While the architects of colonial occupation and Herodian client rule have been building their massive projects, they have rejected the stone that "has become the head of the corner," namely, the people of the land. In Jesus' public work, however, these very stones have become the cornerstone of a new understanding of God's redeeming work and the building blocks of a renewed people of God.[18] Every healing and each exorcism reclaims one of these building blocks: "This was the Lord's doing, and it is marvelous in our eyes" (Mark 12:11).

With this perspective in mind, we can understand Jesus' response to the disciples when they were on the Mount of Olives taking in the magnificent view of the temple. The temple represents the kind of building constructed by rulers, massive public building projects to demonstrate the stability and longevity of their rule. This is how they use stones to secure their future. The disciples are impressed: "Look teacher, what wonderful stones and what wonderful buildings" (Mark 13:1). Jesus' response is unexpected and startling: "See these great buildings? Get a good look, for there will not be one stone left upon another that will not be thrown down" (13:2). The conversation with the disciples contrasts two ways of building for the future: invest in monumental architecture or invest in the people of God, the peasants of the land. Appearances can be deceiving. It looks as though monuments will last forever, while peasants and other assorted castoffs are perishable. The truth turns out to be

18. See ibid., 308–10, for another "political" reading of the parable.

just the opposite of what was expected. No building is imperishable, not even the temple. It can be torn down stone by stone, which is exactly what the Romans did when they razed Jerusalem in 70 CE. But the people of God are imperishable; they will outlast any building. In the Galilee of Jesus' day, the rulers had it all wrong. Antipas rebuilt Sepphoris and turned a ruin into "the ornament of all Galilee" (*Ant.* 18.27), and he built a new capital named Tiberius, "which he established in the best region of Galilee on Lake Gennesaritis" (*Ant.* 18.36–37). Jesus healed the poor, the blind, the lame, the maimed, and the possessed and restored them, incorporating them as building blocks in his own building project, a theme that would find its way into Paul's letters (Eph. 2:19–22).

It can be argued that the parable of the wicked tenants provides us with a glimpse of history from below, a little-tradition reading of the political scene. The rulers who were called to be tenants in Yahweh's vineyard have rejected their role and tried to seize the vineyard through violence. In doing so, they violate the Torah and the covenant of Yahweh. After all is said and done, however, God's justice will prevail. Judgment will fall on the wicked tenants, and the vineyard will once again be given to others who respect Torah and love justice. The judgment scene is, to a peasant listener, an expression of a theology of hope. If the saying from the Psalms was part of Jesus' teaching, it contrasts two kinds of building, one of which was found in the Jesus movement and the other in the monumental buildings of the rulers of Galilee and Judea. Ironically, in pursuing their projects, the rulers of this present age overlooked the most valuable "stones" in their kingdoms, the people they exploited and discarded. Jesus would use these stones to build a very different edifice, a movement that would become the cornerstone of God's renewing work.

ANOTHER VIEW OF THE MESSIANIC BANQUET (LUKE 14:16–24)

The themes of judgment and reversal are found in another familiar parable, the parable of the great banquet. Scott has observed that the struggle to give partisan meaning to history involves "a struggle over the appropriation of symbols" as well as the right to interpret the past and the present and to identify causes and assess blame. These dynamics inform this well-known parable from Luke.

The parable begins with a familiar social script. A wealthy man has prepared a banquet based on the invitations he has issued. Before he prepared his banquet, he sent his servants to invite his social peers to dine with him. Of course, he has invited a few friends who are slightly above him in the social scheme of things, knowing that, if they accept his invitation, they are obligating themselves to extend an invitation to him in return. In this way, he can court wealthier elites as patrons. He will also invite some slightly lower than he in the social scale, guests to whom he can serve as a patron. When they return his invitation, he will attend their banquet, thereby accepting his role as patron to those beneath him in his social class. Issuing invitations is an art, for a host must know who will be likely to accept his invitations and how far above his social location he can go without risking rejection and shaming. Rohrbaugh suggests that the time between the two invitations allows the invited guests to discover the cause of the celebration and the names on the invitation list, both pieces of information that will help them decide whether it is in their interest to attend.[19]

Once people accepted the invitation to a banquet, they were obligated to attend unless some extraordinary circumstances intervened. The host would prepare the banquet based on the number and identity of his guests. When the food was ready to be served, then the host would send his servants to inform his guests that the feast was ready. This is where the parable begins, and this is where the familiar social script takes some strange twists and unexpected turns. The narrative could be divided as follows:

14:16b, 17	invitation (host invites expected guests)
14:18–20	rejection (expected guests reject host)
14:21–23	counterinvitation (host invites unexpected guests)
14:24	counterrejection (host rejects expected guests)

The first twist in the plot comes with the guests' rejection of the servants' invitation confirming that the banquet is ready. Linnemann has argued that the rejections are really not final. The guests are saying that they have an errand or two to run before they show up at the banquet She bases this reading on her understanding of the protocols for organizing a banquet in the ancient world. The invitation brought by the servants essentially announced that the first course was underway, an extended course that allowed the guests time to congregate. After the guests had arrived, the host would close the gate to his courtyard to signify that the main banquet was underway, and anyone arriving after the gate was closed was excluded from the banquet (Luke 13:25–29). Seen in this light, the apparent rejections of the invitation meant only that they would skip the first course but be there for the main banquet. They simply presumed that the banquet would still be available to them when they were ready. This explains why the host says "go out quickly" so that "my house may be filled." He intends to fill his courtyard so that he can close the gate and

19. Richard Rohrbaugh, "The Pre-industrial City in Luke-Acts," in Jerome Neyrey, ed., *The Social World of Luke-Acts: Models for Interpretation* (Peabody, Mass.: Hendrickson Publishers, 1991), 125–49.

surprise the stragglers who presume the banquet cannot begin until they are present.[20] If this were the case, then Jesus told the parable as a criticism of those who presumed that the banquet was for them and assumed that the gate would always be open to them.

The difficulty with this reading has been exposed by Kenneth Bailey, who argues that the guests' responses to the invitation are calculated insults, flimsy excuses intended to fool no one but intended to send a message to the host.[21] What Bailey says of the first excuse applies to all three: "The statement is a bold-faced lie and everyone knows it."[22] Through their excuses, the guests are actually shaming and humiliating the host. No one buys a field without walking every square hectare purchased. A buyer of land will know where the boundary markers are, whether there are disputes, and what water sources might be found on the land. All of this requires an extensive investment of time and energy. It cannot be done during a first course of a banquet. In similar fashion, no one buys five yoke of oxen without having examined them thoroughly from head to hoof. It cannot be done with a cursory glance at the animals; a buyer would want to watch them perform before committing to buy them. The third excuse is the greatest insult of all, for the third guest uses his wife as an excuse, thereby telling the host that he is less important than a woman. In a patriarchal society, this is significant. Notice, too, that the third invited guest abandons even the pretense of cordiality by omitting the phrase "I pray you, have me excused." Thus, the rudeness escalates as we move from the first two excuses to the third excuse. Rohrbaugh argues that the three rejections mean that none of those invited will attend the banquet, since "none will risk cutting himself off from his peers."[23]

Why do the invited guests reject the invitation? Bailey reads the parable in theological terms. Through the public work of Jesus, God has invited Israel to the messianic banquet, but the leaders of the Judeans reject the invitation and issue excuses for their actions. They complain about the patterns of table companionship with toll collectors and sinners. In Bailey's words,

> the parable says that as they reject Jesus (with these unacceptable excuses) they are rejecting the great banquet of salvation promised by God in Isaiah, that is, in some sense, even now set for them through the presence of Jesus in their midst.[24]

20. Eta Linnemann, *Jesus of the Parables: Introduction and Exposition*, trans. John Sturdy, 3rd ed. (New York: Harper and Row, 1966).

21. Kenneth E. Bailey, *Through Peasant Eyes: More Lucan Parables, Their Culture and Style* (Grand Rapids: Wm. B. Eerdmans Publishing Co., 1980), 88–113.

22. Ibid., 95.

23. Rohrbaugh, "The Pre-industrial City in Luke-Acts," 143.

24. Bailey, *Through Peasant Eyes*, 99.

For Rohrbaugh, the excuses mask the real reason why the guests spurn the host, as we would expect in an honor-and-shame society.[25]

The host has been placed in a vulnerable position. He has been shamed by his social peers for reasons that are not clear. Were his peers acting in concert to undermine his power and status through this public shaming? If so, what options does he have? Although the answers to these questions are not clear, his course of action is. The host sends his servants on two errands. The first is to invite the poorer members of the city to attend the banquet by going to the *plateias kai rhymas*. As Rohrbaugh has noted, this phrase describes the wider streets and squares (*plateias*) where communication occurred between elites and nonelites in preindustrial cities just as *rhymas* refers to the narrow, dirty, and cramped side streets and alleys where the poor reside. The second mission takes the servants outside the city walls and gates where the destitute live in the hedge rows (*phragmous*) that line the major approaches (*hodous*) to the city. The first invitation goes to the poor within the city, and the second invitation goes to the utterly destitute outside of the city. Both invitations will create a scandal because they will bring nonelites into the center city where the elites reside. Most nonelites would have been cleaned out of the city center before a banquet was held, but the spurned host brings them back into the center of the city where the elites pursue their lives in as much isolation from the poor as possible.

Bailey thinks that the invitations show a response of "grace, not vengeance," but the host's two invitations to the outcasts seem to be a means of excluding the invited guests who shall not taste "my banquet" (14:24). Just as the guests reject their host at the beginning of the parable, so the host rejects the invited guests at its close. However, the two counterinvitations make an important statement because they represent a notable reversal. At the beginning of the parable, following a normal social script, an elite host invites his social peers to a banquet. If this were heard as a parable about the messianic banquet, the point would be that the host invites his own kind to the feast. Different groups would fill in the guest list according to their theology. So, for example, the Pharisees would envision a gathering of the pure and ritually clean.

Inexplicably, the invited guests reject the invitation and shame the host. In their actions, they act like the tenants of the vineyard studied above, for as the tenants reject their role as tenants, so the invited guests reject their role as guests. The host's response is to open the banquet to those who would normally not be on anyone's invitation list, "the poor, the maimed, the blind, and the lame." The inclusion of the lost means the exclusion of the original guests. So the parable speaks a word of judgment against the invited guests and reminds

25. Rohrbaugh, "The Pre-industrial City in Luke-Acts," 143.

them that the Lord is perfectly capable of opening the banquet to those whom everyone believes will be excluded from the feast.

In short, the parable enters the struggle to appropriate the symbol of the great banquet of salvation for the villagers of Galilee. Like the "poor, the maimed, the blind, and the lame" of the parable, they have been excluded from the centers of power. Yet Jesus depicts a God who is willing to be shamed by the prominent expected guests in order to open the banquet to the least likely people. The parable implicitly criticizes the division of Israel into the elites, who have it all, and the nonelites, who live in poverty and destitution. The rejection of the host's invitation is a rejection of the God who redeemed the people from bondage, made a covenant with them at Sinai, and led them into the land of promise. The "alternate moral universe" disclosed in the parable depicts a world in which the folks at the margins will replace those at the center when the people of Yahweh gather for the great banquet. This provides a view of the great banquet from below. Bailey has suggested that the parable echoes the prophecy of Isa. 25:6–9. But there is a difference between the prophetic and the parabolic texts. Isaiah imagines a great banquet for all peoples, whereas Jesus imagines that the rejection of the host's invitation by the elites opens the way for the poor and degraded to participate in the meal. The themes of inclusion and exclusion imply each other.

VILLAGE HOSPITALITY AND THE REIGN OF GOD (LUKE 11:5–8)

Few parables convey us into the world of the peasant village as quickly as the parable of the friend at midnight. Bailey has proposed a reconstruction of the social scene in the parable that reveals how useful such a reading can be.[26] The interpretation developed here is indebted to Bailey's work. The parable can be divided into two parts:

vv. 5–7	a long rhetorical question
v. 8	a short rhetorical response

The long rhetorical question could be translated as follows:

> Who among you who has a friend (*philon*) will go to him at midnight and say to him, "Friend, lend me three loaves, for a friend of mine has arrived off the road, and I have nothing to set before him," only to hear

---

26. Kenneth Bailey, *Poet and Peasant: A Literary Cultural Approach to the Parables in Luke* (Grand Rapids: Wm. B. Eerdmans Publishing Co., 1976), 119–41.

him answer from within, "Don't bother me; the door is shut and my kids are in bed; I can't get up and get you anything"? (author's trans.)

The question assumes a strong negative response. No one would act like that. Not in our village. What kind of neighbor would act like that? It is shameful!

The scene is a small village or a hamlet, a few peasant houses built around a common well and village oven. Since families take turns baking bread, everyone knows who has fresh bread. This is why the host approaches his "friend" to ask for three loaves of bread. Bread is the most basic staple and the means by which a meal is served. A piece of bread is broken off, dipped in a common dish with salt or other sauces, and eaten. By confessing that he has no bread, he is confessing that he cannot serve a meal to his unexpected guest. Moreover, the neighbor must serve fresh bread. To serve a guest with day-old bread or broken loaves would be as unthinkable as setting a table with used, unwashed silverware. It would be an insult.

Why would the friend awakened in the middle of the night not make flimsy excuses for ignoring the request of his neighbor but rise and provide whatever he needs? Because he is being asked to uphold the hospitality of the village. The neighbor is asking nothing for himself; he is asking for help in hosting a meal for his guest. When a small village receives a visitor, the whole village is the host, not just the family with whom the travelers will stay. So the whole village is responsible for offering hospitality, however inconvenient the time of arrival. The village is obligated to serve an auspicious meal to the guest, who is honor bound to eat the meal offered. Of course, the conversation between the neighbor and his sleeping friend is not exactly a private affair. As the unprepared host calls out to his neighbor, he will awaken everyone else in the village. The friend awakened by his neighbor knows this, and he knows that if he refuses to help, he and his family would be shamed before the village. In fact, he is being honored by his neighbor because he is being asked to contribute an indispensable staple for the meal. If he refuses to respond or responds slowly, others will arise and offer their services in his stead. This is why Jesus says that the sleeping friend will arise and give him "whatever he needs," not just three loaves of bread. Other families in the village will also awaken and hurry to contribute to the meal, for the honor of the village is at stake in the hospitality they offer. The whole affair is a matter of honor. In light of this consideration, sleeping children are a minor inconvenience, and a shut door can easily be opened. They are no obstacles at all, and anyone who would use them as an excuse to avoid the obligation of hospitality would be a shameless fool and a disreputable neighbor. This is why the rhetorical question would elicit such a strong reaction from Jesus' listeners. They know what is at stake.

The problem with understanding this parable surfaces in Jesus' final remark: "I tell you, though he will not get up and give him anything because he is his friend, yet because of his *anaideian*, he will rise and give him whatever he needs." The sleeping neighbor will not arise and give his friend whatever he needs because of friendship but because of his *anaideian* (translated variously as importunity or persistence). Two problems arise: 1) to whom does *anaideian* apply, the sleeping neighbor or the host who awakens him? If it applies to the host who awakens him, then *anaideian* would seem to mean persistence or importunity. But the point of the long rhetorical question is that he would not need to show persistence because the sleeping neighbor would be honored to provide bread for the meal and therefore would act quickly to satisfy the request. If *anaideian* applies to the sleeping friend, then it means "avoidance of shame," as Bailey proposes.[27] The final statement would then read, "Yet because of his desire to avoid shame (before the village), he will rise and give him whatever he needs." Bailey's solution is as ingenious as it is unconvincing. The simple fact is that, in all its uses, *anaideian* means something like "shameless" and is often associated with transgressing or breaking boundaries.[28] It is a negative term that resists being turned into a positive descriptor. What then can it mean in the parable? Or, to put the matter differently, why is the hospitality of the village seemingly characterized as a form of "shameless hospitality"? In whose eyes would their offer of hospitality appear to be something negative and shameful?

At first glance, the characterization does not make sense, since the peasant villagers are upholding the traditions of hospitality associated with Abraham. In the Sodom and Gomorrah episode, Abraham and Sarah's hospitality is contrasted with inhospitable reception accorded the angelic strangers in Sodom (Gen. 18:1–12; 19:1–14). Already noted in the discussion of the parable of the rich man and Lazarus, Abraham would send his steward, Eliezer, to see if the people of Israel were expressing hospitality to strangers and aliens as well as other Israelites in need. Jesus speaks about a judgment that will befall the towns and villages that refuse hospitality to his disciples (Matt. 10:11–15; Luke 10:10–12; cf. Luke 9:51–56), and he envisions the patriarchs, Abraham, Isaac, and Jacob, as hosts of a great eschatological banquet (Q: Luke 13:28–30 par. Matt. 8:11–12). Indeed, Abraham was not only an eponymous ancestor but also modeled the kind of gracious and generous patron whose hospitality anticipated the debt codes of the Torah even before they were given at Sinai.

27. Ibid., 126–32, for his full argument.
28. For a fuller description of these meanings, see Herzog, *Parables as Subversive Speech*, 202–3, 212–13.

The villagers in the parable seem to be practicing this honorable form of hospitality. Why then is it shameless?

The peasants of Galilee lived with a realistic view of their world. They knew that all the goods and services they valued were limited and in short supply. There was never enough to go around. So they cultivated the value of reciprocity in their relations to each other, and they used the resources of the village to help families in need.[29] Kinship and friendship were closely allied themes in peasant life. Each village also maintained a ceremonial fund to be used on special occasions that demanded hospitality, in spite of the sacrifices required to maintain this fund in a world of limited goods and short supplies. When the villagers arise and contribute to the meal for the friend who has come "off the road," they are drawing on the very subsistence resources they must nurture to survive. From the point of view of the elites and their retainers, these peasants were shamelessly wasting their precious resources, expending them on a virtual stranger and getting nothing in return. Their paltry meal was nothing more than a poor imitation of the truly great banquets that nurtured the patron-client relations so carefully cultivated by elites and their retainers. The villagers would have done better to save their precious food for a rainy day, rather than try to imitate a great banquet.

In the last line of the parable, Jesus turned this negative value judgment into an affirmation of the hospitality of the village. The punch line (v. 8) may be spoken ironically. Because "friendship" had been coopted into the system of patronage, it could no longer be appealed to. But the boundary-breaking hospitality associated with Abraham, Sarah, and Eliezer was different. It was as shameless as the Torah's concern for the alien, the stranger, and the sojourner. Every time a village greeted such a guest, their hospitality created a banquet no less important than Yahweh's great banquet itself and a great deal more important than the great feasts in the houses of the elites. The behavior of the villagers was boundary breaking in one other way. According to the Torah, the source of boundary drawing in the first century, only the clean should eat with the clean, yet the peasants were as unclean as their guest who dropped by in the middle of the night. Even though the peasants lived at the margins of the Torah, and perhaps beyond its boundaries, they still lived by their own code of honor and hospitality, embodying a justice that the purity codes could not comprehend.

By extending hospitality the villagers resisted the efforts of their oppressors to dehumanize them and reduce them to creatures obsessed by the desire to

29. For a fuller description of peasant values, see James Scott, *The Moral Economy of the Peasant: Rebellion and Subsistence in Southeast Asia* (New Haven, Conn.: Yale University Press, 1976. See also Halvor Moxnes, *The Economy of the Kingdom: Social Conflicts and Economic Relations in Luke's Gospel* (Philadelphia: Fortress Press, 1988).

survive at all costs. Rather than surrender to the desire to hoard and accumulate, the peasants continued to provide hospitality even when it brought them few, if any, returns. To the outsider, they were wasting their subsistence. To the insider, they were redistributing the wealth of the land in obedience to the wisdom of the Torah. Their ordinary actions had extraordinary consequences.

CONCLUSION

This chapter has explored the village as a place where a "shadow society" could emerge and where an "alternate moral universe" could be created. In addition to his prominent encounters with various kinds of adversaries, usually in public settings, Jesus also taught in the context of village life and reflected the view of history from below common to these settings. Viewed through this lens, Jesus' parable of the wicked tenants (Mark 12:1–12) can be read as a prophetic critique of the ruling class who have arrogated to themselves the role of Yahweh, the true "lord of the vineyard." This parable stands in a long line of prophetic analyses of the abuses of ruling elites. By contrast, the parable of the great banquet affords a glimpse of another kind of great banquet of salvation in which the rejected get invited and the invited get rejected. The parable could be seen as an attempt to appropriate the vision of the messianic banquet for the outcast and disinherited in Israel, the very people among whom Jesus was working.

The parable of the friend at midnight carries us into the world of a small peasant village where the traditions of hospitality associated with Abraham and Sarah and their steward Eliezer continue to thrive, even in a world of limited goods in which peasants live at the subsistence level and often at the edge of destitution. Casting aside any concerns about their future, the villagers provide the kind of meal required by the occasion of a visit from a friend of the village. The ruling elites may regard such displays as a shameless waste of resources, but their judgments do not hinder the villagers, whose hospitality is akin to what will be found in the reign of God.

Jesus is associated with village life, even by his appellation, Jesus of Nazareth. He may well have seen the village as the place where he could teach offstage as a pedagogue of the oppressed as well as the place where he could respond to the challenges posed by his opponents onstage. Whether it functioned as a shadow society that could mock the ceremonies of the elites or as an alternate moral universe that could nurture a prophetic critique of the rulers, the village remained a major part of Jesus' public work even after he left his home town to itinerate in Galilee and possibly Judea.

10

"What is truth?"

(*John 18:38*): *The "Show Trial" in Jerusalem*

THE SUPPER BEFORE THE STORM

Before Jesus was betrayed and captured in Gethsemane, he shared a final meal with his disciples (Mark 14:22–25; Matt. 26:26–29; Luke 22:15–20). Although the historicity of the event has been debated for decades, Sanders includes it in one of his lists of indisputable facts on which one can construct a picture of the historical figure of Jesus. It would take us far beyond the bounds of the current study to explore in detail the meaning of the Last Supper. Discussions of its significance are extensive, particularly in light of the centrality of the event for the worship life of the church. Rather than try to summarize such immense issues, we will explore how this final meal with the disciples relates to the picture of Jesus sketched in the earlier chapters of this book.

To use Freire's language, table companionship seems to have provided a generative theme to describe an important element in Jesus' thematic universe. Following the call of Levi, Jesus sat at table with toll collectors and sinners as a way of profaning the great tradition being promulgated by the oral Torah of the Pharisees. It was as though Jesus were saying that the temple provided neither the model nor the motive for table companionship; rather, it is the covenant love of God who is gathering together the "lost sheep of the house of Israel" (Matt. 10:6) to reconstitute the people of God. The meal that Jesus shared with outcasts was like a covenant renewal ceremony which proclaimed that God was now calling not the righteous, but sinners (Mark 2:17). At the Last Supper, this theme of covenant played a significant role. But how does this reading of the Last Supper relate to the Passover celebration? In the exodus, Yahweh descended into Egypt to gather his people together and redeem them by leading them out of bondage with an outstretched arm and a mighty hand. In his prophetic work in

Israel, Jesus was redeeming the lost and restoring them to the community of
God's people. As Yahweh prevailed with his mighty arm and hand, so Jesus casts
out demons by "the finger of God" (Luke 11:20). Both meals celebrate the
redemption of the lost and the gathering of the exiled. This exodus theme echoes
throughout the public activity of Jesus whenever he looses those bound by Satan
(Luke 13:10–17), exorcizes those possessed by demons (Mark 1:21–28), or heals
those in bondage to disease (Mark 2:1–12). In these ways, Jesus continues the
prototypical work of Yahweh first revealed in the exodus, the work of liberation.

Scholars have debated whether or not the Last Supper was a traditional
Passover Seder. In light of what we know of Jesus' activity, we would be sur-
prised if it were just that and nothing else. In spite of Luke's determined effort
to cast the meal as a Passover celebration, the truth is that it both is and isn't a
Passover meal. It combines tradition and transformation, a combination also
found in the parables of Jesus that deal with meals. The parable of the great
banquet (Luke 14:15–24), for instance, presents a traditional banquet whose
meaning and purpose is transformed when the invited guests reject the generosity of the host, thereby opening the banquet to the most unexpected guests.
How could a banquet planned in the usual way become so unusual? In similar
fashion, Yahweh liberated a group of slave laborers from Egypt and transformed
them into a people of the promise. Who could have anticipated such a move?

The greatest reversal associated with these meals is who is on the invitation
list and who is not. In the parable of the rich man and Lazarus (Luke 16:19–31),
the rich man feasts sumptuously every day, but it is the poor beggar, Lazarus,
who appears as the guest of honor reclining on Abraham's bosom. Jesus
addresses this theme of reversal in his teaching.

> There will be weeping and gnashing of teeth when you see Abraham
> and Isaac and Jacob and all the prophets in the reign of God and you
> yourselves thrown out. Then people will come from the east and the
> west, from north and south, and will eat in the reign of God. (Q: Luke
> 13:28–29 par. Matt. 8:11–12)

In each case, the reversal provides an opportunity for the outcasts while
excluding those who presume they will be at the party, a lesson that applies to
the Last Supper itself. Who is sitting around the table when the Lord renews
the covenant with Israel? The ruling elites? The high priestly families? Those
who orchestrate and control the pilgrimage festival called Passover? No. None
of them are present. Who is present then? A group of what Crossan would call
"nuisances and nobodies."[1] A popular prophet who works the edges and the

---

1. John Dominic Crossan, *Jesus: A Revolutionary Biography* (San Francisco: Harper
Collins, 1994), 54–74.

margins and a few of his misguided followers. From a certain point of view, it is just another gathering of toll collectors and sinners. How can anyone conduct a covenant renewal meal without the assistance of the temple and its system? It was a bold move.

An ominous foreboding surrounds the meal. On the one hand, the renewed covenant is associated with the pouring out of blood and betrayal (Mark 14:18–21, 24; Matt. 26:21–25, 28; Luke 22:20, 21–23) while it is associated with fulfillment in the reign of heaven, on the other hand (Mark 14:25; Matt. 26:29; Luke 22:18). In this regard, the Last Supper consciously echoes the covenant renewal ceremony in Israel, which alternates between blessings and curses (Deut. 27–28). The same mixture of hope and threat informs the Last Supper. When read in this way, the supper not only represents a calm before the storm but anticipates the events that will transpire shortly. Even at table with his disciples and followers, Jesus challenged the ruling elites who controlled the festival. He must have known that elites do not allow challenges to their hegemony to pass without retaliation. This is why they recruited a disaffected disciple and turned him into an informer and a betrayer. It was a common pattern. In this case, Judas's betrayal made the show trial possible.

THE SHOW TRIAL IN JERUSALEM

In many ways, this is the most sensitive chapter in the book because the trial of Jesus has been the source of such bitter animosity and contention. Christians have used the trial to blame Jewish authorities for Jesus' death and justify varied forms of anti-Semitism and anti-Judaism. In recent times, the debate about the trial of Jesus has been renewed in the conversation between Raymond Brown and John Dominic Crossan. In 1994, Brown published a two-volume study entitled *The Death of the Messiah: From Gethsemane to the Grave. A Commentary on the Passion Narratives in the Four Gospels*, in which he argued for the accounts as "history remembered." A year later, Crossan published a response to Brown's study (and a rebuttal of it) entitled *Who Killed Jesus: Exposing the Roots of Anti-Semitism in the Gospel Story of the Death of Jesus*, in which he argues that the trial narratives were examples of "prophecy historicized." In essence, this means that the Gospel narratives seized upon some prophetic texts from the Hebrew Bible, such as Isa. 50:6, and fashioned a narrative based on them to demonstrate that Jesus' death was the result of the fulfillment of prophecy and, therefore, had divine sanction. Both of these works are sophisticated and nuanced studies that cannot be summarized in a paragraph, but each study, in its own way, opens the Pandora's box associated with this subject.

The discussion in this chapter will differ from both of the approaches mentioned above by asking how the so-called trial materials can be understood in the context of advanced agrarian societies and aristocratic empires. The first problem that we have to face is a familiar one, namely, anachronism. When we speak of the "trial" of Jesus, we often assume a system of jurisprudence very much like our own. This would include specification of charges or an indictment, the right to legal counsel, the presumption of innocence until proven guilty, the right to call witnesses, the right to examination and cross examination of witnesses, rules for the introduction of evidence, the impaneling of an impartial jury of one's peers, an impartial judge to oversee the trial, the right to a change of venue in order to ensure a fair trial, and many other provisions as well. This is, in part, what we mean when we speak of a trial.

None of this applies to the trial of Jesus, and that is why this study will speak of a "show trial" in Jerusalem. What is a show trial? A show trial is one way of processing deviants in an authoritarian society. Jesus was not tried to determine his innocence or guilt. In that sense, there never was a trial of Jesus, and it is probably anachronistic to speak about "the trial of Jesus." But he was subjected to a show trial, which is a form of political theater. In her essay on theaters in the Roman world, Mary Boatwright noted that, in addition to drama, musical events, and athletic contests, theaters were used "as venues for public trials and meetings."[2] Horsley has noted that theaters were used for political purposes in Caesarea and Sepphoris.

> When needed, they could also be used for the rulers' special purposes such as the "demonstration effect" of a public political trial of dissidents who had dared to demonstrate against their native ruler's collaboration with Roman domination (*Ant.* 17.155–167).[3]

How does a show trial differ from what we call a trial? In a show trial, the guilt of the person to be tried has already been determined, usually on political grounds. In a show trial, there is no weighing of evidence, nor does the condemned person have counsel, legal or otherwise. The show trial is conducted under the supervision of the state; there is no independent judiciary. The purpose of the trial is not only to execute a subversive but to publicly shame and humiliate an enemy of the state so as to discredit and degrade everything he represents. The procedure follows the political script determined by ruling elites. The "witnesses" called to testify have been coached on what to say. The entire event is a piece of political theater governed by the "public transcript"

---

2. Mary Boatwright, "Theatres in the Roman Empire," *BA* (1990): 184–92.
3. Richard A. Horsley, *Galilee: History, Politics, People* (Valley Forge, Pa.: Trinity Press International, 1995), 180.

of the elites. Indeed, a show trial will be scripted and choreographed to con-form to the public transcript of the ruling class. In this context, public theater provides an appropriate setting for a show trial.

Show trials are one way to process deviant figures who have challenged the rulers' construction of reality and to destroy their influence lest its corrosive effects continue. The priestly rulers in Jerusalem and their allies used their authority and their reading of the Torah to generate rules to govern the lives of the ruled. Rule makers, such as the priests, create the need for rule enforcers, who monitor compliance and ensure obedience to the laws being generated by the ruling class (a form of the great tradition). When Jesus challenged the scribal Pharisees, he was locking horns with the rule enforcers of the temple. Jesus, the reputational leader, attempted to dislodge the norms that were being propagated from the temple, and in doing so, he ran afoul of the high priestly aristocrats and called into question a group that could not afford to ignore his affront. If the high priestly houses were in the precarious position that Good-man has outlined (see chapter 3), their tolerance would be limited. This dilemma alone would have been cause enough to initiate the deviance process that we call the trial of Jesus.[4] Jesus simply posed one problem too many.

The first step in a deviance process involves negative labeling, a tactic that can be traced to the beginning of Jesus' public activity.[5] The most obvious pas-sage where negative labeling occurs is the Beelzebul controversy in which Jesus is accused of being in cahoots with the devil: "He has Beelzebul, and by the ruler of demons, he casts out demons" (Mark 3:22, but see 19b–30; Matt. 12:22–32; Luke 11:14–23). His habit of sharing table companionship with out-casts led to the charge that he was a friend of toll collectors and sinners (Mark 2:16). The scribes in Capernahum call Jesus a blasphemer (Mark 2:1–12). After Jesus is apprehended in Gethsemane, the process escalates. Witnesses come forward to denounce him (Mark 14:57–58; Matt. 26:61), although they have not been coached well enough, so their testimony conflicts, but still the charges grow more serious. Ominously, Jesus is charged with blasphemy (Mark 14:63–64; Matt. 26:65) and with threatening to destroy the temple itself (Mark 14:58; Matt. 26:61).

The second step in the process escalates from negative labeling to denun-ciation, whose purpose is to turn the person into a stereotype of a deviant. So "the person accused of deviance must be made into an instance of what he or

---

4. See Erdwin H. Pfuhl Jr., *The Deviance Process* (New York: Van Nostrand Reinhold Co., 1980); Bruce J. Malina and Jerome Neyrey, *Calling Jesus Names: The Social Value of Labels in Matthew* (Sonoma, Calif.: Polebridge Press, 1988).

5. For a more extensive discussion of labeling, see Malina and Neyrey, *Calling Jesus Names*. They are indebted to the work of Pfuhl, *Deviance Process*.

she is alleged to have done: from devious doer to deviant; from crime perpe-
trator to criminal."[6] Denunciation serves a two-fold purpose; it both destroys
the person's identity and replaces it with a more sinister identity. Paulo Freire
would say that the authorities are dehumanizing the figure about to be placed
on show trial to justify the brutality to which he or she will be subjected. It is
at the denunciation stage that an ad hoc "official" body needs to be convened.
Was it the Sanhedrin? If not, what ad hoc body was convened? We will return
to these questions later in this chapter. For the moment, it is enough to know
that such a body was a necessity, for there must be some formal body representing properly sanctioned authority to whom the denunciation is directed.
The body convened would be essentially a "deviance processing agency," but it
also provides an aura of legitimacy and authority of the ruling class to the proceedings. This process can be observed in Mark 14:55–65 and Matt. 26:59–68.
Mark and Matthew describe this body as "the whole council" (*holon to synedrion*)
whereas Luke describes the group as "the assembly of the elders of the people"
(*synēchthē to presbyterion tou laou*), which included chief priests and scribes who
led Jesus away from the gathering of the elders to "their council" (*to synedrion
auton*). Luke seems to distinguish the gathering of elders from a more formal
body, neither of which must necessarily be the Sanhedrin. The descriptions
assume that Jesus was presented to some formal body for denunciation.

When done successfully, the result of the process of denunciation is to create a "retrospective interpretation"of the deviant's life to demonstrate that he
or she is not on trial for a single offence but for a pattern of activity that proves
him or her to be a perverse and dangerous character,[7] a chaotic threat to the
order of society and creation. This whole process will culminate with the identification of a master status for the person on trial that may result in the assign-
ment of a master label or a cluster of related labels. In the Gospels' account of
the show trial, either blasphemer or fraudulent king of the Judeans seems to
be the status chosen. Malina and Neyrey believe that "Jesus's master status,
then, is that of a deviant, a blaspheming temple-profaner and a presumptuous
fraud."[8] Other charges would be read in this light.

In the Gospels, three charges are brought against Jesus. First, he was
accused of undermining the payment of tribute to Caesar. A member of the
kangaroo court that confirmed Jesus' guilt (it is very unlikely that it was the
Sanhedrin, as we shall see) declared, "We found this man perverting our

---

6. See Pfuhl, *Deviance Process*, 160–69. See also the unpublished paper by Bruce
Malina, "Interpreting the New Testament Anthropologically: Some Examples," given
at the Catholic Biblical Association, 17.
7. See Pfuhl, *Deviance Process*, 176–78; Malina and Neyrey, *Calling Jesus Names*, 86.
8. Malina and Neyrey, *Calling Jesus Names*, 88.

nation, forbidding us to pay tribute to Caesar"(Luke 23:2a, b). Second, Jesus was accused of threatening to destroy the temple (Mark 14:58; Matt. 26:61; Mark 15:29; Matt. 27:40). This charge would include the charge of blasphemy. Third, he was charged with claiming to be a king or anointed one (messiah) (Luke 23:2c). Were the charges true? The first charge concerned refusal to pay tribute. As argued earlier in this study (chapter 8), Jesus may well have opposed the payment of tribute even though he expressed that opposition through an ambiguous and coded hidden transcript. So there is surely a sense in which the accusation is true. In similar fashion, Jesus did enact a symbolic destruction of the temple and undermined the role of the high priests as brokers of God's favor through the temple system (chapter 7), as is evident in his forgiveness of debt or sins. Seen in this light, he is a blasphemer, a charge the scribes saw very clearly (Mark 2:1–12). Jesus' form of blasphemy was related to his roles as reputational leader and broker of the reign of God. As a reputational leader, he did indeed attempt to dislodge the norms of temple and Torah, and as a broker, he did mediate God's forgiveness of sins without benefit of the temple. In both roles, Jesus ignored or transgressed serious boundaries with a total disregard for the powerful institutions involved. As a threat to temple, priesthood, and sacrificial system, he attacked what some held to be sacred, and therefore he was branded as a blasphemer. So there is a sense in which the second charge brought against Jesus is also true, seen from the point of view of the rulers and their retainers.

But while both of these charges contribute to a reading of Jesus as a dangerous deviant, it is the final charge, his claim to be an anointed figure, that weighed most heavily against him. Historically speaking, what does it mean that Jesus is accused of saying that "he himself is the anointed one [*christos*], a king [*basilea*]" (Luke 23:2c)? This is where the danger of anachronism is greatest, for it is tempting to read into this third charge the claim of Christian theology that Jesus is the Messiah. When we do this, we set up a volatile reading of the trial in which the Jews kill the messiah, a reading which has led to countless pogroms and abuses of Jewish people. Some Jewish scholars argue that there does not seem to have been any "messianic" template that described a long-awaited redeemer. Jewish scholars have called this construct into question, and if their work is correct, then it is simply historically erroneous to think that the use of the description "anointed one [*christos*]" could apply to Jesus in the same way it would subsequently be applied to him by the early church. It is historically more likely that Jesus is being accused of assuming the role of popular kingship studied so well by Horsley and Hanson.[9] A popular

9. See Richard Horsley and John Hanson, *Bandits, Prophets and Messiahs: Popular Movements in the Time of Jesus* (New York: Winston Press/Seabury, 1985), chap. 3.

king was acclaimed by the people, not appointed by regnant political authorities like Caesar when he legitimated the house of Herod. In John 6, we have
a partial memory of just such a moment. After feeding the multitudes, Jesus
"realized that they were about to come and take him by force to make him
king," so he withdrew and avoided the anointing (John 6:15).

Having noted the charges lodged against Jesus, it is important to emphasize that they are really irrelevant and unimportant to the show trial, for the
show trial is a form of a "status degradation ritual,"[10] and, as such, its power
derives not from proving charges but from shaming a deviant, dehumanizing
an enemy of the state, and denouncing everything he or she embodied. This
explains why mockery and abuse are part of the show trial. Jesus is mocked as
a false prophet (Mark 14:65; Matt. 26:67–68; Luke 22:64) and as a fraudulent
king of the Judeans (Mark 15:17–19; Matt. 27:28–30). By applying honorable
labels (prophet, king) in sarcastic fashion, the rulers further debase and dismiss
Jesus as a marginal fraud, helpless to prevent his own destruction. If the titu-
lus on the cross is our guide, it summarizes Jesus' life in a kind of retrospective interpretation, invoking the story line of popular kings, all of whom were
captured and executed. The degradation ritual also mocks the hopes of those
who believed that this popular prophet would bring the "reign of God." The
show trial must crucify the deviant and crush the hope of his followers

Who then officially sanctions the show trial? What body is convened
to receive the denunciations of the rule enforcers? James McLaren has studied over twenty episodes of ancient decision-making processes (from the
Hasmonaean period through the first Jewish Revolt, a span of about two
hundred years) in which Jews were involved. In every case, the decision
making was really in the hands of the ruler and a very few members of the ruling class, a cadre including the ruler and some inner circle of his political
friends and allies.[11] The equivalent of congressional bodies or deliberative
assemblies, like a Sanhedrin, simply didn't play a role. The task of the small
cadre was to rubber stamp what the ruler and the power brokers of the ruling
class wanted to happen. They had no independent will of their own. McLaren's
findings accord with Lohse's description of Herod the Great's treatment of the
Sanhedrin:

> When Herod became king, he could not be high-priest or preside over
> the Sanhedrin because he was not of priestly descent. . . . But, in fact,
> he dispensed royal justice without bothering in the least about the

---

10. For a discussion of status degradation ritual, see Malina and Neyrey, *Calling Jesus
Names*, 69–91.
11. James S. McLaren, *Power and Politics in Palestine: The Jews and the Governing of
Their Land, 100 B.C.–70 A.D.* (Sheffield: JSOT Press, 1991).

priesthood or the High Council. *Ant.*, 14.167; 15.273f.; 16.1–5. The power of the Sanhedrin remained *de iure* but *de facto* the ruler alone exercised the *ius gladii* (=death penalty power).[12]

Herod could do even worse. The Sanhedrin accused him of killing Ezekias and other social bandits before they were tried and condemned by the Sanhedrin because the Torah "forbids us to slay a man, even an evildoer, unless he has first been condemned by the Sanhedrin" (*Ant.* 14.167). After he came to power, Herod had every member but one of that Sanhedrin slaughtered and packed the body with his own supporters (*Ant.* 14.175–76). All of this indicates that it is unlikely that the Sanhedrin would have been convened on a matter as politically charged as the show trial of Jesus and, even if they were, it would have been for the express purpose of confirming what the rulers had already decided.

How does all of this apply to the trial of Jesus? McLaren identifies three groups of actors in the trial and categorizes them by the degree of likelihood that they participated in the trial.

certain:	chief priests; Caiaphas; Pilate
probable:	the elders, rulers, or scribes; captain of the temple; high priest's father-in-law
doubtful:	Pharisees; Antipas; the Sanhedrin

The certain participants are all members of the upper echelons of the ruling elites in Jerusalem and the temple as well as the Roman prefect, the highest-ranking Roman official in Judea. The probable group includes most of the supporting cast (the elders and temple officials) or retainers (scribes) who serve the interests of the ruling class. The doubtful group includes a political faction of laity (Pharisees) who were not involved in the show trial, a ruler without jurisdiction but with an undeniable interest in Jerusalem (Antipas), and the official Sanhedrin. Since Jesus was being executed at the time of a major pilgrimage festival, both Roman authorities and their collaborators, the high priestly families and the lay aristocrats, would perceive it as being in their interest to get the job done as quickly as possible, involving as few as possible. This means that it is quite likely that the ruling elites convened some form of kangaroo court, that is, an unofficial body with an official aura of authority, to deal with the official denunciation and condemnation of Jesus. Since it appears that this court of opportunity met in the high priest's house, it is unlikely that it included all seventy-one members of the Sanhedrin. That this group included some members of the Sanhedrin is certainly possible, perhaps even probable, but it is highly unlikely that the leaders would have convened the

12. Eduard Lohse, *synedrion* in *TDNT* 7:865.

whole Sanhedrin. If they did, then they would be forced to give the impression that they were adhering at least to some of the rules of the Sanhedrin, even if they might not be identical with the procedures enumerated in the Mishnah tractate on the Sanhedrin.[13] This would include hearing witnesses bring charges and debating them, a forum that could not be controlled by the leaders as effectively as a selected group of social peers willing to do their leaders' bidding. If the traditions about Joseph of Arimathea contain any historical echoes (Mark 15:42–47; Luke 23:50–56), they witness to the possibility that some members of that body may have objected to the show trial of Jesus. In his article on the Sanhedrin, Lohse lists five rules that were broken or abrogated in the show trial of Jesus.

1. Capital cases were to be tried by day, not at night.
2. No proceedings were to be held on feast days or the sabbath, yet Jesus was tried on the eve of Passover.
3. A death sentence was never passed on the day of the trial but on the following day, yet Jesus was condemned on the day of his trial.
4. Blasphemy applies to pronouncing the divine name, yet Jesus never did at his trial.
5. The venue of the trial was in the house of the high priest, but the Sanhedrin was supposed to meet in its assembly hall.[14]

To summarize, the evidence points to the fact that Jesus was not tried by the Sanhedrin but by an informal kangaroo court, doing the bidding of the high priestly houses, especially the will of the high priest Caiaphas. No doubt the whole procedure was justified by an appeal to political expediency and the self-interest of the rulers: "You do not understand that it is better for one man to die for the people than to have the whole nation destroyed" (John 11:50). Sanders judged the interrogation by Caiaphas to be one of the indisputable facts on which he could build a picture of Jesus (chapter 1). Finally, McLaren's view supports the interpretation proposed here:

> It is important to acknowledge that the execution of Jesus was instigated by a powerful, select group of Jews. The action was formal and legitimate because the Jewish protagonists were influential men of high public standing, able to manipulate the situation to their advantage, and obtaining Roman support.[15]

13. See Herbert Danby, *The Mishnah*, trans. and annotated by Herbert Danby (London: Oxford University Press, 1933), 382–400. The critical issues surrounding the functioning of the Sanhedrin (even whether there were one or two Sanhedrins) are complex and cannot be dealt with in this study.
14. Lohse, *synedrion*, *TDNT* 7:868.
15. McLaren, *Power and Politics in Palestine*, 97.

McLaren has identified the chemistry needed to concoct a successful show trial.

It is critically important to note that none of the Jerusalem authorities acted as they did because they were Jews. Indeed, the Greek word *ioudaios* is better translated as "Judean" rather than as "Jew." The latter translation invites anachronism and buries the first-century conflict behind a modern reading that sees Jews as killers of the Christian, Jesus. The Judeans who collaborated with the Roman prefect acted as urban elites colluding with their colonial overlords to execute an increasingly effective prophet of the people, pedagogue of the oppressed, exorcist, healer, and reputational leader who claimed to broker God's coming reign, so that they could eliminate a potential threat to the stability that Rome had so carefully cultivated through its alliances with the high priestly houses in Jerusalem and the house of the Herods in Galilee. In preparing a show trial, they acted very much like their counterparts in other areas of the empire would have acted under similar circumstances. To suggest that they acted as Jews trying to extirpate a nascent Christian movement is untrue and misleading to the point of being vicious. No attempt to understand the events of the show trial in Jerusalem should give any comfort to those who twist the meaning of these events to serve an anti-Semitic or anti-Judaic agenda.

The way that the materials in the Gospels cohere with the framework and process involved in a show trial should also caution us against dismissing the Gospel narratives as "prophecy historicized." They may convey important historical information about the dynamics surrounding the death of Jesus. Just because the show trial narratives have been put to mean ends does not, in and of itself, discredit them or prove that they are unhistorical. In this regard, Ellis Rivkin has proposed a solution to the question "Who killed Jesus?" It would be more accurate, he argues, to change the question altogether. The issue is not "who killed Jesus" as much as it is "what killed Jesus." His answer is astute though finally unsatisfactory:

> For it emerges with great clarity, both from Josephus and from the gospels, that the culprit is not the Jews, but the Roman imperial system. . . . It was the Roman imperial system that exacted harsh tribute. It was the actions of Roman governors that drove the people wild and stirred Judea with convulsive violence. And it was the Roman imperial system that bred revolutionaries and seeded charismatics.[16]

The difficulty with this explanation is that it does not explore fully enough either the complexities of colonial occupation or the range of Jewish responses

16. Ellis Rivkin, "What Crucified Jesus?" in James H. Charlesworth, ed., *Jesus' Jewishness: Exploring the Place of Jesus within Early Judaism* (New York: Crossroad, 1991), 253.

to Roman imperialism. As this study has argued, the high priestly houses and lay aristocrats actively colluded with Rome and benefitted from their collaboration. The same could be said of Herod Antipas and the Herodians as well. This is why it is necessary to distinguish the variety of Jewish responses to Roman occupation and to note who worked with Rome to dispense with Jesus. McLaren's study does exactly this by noting who was involved and who was not. He concludes that a fairly small cadre of the ruling elites cooperated with the Roman prefect but that larger bodies like the Sanhedrin and political factions like the Pharisees did not. What killed Jesus was indeed the Roman imperial system, but it was an indispensable element of that system to impress local elites into the role of collaborators with Rome in disposing of threats to their mutual security and challenges to their rule. It is impossible to deal with the "what" without including the "who." Nevertheless, Rivkin is certainly correct when he argues that

> it was not the Jewish people who crucified Jesus and it was not the Roman people—it was the imperial system, a system that victimized the Jews, victimized the Romans, and victimized the Spirit of God.[17]

It is true that it makes as much sense to blame the Jews for Jesus' death as it does to blame Italians living in Rome (Romans?). But the essence of the imperial system was to divide conquered people into those who cooperate with Rome and those who do not; the system rewarded those who cooperated with Rome and turned them against their own people. This means that local high priestly elites victimized their own people in order to maintain their standing with Rome. This victimization was most clearly present in the economic exploitation of the peasants of the land. Consequently, it would not be accurate to depict an impersonal system victimizing all groups equally, a first-century version of equal-opportunity victimization. To understand the dynamics of the first century requires that we take a more differentiated approach. This is why Rivkin's explanation is finally unsatisfactory although it does rightly focus on the systemic dynamics involved in the execution of Jesus.

While speaking about the role of the imperial system, it may be useful to examine the actions of Pilate. There is a general consensus that the Gospels increasingly shift responsibility for Jesus' death away from Pilate and place it on the shoulders of the Jewish leaders. Pilate seems to believe that Jesus is innocent but cannot figure out how to save him from the crowd and their leaders. Three times in Luke, Pilate declares Jesus innocent of any crime (23:4, 14b, 22), and twice he offers to "chastise him" and release him (23:16, 22b). When he is unable to persuade the leaders or the crowd, he washes his hands,

17. Ibid., 257.

declaring, "I am innocent of this man's blood; see to it yourselves" (Matt. 27:24), a remark that implies that he is placing in their hands the *ius gladii*, that is, the power to execute.

In this interaction between Pilate and the high priestly authorities, the crowd plays a critical role. A great deal has been made about the fickle nature of the crowd that greeted Jesus with acclamations when he entered the city (Mark 11:1–10; Matt. 21:1–9; Luke 19:28–40) and then turned into a frenzied mob screaming for his crucifixion (Mark 15:13; Matt. 27:22b; Luke 23:21). The crowd is vacillating only if it is the same crowd, a very dubious assumption. The crowd that accompanied Jesus from Galilee to Jerusalem for the Passover was most likely a crowd of Galilean pilgrims, but the crowd that assembled in the upper city by Pilate's palace was a crowd of clients indebted to their powerful patrons, who had coached them what to say. Indeed, Mark (15:11) and Matthew (27:20) indicate that the chief priests coached the crowd of their clients what to say when Pilate offered to release Barabbas and what to say when Pilate tried to release Jesus. The outcry "Crucify him! Crucify him!" was not a spontaneous demonstration but a public transcript written by the rulers.

It certainly is possible that Luke is whitewashing Pilate, the Roman prefect, although that is not an easy job. Other ancient authorities depict Pilate as brutish, boorish, violent, and shortsighted, with no concern for issues of justice. In his *Embassy to Gaius*, Philo says of Pilate that it would not be wise to "expose the rest of his conduct as governor by stating in full the briberies, the insults, the robberies, the outrages and wanton injuries, the executions without trial constantly repeated, the ceaseless and supremely grievous cruelty" (302). If we add this description to the incidents reported by Josephus in which Pilate seemed to take pleasure in provoking and insulting the Judeans and their leaders, we do not discover a figure overly concerned for the pursuit of justice. In fact, he was noted for "the executions without trial," a reference to the perfunctory use of show trials to execute enemies of the Roman imperium. This fact alone casts a shadow of suspicion on the Barabbas episode in Jesus' show trial. Pilate does not seem like the kind of prefect who would at a feast free a social bandit or a sicarius for which he had no respect. Passover was not a Roman celebration!

In light of what is generally known about Pilate's character (or lack thereof), is it possible to interpret his actions during Jesus' show trial in a way that differs from the usual reading? Do the Gospels provide any other clues? They do, but a critical clue is found in the Gospel of John, normally not used as a source in studies of the historical Jesus. Earlier in this study, we did note that there were some exceptions to the general tendency not to use John for historical reconstruction. The show trial is one of them. After Jesus' interrogation by Caiaphas, the Judean leaders take Jesus to Pilate, but only John records the following:

> Then they led Jesus from the house of Caiaphas to the praetorium. It
> was early. They themselves did not enter the praetorium, so that they
> might not be defiled, but might eat the passover. (John 18:28)

The "praetorium" carried a cluster of meanings related to Pilate's palace in
Jerusalem. Gealy summarizes its range of meanings as follows:

> Since the governor's palace, the open court (atrium) within or before
> the palace where the judgment seat or bema was set on a mosaic floor
> or "pavement" (John 19:13) made for the purpose of public hearings
> and the barracks were part of the same establishment, "praetorium"
> seems to have been a term designating either the whole or the part.[18]

Given what is known of Pilate's utter disregard for Judean sensibilities, he
could not have viewed their refusal to meet him on his ground in a positive
light (*Ant.* 18.56 par. *War* 2.169; *Ant.* 18.60–62 par. *War* 2.175–76). He knows
that they would consider themselves defiled if they set foot in his praetorium.
However, he can turn this to his purposes. First, he examines Jesus in the praetorium out of sight of the temple authorities so they cannot know what he is
doing. Then he comes out to them, ostensibly to determine their accusations
more clearly but actually to dismiss the case and turn it over to the Judeans.
"Take him yourselves and judge him by your own law" (18:31). He says this
not because he believes Jesus is innocent but because he wants to rub their
noses in the fact that they cannot execute their prisoner. "It is not lawful for
us to put anyone to death" (18:31). This isn't news to Pilate; he knows it very
well. He is toying with the Judeans to remind them of their dependent condition. Although Pilate's second interrogation of Jesus is a vehicle for Johannine
theology (18:33–38a), it issues in the same result. Pilate dangles Jesus before
them: "I find no case against/grounds for accusation against him" (18:38b,
author's trans.). His willingness to mock and scourge Jesus (19:1–7) leads to a
third trip into the praetorium, where Pilate continues to trifle with the high
priestly leaders. Even allowing for Johannine and Lukan theologies, which are
clearly present, Pilate's behavior need not be read as a tireless effort by an advocate for justice to right the wrong in the case of Jesus of Nazareth versus the
temple authorities. He uses the high priests' desire to execute Jesus as a weapon
against them, and he does not release Jesus to them until he has used him to
reinforce the role of the prefect and the preeminence of Roman power. When
he finally moves out to the atrium and sits on the bema or judgment seat, he
asks, "Shall I crucify your king?" (this must be said sarcastically), the chief
priests answer, "We have no king but Caesar" (19:15). He has made his point;

---

18. F. D. Gealy, "Praetorium," in *IDB* 3:856.

the colonial collaborators have cried "uncle." After he has accomplished this goal, he can crucify Jesus with impunity, and he does. He was neither friend nor defender of Jesus. He simply used Jesus to reinforce the brutal realities of Roman domination and, in this case, uses the arrangement of the praetorium to his advantage because it allows him to separate Jesus from his accusers and keep the chief priests dangling on a string.

The actions following Jesus' formal condemnation reveal the true purpose of the show trial. The process of degradation begins in earnest as soon as the deviant has been exposed and labeled. It will include displays of contempt (spitting), mockery ("prophesy who struck you," or using a crown of thorns), violence (beatings, scourging), and degrading assaults (striking his head). The mockery will attempt to discredit and defame his popular standing as a prophet (Mark 14:65; Matt. 26:67) and an anointed leader (Mark 15:17–20; Matt. 27:28–31). The violence directed at the deviant will escalate as it leads to the crucifixion itself.[19]

CRUCIFIXION

Crucifixion was not used sparingly in the ancient world. Both before and after the first Jewish Revolt, Josephus reports the use of mass crucifixions (*War* 2.306–8; 5.447–51), including more than three thousand in one day. Citing material from Josephus and the Dead Sea Scrolls, James Charlesworth concludes that "we know that from the time of Herod the Great until the destruction of Jerusalem in 70 C.E., the Romans crucified thousands in Palestine"[20] (*Ant.* 17.295; 20:102). Crucifixion was reserved primarily for slaves, subversives, and the poor, though it could be used to execute deserters from the military. Around 1970, archaeologists recovered the bones of a Jewish male named Jehohanan (his name was on the ossuary in which his bones had been interred), who was crucified, sometime during the first century, when he was in his mid- to late twenties. From an examination of his bones, archaeologists were able to reconstruct the manner of his crucifixion. His arms were lashed to the crossbeam, not nailed to it. Then his legs were spread and laid against the sides of the upright beam and a nail was driven through each heel bone. In Jehohanan's case, when the nail was driven through his right heel, it bent on a knot in the

19. For a study of crucifixion, see Martin Hengel, *Crucifixion in the Ancient World and the Folly of the Message of the Cross* (Philadelphia: Fortress Press, 1977).

20. Joe Zias and James H. Charlesworth, "Crucifixion: Archaeology, Jesus and the Dead Sea Scrolls," in James H. Charlesworth, ed., *Jesus and the Dead Sea Scrolls* (New York: Doubleday, 1992), 279.

olive wood, making it impossible to remove the nail from the heel bone and the wood. His legs were broken to hasten the time of his death by asphyxiation. Had they not been broken and were he a healthy male in his twenties, it might have taken two to four days before he died on the cross. When his body was taken down, his family had to take the nail and the wood which were attached to the heel bone, a fortunate coincidence that would later provide archaeologists an insight into how Jehohanan was crucified.[21]

Knowing how Jehohanan died does not necessarily tell us how Jesus was crucified because crucifixion was done in many ways. During the final days of the siege of Jerusalem, many of the poor tried to escape the city but were captured by Roman troops who tortured and crucified them. Josephus reports that "the soldiers out of rage and hatred amused themselves by nailing their prisoners in different postures" (*War* 5.451). Impaling also accompanied crucifixion, either to add to the suffering and pain of the crucified or to hasten death if circumstances warranted. John's Gospel (19:31–37) reports that Jesus was impaled, but it does so after Jesus' death and in order to fulfill scripture, so the event is somewhat suspect as history.

The crucified were executed in public places where their humiliation could be witnessed by all who passed by. The supposed point of it all was deterrence, but Crossan frames the issue in broader terms when he says, "Roman crucifixion was state terrorism; . . . its function was to deter resistance or revolt especially among the lower classes."[22] The use of this torturous style of execution was also consistent with the Romans' use of power and violence to maintain control over their subject peoples. Even more ominously, it reflects their willingness to unleash the sadistic impulses of their legions against civilian populations. It evidently never occurred to the Romans that if crucifixion was supposed to act as a deterrent, it was not working very well, for it only seemed to encourage new forms of resistance to imperial rule. Crucifixion only led to more crucifixions; it did not deter rebels, social bandits, prophets, or other subversives from doing their work. All of the ancient writers who mention crucifixion agree that it was a horrific and terrible way to die. As Crossan has argued rather convincingly, crucifixion was one of three supreme punishments in the Roman world and should be grouped with being burned to death or being thrown to the wild beasts because, in each case, there would be no remains left to bury.[23] Crucifixion did not end with the death of the crucified; their bodies were left on the cross to rot or until the wild dogs and vultures

21. Ibid.; see the artist's rendering of the crucifixion of Jehohanan following p. 152.
22. Crossan, *Jesus: A Revolutionary Biography*, 127.
23. Ibid., 126–27.

had devoured what was left of the victims. Denying burial was the ultimate form of shaming in first-century Palestine. Crossan expresses the significance of this outrage in his own eloquent way:

> Without minimizing the extended and excruciating pain, which was temporal, the shame of nonburial, which was eternal, was equally feared. In the ancient mind, the supreme horror of crucifixion was to lose public mourning, to forfeit proper burial, to lie separate from one's ancestors forever, and to have no place where bones remained, spirits hovered, and descendants came to eat with the dead. That is how Jesus died.[24]

As the retrieval of the bones of Jehohanan makes clear, some victims of crucifixion were evidently retrieved from the cross. The Gospels report that this is what happened to Jesus. Although Crossan does not share this view and believes that Jesus' body was left to the dogs at the foot of the cross, he has unwittingly revealed why the women accompanied Jesus to Golgotha and remained at a distance to watch over him in his final hours. As an act of honor and respect, they were present to scare away the scavengers and vultures and to protect Jesus' body until it could be taken off the cross. It took political pull to save the body of a crucified seditionist, and this is exactly what Mark and Luke report about Joseph of Arimathea, "a member of the council" (*bouleutēs*, Mark 15:43; Luke 23:50). Presumably, this refers to the Sanhedrin, although that is not certain. He is highly placed enough to secure Jesus' body from the cross and lay it in a tomb. Crossan's remarks reveal how important an action this is and how devoted the women must have been to risk being associated with a crucified criminal. Theirs was an act of courage.

CONCLUSION

Both evidence and inference point to the fact that Jesus was executed by a small group of ruling Jerusalem elites collaborating with the Roman prefect Pontius Pilate, who alone held the power to execute Jesus (the *ius gladii*). His execution was the consequence of a show trial, not a proceeding by the Sanhedrin, and it was done for reasons of political expediency, perhaps even political necessity. The purpose was not just to execute Jesus but to subject him to a status-degradation ritual that would undermine and destroy everything he represented in the eyes of his followers and the crowds that accompanied him in

---

24. John Dominic Crossan and Jonathan L. Reed, *Excavating Jesus: Beneath the Stones, Behind the Texts* (San Francisco: Harper Collins, 2001), 247.

Galilee. The descriptions of the trial found in the Gospels fit well with the process and purpose of a show trial.

Crucifixion was a brutally painful and humiliating way to die. Its purpose was, so the Romans believed, to deter other prophets and subversive figures from sowing discord and fomenting discontent. This meant that the form of execution would be public, and it would deny burial to those crucified as a final, ultimate insult. This is most likely the reason why the women accompanied Jesus and remained at a distance. They wanted to preserve his body from what Crossan calls "the dogs at the foot of the cross." A member of the Sanhedrin who may have heard about the actions of the kangaroo court in condemning Jesus intervened with Caiaphas to claim the body of Jesus and bury him in a family tomb. This permitted his associates and followers to provide an honorable burial for Jesus, an outcome not commonly procured for the victims of crucifixion.

In commenting on the death of Jesus, Marcus Borg argued that

> Jesus died as a martyr, not as a victim. A martyr is killed because he or she stands for something. Jesus was killed because he stood against the kingdoms of this world and for an alternative social vision grounded in the kingdom of God. The domination system killed Jesus as the prophet of the kingdom of God. That is the political meaning of Good Friday. [He was] a social prophet who challenged the domination system in the name of God.[25]

The earlier chapters of this book have attempted to express what Jesus stood for and what he opposed. They have also provided glimpses of Jesus as contextual theologian relating God's new work for a new day. This is a promising place to begin our understanding of Jesus' death, but it cannot be the final word. That will have to await the Epilogue.

---

25. Marcus Borg, "Why Was Jesus Killed?" in Marcus Borg and N. T. Wright, *The Meaning of Jesus: Two Visions* (San Francisco: Harper Collins, 1999), 91.

Epilogue or Prologue?

In my end is my beginning
—*T.S. Eliot, "East Coker"*

If the truth be known, every study of the historical Jesus is a Christology in disguise. There is a reason why that is the case. After the women accompanied Jesus to the cross and kept their faithful vigil, and after Joseph of Arimathea had gone to Caiaphas to bargain for the body of Jesus, they were able to claim Jesus' body and provide him with a hasty but honorable burial as the shadow of the sabbath suspended their efforts. Theirs was an important act of devotion that ensured Jesus would be "gathered to his ancestors." Indeed, Joseph of Arimathea followed an ancient custom when he buried Jesus in a cave, much as Isaac and Ishmael buried their father, Abraham, with his wife, Sarah, "in the cave of Machpelah in the field of Ephron . . . east of Mamre" (Gen. 25:9).

But just as there was something different about Jesus' life, something that set him apart from other prophets, healers, exorcists, teachers, leaders, and brokers, so there was something about his death that was different, too. Not that the high priestly houses recognized it, nor the minions of Herod for that matter. Only three short days after they believed that they were done with Jesus of Nazareth ("Can anything good come out of Nazareth?" [John 1:46]), just three days later, they had to deal with him again. Matthew got it and structured his insight into the design of his Gospel. In the beginning, the powers that be in Jerusalem, Herod the Great, his courtiers and soldiers, try to prevent the birth of the child. Warned by the magi, Herod slays the children in Bethlehem but misses the child he had intended to kill (Matt. 2:1–12, 16–18). At the close of his Gospel, the powers that be try to prevent the resurrection and fail. The temple authorities ask Pilate to station guards at the tomb (Matt.

231

27:62–66; 28:11–15). In his weary response to them, even Pilate seemed resigned to the fact that he had reached the limits of his power. So he passed the buck to the temple police: "You have a guard of soldiers. Go, make it as secure as you can." The principalities and powers failed to prevent the life of Jesus; now they will fail to seal his death.

The theophany described by Matthew (28:1–8) conveys an ironic reversal. When the angel of the Lord descends amidst earthquake, wind, and fire, "the guards became like dead men," and the dead man was raised to life. Just like when Jesus touched a leper, and the leper was cleansed but Jesus did not contract the disease. What is going on here?

One answer that fails to do justice to the meaning of resurrection but can still be helpful is this: God was honoring Jesus after the great shaming and humiliation of the show trial. Just as the woman in Simon's house was stirred to reverse each insult directed at Jesus, so God reverses and rejects the degrading show trial and death visited upon "the son." Life replaces death; honor replaces shame; nurturing care replaces physical abuse; acclamation replaces denunciation; the Last Supper gives way to the first supper in Emmaus (Luke 24:13–35); and the agony of crucifixion yields to resurrection life. The appearance of the risen one encourages the reemergence of the Jesus movement. This dynamic is captured in the "great commission" passage (Matt. 28:16–20), the Johannine pentecost (John 20:19–23), and the Lukan ascension (Luke 24:44–53). The entire event that we speak of as resurrection could be captured in the angel's question at the empty tomb, "Why do you seek the living among the dead?" (Luke 24:5). Having spent his life confusing boundaries and transgressing them (or transcending them), Jesus now confuses the boundary between life and death, a theme Paul would pick up in his letters (2 Cor. 4:7–12).

What seems central in relating the resurrection to the public activity of Jesus is this: the resurrection placed God's seal of approval on Jesus' public activity and its emphases on justice, judgment, compassion, and mercy. Now they can no longer be ignored as irrelevant to the "good news" or shuffled aside as of secondary importance. In the light that the resurrection casts on the public activity of Jesus, it is clear that God's redemption includes justice; the gospel includes the social gospel. No realm of human life is left untouched from the rulers to the beggars. It is also true that the "good news" does not mean one thing for all. The good news is bad news when announced to the ruling elites, as the rich ruler discovered (Mark 10:17–31), but it is unspeakably liberating when it leads to the forgiveness of sins, as the paralytic discovered (Mark 2:1–12). Just as the empty tomb was good news to the women but bad news to the powers that stationed guards at the tomb, justice and judgment go hand in hand.

The event that we call the resurrection blurs a number of lines. Jon Sobrino has explored the blurring of the line between theology and history:

> It is impossible to write a history of Jesus without producing theology about him, but it is true also—and this is the specific contribution of the Gospels—that it is impossible to produce a theology about Jesus without writing a history of him. . . . There are two important lessons. . . . The first is that we cannot turn the figure of Jesus into theology without turning him into history and telling the story of his life and fate. Without this, faith has no history. The second is that we cannot turn Jesus into history without turning him into theology as good news. . . . Without this, history has no faith.[1]

The Gospels themselves witness to this inextricable blending of faith and history since it permeates their narratives and, insofar as their narratives serve as source material for constructing and reconstructing the historical figure of Jesus, they will hand their legacy to future generations, including this study. The figure of Jesus who appears in the earliest Gospel, the Gospel of Mark, was already a composite figure, a combination of the historical one and the risen one. Mark did such a skillful job of blending them into his portrayal of Jesus that we have not been able to separate them to this day. So Schweitzer was right when he suggested that the only way to sketch a portrait of the historical Jesus is to make and try out hypotheses, such as this study of Jesus has attempted to do.

This leaves us in an ambiguous and confusing situation. Is this an epilogue, a final look backward at the historical Jesus whose life ended on a cross, or is this a prologue, a first look ahead to the resurrection of Jesus whose life begins at the empty tomb? Is this an end or a beginning? I suppose the answer is—Yes!

---

1. Jon Sobrino, *Jesus the Liberator: A Historical-Theological View*, trans. Paul Burns and Francis McDonagh (Maryknoll, N.Y.: Orbis Books, 1993), 60, 63.

Index of Ancient Sources

Index of Subjects